Penguin Education

Psychedelic Drugs

Psychological, Medical and Social Issues

Brian Wells

Psychedelic Drugs

Psychological, Medical and Social Issues

Brian Wells
With a Foreword by Humphry Osmond

Penguin Education

Penguin Education
A Division of Penguin Books Ltd,
Harmondsworth, Middlesex, England
Penguin Books Inc., 7110 Ambassador Road,
Baltimore, Md 21207, USA
Penguin Books Australia Ltd,
Ringwood, Victoria, Australia

First published 1973
Copyright © Brian Wells, 1973

Made and printed in Great Britain by
C. Nicholls & Company Ltd
Set in Monotype Times

Contents

For Tricia

Foreword

It is a pleasure to be able to write a foreword to this excellent book. Excellence lies in the eye of the beholder and no doubt there will be some whose attitudes towards it will resemble that of one of the Deans of Harvard University. In the late 1960s this eminent gentleman was traversing Harvard yard when he ran into Professor Richard Evans Schultes, the great ethnobotanist, who directs the Harvard Botanical Museum. Schultes has contributed more to our knowledge of psychoactive plants than anyone in the world today. He is the proper successor to the great Spruce and other botanical explorers of Amazonia. The Dean was naturally glad to see his distinguished colleague once more back from the jungles and mountains of South America, and asked him in an absent-minded way: 'And what have you found this time Dick?' To which Dr Schultes replied: 'We found three more hallucinogenic plants.' The Dean clasped his head and moaned 'Don't we just need them here,' and slunk away. Harvard was at the height of its troubles then.

Early in 1973 I was at a meeting where Schultes enlivened the assembly by telling us that when he first went to Central and South America only about half a dozen hallucinogenic plants were known. After his most recent expedition, and those of his pupils, he has now brought the number to eighty-eight. Schultes has the enthusiasm of great specialists, but his discoveries underline the theme of Brian Wells' admirably compact and sensible book, for at one time or another many of us have been troubled by the results of these powerful substances when used ineptly or clumsily, and have wished that they would disappear. The evidence is that they are not going to do so.

They seem to be an ancient, long-sustained and general interest of humankind which, until recently, could only be satisfied sporadically, uncertainly and often dangerously. Dr Schultes told us of the mescal bean (not to be confused with peyote or mescal button, as it is called), a most powerful and dangerous hallucinogen of which he found many splendid examples growing as ornamental trees when on a Southern campus recently. He photographed them but did not discuss them in his lectures. Due to the presence of cytosine this particular hallucinogen has something of the property of Russian roulette, and is favoured by only the most courageous.

Quite recently Schultes' pupils have discovered a psychedelic petunia growing somewhere in the Andes. His work shows that these substances have been with us since the beginning of history, that they are likely to stay with us and will probably become more abundant. Our enormous knowledge of synthetic chemistry, psychopharmacology and enzymology makes it improbable that we will be able to prevent their use by those who wish to use them unless we are prepared to set up a police state of the most oppressive kind, or can persuade people to abstain in some other way. History suggests that policemen are not at their best or most effective when trying to prevent people from doing things which they are inclined to do, and which others do not consider grossly immoral or socially dangerous. In other words, as this book suggests, we shall probably have to learn to live with these substances just as we have learned to live with alcohol, tobacco, and some of those sports which were once considered to be bloody and brutal, like that disruptive minor form of warfare, known as 'footeball', which caused moralists great distress in the sixteenth and seventeenth centuries, being considered not a safety-valve against riot but an incitement to rioting.

Should we then shrug our shoulders and act as if there was nothing to worry about? Certainly not, there is plenty to worry about, and Brian Wells has raised most of the really important questions here. It is unfortunate that once again medicine and society fell into that old trap of trying to reinforce moral disapproval of those who take psychedelics, with medical warnings about the dreadful fate which would befall them. We have done this repeatedly and it always fails, but that doesn't prevent us from trying once more. Just how devoted we are to this kind of thing is shown by that completely fictitious sun-gazing episode in which a rather pathetic blind official in Pennsylvania concocted a story of six young LSD takers who blinded themselves by gazing at the sun. This story became incorporated in official statements about the dangers of LSD even though the episode itself was wholly false.

The great differences of opinion among those who study the effect of LSD on chromosomes has been even more remarkable. The late Dr Walter Pahnke of Springrove Hospital, Maryland, told me that in their study of alcoholics, who were being treated with LSD, it was his task to take over samples of blood before and after treatment to a well-known cytologist at the National Institute of Mental Health. After he had delivered one sample the scientist rang him up saying: 'We must stop this, it is far too dangerous to continue. The chromosomes are in such very poor shape.' My old friend reminded him gently that perhaps before stopping the experiment they should find out whether they were dealing with an alcoholic who was receiving the LSD treatment, a member of the comparison group, or pre-treatment patients who had not received any. The cytologist agreed and was chastened to discover that the sample he had received was from a pre-treatment patient. Their follow-up suggested that, if anything, chromosomes were somewhat improved by LSD treatment; but this should not be taken seriously, for in addition to the LSD they had been having a better diet, and living under better conditions than they had been doing before admission to hospital. This does suggest, however, that we should be wary of leaping to conclusions, and should avoid trying to scare away intelligent young people who are perfectly well aware of the errors which have been made.

I am not suggesting that there may not be physical dangers, which we are still unable to evaluate. The author deals with these sensibly, but I think there is one matter that he has not, perhaps, emphasized sufficiently. This is, even supposing we were able to produce a wholly safe, totally reversible psychedelic, it still seems doubtful to me whether this should be employed by the young, whose perceptual worlds are still unstable. One of the main tasks of growing up consists of learning to be relatively emotionally stable in a relatively stable perceptual world. It is we who make that stable world and it is sometimes very difficult to achieve this. I believe that many young people have been distracted by psychedelics from this major task, which is to learn something about the world in which they find themselves, its customs and its folkways, and relate what they have learned to their own personal temperamental equation in the best way possible. Some cultures have managed to incorporate psychedelics in their *rite de passage*, but this is certainly not true of Europe and the United States today.

However, when we come to the middle aged and the elderly, the situation is wholly different. They are frequently far too set in their ways in a world which is changing rapidly. They are likely to suffer for these rigidities. Some people have become stodgy by their twenties, but many people by their forties are beginning to become like T. S. Eliot's clubman cat, Bustopher Jones, with his comforting thought, 'it will last out my time'. With our increased expectation of life this is fortunately not true; we need to find ways of keeping people flexible enough to live in a constantly changing world which can become increasingly unfamiliar, threatening and even hostile, for those who are unwilling or unable to recognize that things just will not stand still.

It has seemed a curious irony to me that psychedelics became popular with the wrong people, at the wrong time, in the wrong way. The headstrong young approached them with a careless rapture and were often indiscriminating and prepared to take anything; consequently, many avoidable misfortunes occurred. However, they seem to be learning by employing the method scorned by Bismark, who said: 'Fools say they learn by experience; I prefer to learn by other people's experience.' I have the impression now that they are a good deal more cautious and misfortunes are consequently becoming fewer, which is what one would expect.

Regarding the term psychedelic; it was intended as a neutral term to replace psychotomimetic, hallucinogenic, fantastica, etc. Aldous Huxley and I corresponded about this; he wrote to me on 30 March 1956:

About a name for these drugs – what a problem! I have looked into Liddell and Scott and find that there is a verb *phaneroein*, 'to make visible or manifest', and an adjective *phaneros*, meaning 'manifest, open to sight, evident'. The word is used in botany – phanerogam as opposed to cryptogam. Psychodetic is something I don't quite get the hang of. Is it an analogue of geodetic, geodesy? If so, it would mean mind-dividing, as geodesy means earth-dividing, from *ge* and *daiein*. Could you call these drugs psychophans? Or phaneropsychic drugs? Or what about phanerothymes? *Thumos* means soul, in its primary usage, and is the equivalent of Latin *animus*. The word is euphonious and easy to pronounce; besides it has relatives in the jargon of psychology – e.g. cyclothyme. On the whole I think this is better than psychophan or phaneropsychic.

Phanerothyme – substantive. Phanerothymic – adjective.

To make this trivial world sublime,
Take half a gramme of phanerothyme.

I thought and still think that this is a most beautiful word, but it seemed rather difficult, so after considering such possibilities as psychephoric – mind-moving; psychehormic – mind-rousing; psycheplastic – mind-moulding; psychelytic – mind-releasing; psychezymic – mind-formenting; psycherhexic – mind-bursting forth, my choice is psychedelic – mind-manifesting (Osmond, 1957), because it is clear, euphonious and uncontaminated by other associations.

I thought one of these terms should serve and, therefore, replied to Aldous with this couplet:

To fathom Hell or soar angelic,
Just take a pinch of psychedelic.

I had no idea then how widely this word would come to be used.

What can we expect for the future of psychedelics? Who can tell? But there are some things which seem unlikely. Establishments do not change their points of view quickly or dramatically; what is likely to happen is that people will become slowly less excited and distressed regarding psychedelics, and this will coincide with wiser, more sensible and more cautious use. As the Establishment sees it, the beastly things will have apparently gone away; those who enjoy using them will, if they are wise, not prod their elders too much or say 'I told you so' too often. In the next few decades we can expect simple ways of producing psychedelic substances, probably on a domestic basis, but also fairly simple ways of preventing their more harmful effects. In fifty or sixty years they will probably be incorporated in Western cultures, and historians looking back will wonder what all the fuss was about. They will also, I am sure, wonder why my old friend Aldous Huxley's good advice was not taken, but then it is the fate of the wise and prophetic seldom to have their advice taken.

Let us hope that we will learn to use these remarkable substances wisely and well rather than simply as trivial entertainments. Meanwhile those of us who would become a little more unblinkered would do much worse than read this concise, admirable and well-researched book.

Humphry Osmond
Director
Bureau of Research in Neurology and Psychiatry
Princeton, New Jersey
May 1973

1 Prospect

Despite all the research that has been done, and the great deal more that has been written, the psychedelic drugs still remain an enigma. They have been hailed as of enormous social, medical, and religious value – and also as the most destructive, pathogenic, and misleading discovery of all times. Their possibilities for good and ill are obviously very great and, whilst scientists continue to evaluate them as part of their job we must also, as citizens, engage in the even more onerous task of deciding what future, if any, such mind-altering drugs are to have in our society. Scientists give us the facts but we must collectively take responsibility for making the decisions which effect either the course of society's development or the freedom of the individual. Both are involved in the case of the psychedelics.

Yet the content of this book is intended to be more than just a starting point for airing a social issue: it is also meant to provide a *key* to the vast and scattered literature which refers to the divers substances we term 'psychedelic'. The surprising range, as well as the sheer volume, of what has been written is already far beyond the compass of any such modest guide as this, but it is hoped that the selection made may at least serve as an orientation to the many intriguing facets of the subject.

The basic material with which we are concerned, the drugs themselves, tends also to resist brief simplifications. The defining criteria have to be psychological as there are no comprehensive pharmacological ones – despite the fact that there is either a natural or synthetic molecular similarity between *many* of the drugs. In fact, the list of psychedelically active materials is dauntingly large and would take us far beyond anything that would be manageable within a single volume. Moreover, even if one did appraise the full list, it would still be incomplete and out of date before it could be published as new additions are being made all the time. Even if this was not so, there would be very little point in attempting such a coverage as only a fraction of the materials known to be active have any users.

However, drugs which *are* readily available and widely used get a degree of attention roughly commensurate with their place in the scheme of things and consequently it is LSD-25, mescaline, psilocybin, and cannabis which will claim the greater part of our attention. Of these, cannabis tends to be the odd man out as it is pharmacologically more dissimilar from the other drugs than they are from one another and, in the doses which are currently usual, its psychological effects tend to be different too. As a socially used smoking mixture, its effects are typically those of a euphoriant which simply makes the user feel 'good' or 'high'. Yet in large doses it can, and does, also produce very powerful effects of a distinctively psychedelic type. It is therefore appropriately grouped under the same rubric with such different chemicals as mescaline and LSD.

Inevitably, in compiling any general work like this, it becomes necessary to write something on the history of the subject for, despite what is said by the press and other mass media, the psychedelics are *not* a brand-new phenomenon. Nor are they easily legislated out of existence – as is obvious from the way they have survived innumerable attempts to suppress them. They have already accompanied mankind through his social evolution for many millenniums and will, no doubt, still be around in many more to come – whatever our views, decisions, or sanctions, which can hardly be more pronounced than in previous times. However, setting a historical perspective need not necessarily involve a separate narrative and so, rightly or wrongly, I have departed from this more conventional course and have chosen to fit the allusions of history into individual chapters. Thus historical accounts of the effects of these drugs on religious experience, sexuality, aggression, etc., are fitted into the chapters which specifically review those aspects of psychedelic drug action.

Even so, it is perhaps worth drawing attention to a few of the more salient historical events which, in addition to suggesting some sort of perspective, also indicate some of the weaknesses inherent in these accounts. In fact, the very first point which should be made concerns the doubtful *validity* of these historical records for, apart from questions of the credibility of the narrative, there is usually also the real difficulty of being certain that the drugs described in ancient accounts are the same ones as are used today – whether or not the terms used by the translators are the same. This is not to dismiss or diminish the importance of the historical records, for very *similar* drugs were certainly in use; it is simply to caution that there is sometimes a lack of precision in mapping the historical course of any particular substance.

There is also the problem that some of the very old sources are legendary rather than historical. For example, it is often stated that cannabis appeared in the pharmacopoeia of the Emperor Shen Nung in 2737 B.C. Though a Shen Nung may well have ruled at about that time, and although cannabis has been known to exist in China for many millenniums, this apparently precise reference is based on legend rather than clear historical sources. But, though it is certainly true that cannabis use has a very ancient medicinal tradition throughout the Eastern world, it has no less a distinguished record for spiritual inspiration. It has, for example, been identified by many scholars as the 'heavenly guide' referred to in the Hindu *Atharva-* and *Rig-Vedas*. And, by way of apparent paradoxes for us to try and reconcile, the psychedelics also appear on the pages of history in quite the opposite role: causing the fanatical and wild conduct of such people as the Norse 'Berserkers' and the Persian 'Assassins'. Which drugs were implicated, and the probable degree to which they were responsible for the behaviour which occurred, will be the subject of much more detailed treatment later.

In spite of the fact that there is a flourishing use of psychedelics in the Americas, as manifest in the use of a bewildering range of snuffs, edible fungi, and smoking mixtures, the evidence here tends to be anthropological rather than historical. This is largely, but not entirely, due to usage being most prevalent amongst preliterate peoples who have never kept any records of their history and customs – apart from a virtually undatable verbal tradition. Such fragments as do exist tend to date from relatively recent times and derive from the early travellers and anthropologists who generally concluded that the practices which they observed *seemed* to be of fairly ancient origin. Our only hope of unequivocal records lies with the advanced and literate peoples of that continent, but, alas, most of the historical record has now been lost due to the zeal of the early Christian missionaries who persecuted the members of indigenous cults and destroyed their artifacts and records lest the heathen tradition should compete with Christianity.

Africa, too, gives some evidence of having a native tradition in the use of psychedelic drugs but, because of the severe effect of climatic conditions on man-made artifacts, and of the dearth of written languages, most of our knowledge from this part of the world is also of relatively recent origin. We have, for example, excellent accounts of the pervasive influence of hashish on the tribal life of the Baloubas of the Belgian Congo, but this only dates back as far as the nineteenth century, and even this type of evidence is fragmentary for anywhere other than the northern part of Africa.

In the north the position is very much better because of the less humid climates and the variety of advanced cultures and written languages. Here, the record clearly shows that cannabis ('hashish') was a culturally well-established drug throughout much of northern Africa by the time of Mohammed and, although he banned the use of alcohol as being inimical to the spiritual life, hashish was not so proscribed and thus continued in an unbroken tradition. Evidence will also be presented later to show that other psychedelics, like flyagaric, were also important religious materials before the dawn of the Christian epoch.

In fact, there is clear evidence that the psychedelic drugs are known in every corner of the earth and have been so for a very long time. They were present in the classical cultures which moulded our own and have been found in every environment from the scorched desert to the northern tundra, and from jungles to plains. But their real history, so far as our own culture is concerned, begins in the nineteenth century. At about this time, some of the more adventurous literati began experimenting on their consciousnesses with drugs brought mainly from Egypt, the Middle East, and India. Opium already had its own well-established and rich literary tradition but the mid-nineteenth century, with the introduction of cannabis, saw the birth of another – the psychedelic. Much of the original impetus came when the French physician Dr Moreau de Tours provided his literary friends with a supply of *dawamesc*, a sweetmeat form of cannabis, which he had brought from Algeria.

A strange club, 'Le Club des Hachichins', was subsequently established in Paris at Pimodan House – a sepulchral structure sited on the Ile Saint-Louis by the Seine, and here the members joined together to eat large quantities of cannabis-based confectionery. Amongst their members were extremely gifted bohemian writers, men like Baudelaire and Théophile Gautier, who through their glittering accounts of what followed did much to promote both a new literary tradition and also a wider interest in such mind-altering drugs.

In the United States, too, writers like Bayard Taylor and Fitzhugh Ludlow began to propagate accounts of their own ecstatic states and psychedelic experiences due to cannabis use. This tradition has evolved principally around the smoking of cannabis in the dried-plant form (marijuana or marihuana). Other consciousness-changing substances like nitrous oxide also began to be popular and a substantial addition to the lore was made in 1902 by William James, the distinguished American psychologist, who published a widely read and controversial book dealing with the religious significance of experiences deriving from the use of psychoactive drugs. Curiously, in view of his subsequent influence on psychedelic thought and thinkers, James himself had little contact with psychedelics. He knew of, and was interested in, the Indian peyote ceremony but when he took the substance himself, its only effect was to make him violently sick! Nevertheless, his experiements with nitrous oxide and other substances, including alcohol, led him to come out very strongly in support of the view that chemicals are capable of evoking enriching and mystical states of consciousness. And, as his conclusions were expressed in very positive terms, he was quite predictably the target of a good deal of hostile attention and publicity which, just as predictably, added substantially to public knowledge of drugs and their exotic possibilities.

But by far the most significant contribution to popular knowledge of the non-opiate psychoactive drugs came in 1954 with the publication of Aldous Huxley's book *The Doors of Perception* – an account of the way in which mescaline had thrilled and enhanced the author's perceptions of the world, as well as illuminating his earlier religious and philosophical beliefs. This book turned out to be what is arguably the most important single event in the unfolding of the psychedelic movement and must rank with the earlier, though then somewhat obscure, chemical advances that had been made by Hofmann and Stoll in the synthesis of L S D-25.

Indeed, the synthesis of L S D-25 was originally a routine stage in the development of drugs to control the activity of unstriped muscles, particularly in relation to the pregnant uterus. However, the new drug did not appear to be particularly promising and it was duly superseded by other, more successful, ergot alkaloids. Not until five years after L S D-25 had first been synthesized was it discovered that it had such remarkable psychological properties. Then the hunt was on.

Laboratories began work on a whole new range of psychedelic materials and medical circles started to become really interested in their psychiatric possibilities. These new drugs were thought not only to have a real therapeutic potential but, more importantly, to suggest the biochemical basis of the psychoses – especially schizophrenia. But the popularization and abuse of these substances was probably responsible, much more than any contra-indications for their use, for their falling into professional disfavour. Within a little more than a decade, from the early fifties to the mid-sixties, they had risen to a position of high scientific and clinical promise only to fall to a state where they were regarded as the hall-mark of pseudo-science and the harbingers of unprecedented social evils. The time-scale for cannabis is somewhat different from that of other drugs closer in type to L S D, but the picture is much the same.

The disgrace of the L S D-type drug is, as we have said, closely connected with the way in which it became popular amongst young people – and especially amongst students. The public and professional decline of these drugs, though not in the sense of any reduction in their use, is perhaps best exemplified in the events surrounding Timothy Leary and his colleagues at the

University of Harvard. Dr Leary, a professor of psychology, being exceptionally enthusiastic about the potential of these drugs for expanding the individual consciousness and for favourably modifying social attitudes, conducted a range of unusual experiments whilst also vigorously seeking converts to his views amongst young people. He has since tended to see himself as a sort of latter-day Socrates – unjustly accused and condemned by senile and reactionary 'elders' for allegedly corrupting the young by encouraging them to question the prevailing ways of looking at the world.

Whatever one's own views about Leary's interpretation of events, he was certainly bitterly opposed for his interests, beliefs and some of his unconventional activities; so much so, that he was dismissed from his post. But his popularity with the young, and his great literary energy and ability, soon made him an important cult figure and when, after a period of quite undeniable and unremitting harassment, he was committed to prison for ten years on the charge of possessing a small quantity of marijuana, he became a martyr and charismatic symbol for many young people. He later escaped from prison and fled to North Africa and thence to Switzerland where, though in virtual retirement, his publications still give him considerable influence as a 'high priest' of the psychedelic cult.

And this really brings us completely up to date; the storm still rages and we have as much reason as ever to be concerned about the effects of psychedelics on our society for, illegal or not, they are probably in more widespread use now than ever they were before. Moreover, the influence of these drugs is much greater than their direct influence on the people who actually use them. The psychedelic movement has, through the work of artists, designers and writers, and through the influence of pop music, achieved an astonishing degree of cultural diffusion – even allowing for the very powerful help given by the mass media. But, though a great deal of diffusion has taken place, so, too, has a great deal of dilution and distortion. So much so, that the very *meaning* of many of the key terms in these issues of constant public debate are frequently hard to determine.

Unfortunately, both the descriptive words 'psychedelic' and

'drug' have associations and connotations which prejudice the ways in which they are perceived. Already, 'psychedelic' is being used to describe anything in youth culture which is colourful or unusual and fashionable. Indeed, marketing people have already seen the potential of the word to sell everything from clothing and records to fabrics and light-fittings – and the qualities of psychedelic art have been particularly exploited by the packaging world. Yet what *is* 'psychedelic' and what are its appropriate connotations? The answer to this question is really what the rest of the book is about and so it would be impracticable to try to give a satisfactory answer in the opening remarks, but one or two scene-setting comments may not be too out of place.

In 1957, Dr Humphry Osmond formally proposed the word 'psychedelic', using Greek roots, and produced a word to signify something which is 'mind-manifesting', or capable of having *profound* effects upon the nature of conscious experience. It is difficult to be precise about such a defining characteristic, as it could equally be said to apply to otherwise quite neutral substances which have strange effects in either deficiency or toxic quantities. The definition is therefore somewhat fluid and dependent upon the context of discussion and this, inevitably, has been a source of considerable criticism of both the concept and the term. But whatever criticism can be levelled at the term 'psychedelic' can also, *mutatis mutandis*, be levelled against such suggested alternatives as 'fantastica' or 'psychotomimetic' and 'hallucinogenic' drug.

'Psychotomimetic', or psychosis mimicking, has been a very strong contender as a descriptive term but has lost a good deal of ground in recent years as research workers have demonstrated that, in many ways, the comparison is facile as there are many crucial points of difference between psychotic experiences and those induced by these drugs. For example, the 'hallucinations' created by these chemicals differ profoundly from the 'real' ones of psychosis in that normal people under the drug influence, whether enchanted or terrified by the experiences and images which occur, nevertheless *generally* remain in reality-contact and quite aware that they are reacting to a drug state. Thus the 'hallucinations' evoked by psychedelics are usually of a somewhat different order from those occurring in psychosis and should, in most cases, more correctly be referred to as 'pseudo-halluc-inations'.

However, it would be unduly pedantic, and quite unrealistic, to expect that all references to these hallucinatory types of phenomena should be specified as 'real' or 'pseudo'. Notwith-standing the fact that the use of the generic term 'hallucinogen' is potentially misleading and must ultimately result in taxono-mic incongruities, most writers still find it convenient to use the term 'hallucination' in a broad descriptive sense to refer to the perceptions experienced by one person and conveying to him an immense sense of reality (though not necessarily an acc-eptance of the real nature of the things seen or heard) but which cannot be accounted for in objective terms by other people. Never-theless, despite the semantic utility of the term 'hallucination', the category designation of 'hallucinogen' is still probably sub-ject to more serious objections than those attending the term 'psychedelic' – which has the additional advantage of conveying an appropriately richer connotation whilst also retaining the most *neutral* meaning amongst the widely acceptable terms. But, having established the author's own reason for preferring one term rather than another, it should perhaps be said that the 1971 Canadian Government Commission of Inquiry held that the proper classification for LSD was in the category *psychedelic-hallucinogen*! Of course, in practice the two terms thus conjoined both refer to the same substances and are used quite inter-changeably and so, as no clear-cut taxonomy seems to exist, our usage must be a matter of preference rather than precision.

'Drug' too is a word which, unless one is careful, conjures up a very prejudicial image of disease, addiction, and destruction. The associations are too well known and too sombre to need any further comment but it is just worth making the point that the word 'drug' is of such a wide applicability as to make it virtually meaningless in either a practical or a definitional sense and, in fact, it may be used to refer to a whole host of perfectly innocuous and commonplace domestic materials. Consequently, care should be taken that the use of 'drug' with 'psychedelics' does not lead us into thinking that there is necessarily any basic similarity between these substances and others such as the opiates, barbiturates, and amphetamines.

Neither should the fact that this sort of grouping together of drugs is regularly done for control and legislative purposes prejudice our approach to the psychedelics; research on these substances has still hardly begun and we must be very careful to sift the *evidence* concerning their effects before being driven to hasty classifications and conclusions. Unfortunately though, and due mainly to current severe legal restraints in further empirical research with human beings, there is a real hiatus in many areas of knowledge and many able workers have become so discouraged that they have given up this line of approach completely in favour of others which are not frustratingly circumscribed.

In consequence, most of the current work actually being done has to depend upon observations of the effect of illegal use which, as we shall see, raises really grave problems of experimental control and representative sampling. Even so, the pursuance of this type of investigation is no less important than that done in the laboratory as the psychedelics are not only important in a pharmacological sense, but also in their role as drugs of abuse and elements in a social revolution. And, if methodological problems are raised for psychologists and pharmacologists, they are not alone in this. For example, philosophers, religious writers, and theologians must question the status of the experiences derived from psychedelic drug use. They must decide whether the states induced are distinguishable from those claimed as truly 'mystical' and decide also whether, as many users have claimed, the drugs act as external aids like the microscope to reveal a whole new dimension of reality. As we shall see, there is plenty of fascinating material relevant to such discussions.

Inevitably though, where the issues involved cut across so many strongly held beliefs, attitudes, and prejudices, it is difficult to be completely impartial. We are *all* subject to our own idiosyncrasies and are all likely to select the evidence which we feel reflects the most reasonable position on any given issue. In my own case, I have sometimes been criticized by colleagues for drawing attention to the positive aspects of the psychedelics. But I sincerely believe that there *are* positive benefits to be derived and that, whatever the final balance may be, it would be partial and misleading not to take account of them. After all, millions of people choose to use these drugs and they must be presumed to do so for, to them at least, good reasons. So, in taking this line, I have attempted to give due weight to all sides whilst accepting and cautioning that a totally neutral position is not possible – even in the task of collating and summarizing the evidence.

Having issued this caveat, it should also be said that the business of achieving an unbiased account of the problem is made doubly difficult because the literature itself lacks balance. Most of what is published in the more august journals is of a distinctly negative character – no doubt reflecting to some degree the fact that much professional and financed research is, of course, medical in nature and thus primarily concerned with the drug casualties and other pathological factors. By the same token, the pharmacologists also tend to emphasize possible contra-indications and thus the content of both medical and pharmacological journals, or a large part of the relevant and available source of scholarly technical communications, tends to be mainly concerned with presenting evidence of the pathological effects.

Much other appropriate evidence, the experience of publicity-avoiding users who do *not* get involved with either the police or psychiatrists, finds expression only in the experience of the social epidemiologist and the writings of those observers who manage to penetrate psychedelic-using circles and who, not infrequently, have been known to do so on the basis of participation. One's natural caution should be aroused at handling this sort of material but data it undeniably is, and it represents a useful and naturalistic source of information – though one which we are no more obliged to accept at face value than any other.

In the course of analysing our sources of data we shall come across a vast range of users from the Eastern contemplative to the Western Christian theologian; from the acute psychiatric casualty to the adjusted 'psychenaut' introspectively exploring the inner space of his mind; from the research subject and the creative artist to the representatives of cultures both primitive and defunct. All these, and more besides, are necessary to tell the story of psychedelics. Inevitably, the experiences and outcomes recorded tend also to have a very wide range and so it will not be possible to make any categorical statements about *the* drug effects. The psychedelics are not specifically acting drugs; rather, as we shall see, their effects depend upon an *interaction* between the drug itself and the make-up of the individual, his motivations and expectations, and the setting in which he takes the drugs. But, having said this, let us now look at the basic features of these drugs and at some of their more common psychological effects. We shall then be in a much better position to appraise the exotic range of their manifestations.

2 Minor Psychedelics

Contrary to what is popularly believed, the number of known psychedelic substances is not limited to three or four but is to be reckoned comfortably in three figures – and the tally continues to grow. Inevitably then, it would not be practically possible to give an account of all psychedelic materials and so some sort of selection, from the better known and most available, must be made. Other drugs will be introduced later, in the context of their special properties or uses.

The purpose of this chapter and the next one is to set out in brief fashion the main agents and their principal features whilst carrying forward much specific material relating to their effects in such areas as therapy, sexuality, and aggression for fuller treatment in the appropriate sections. In presenting this overview of the drugs it is convenient to follow the pattern set by the American psychologist Charles Tart (1969) of dividing substances into 'minor' and 'major' psychedelics in order to impose some sort of grouping and thus simplify the distinctions between the many drugs involved.

The minor psychedelics then are typified by four characteristic qualities.

1. Users report that they retain a fair amount of volitional control whilst experiencing the drug effects.

2. The duration of the effects is usually relatively short.

3. After-effects generally do not occur, or are mild.

4. The experience is seldom so powerful as to induce the user to become a proselytizer in the same way that LSD users tend to look for converts.

The opposite effects, naturally, tend to typify the major psychedelics. Now Tart would be the first to insist that the above are not 'criteria': they are not inflexible defining features, simply generalizations which have a broad validity and serve as a first attempt at a taxonomy based on psychological effects.

The substances which Tart would see included in the 'minor' grouping include marijuana, shrubs like broom – Scotch, Spanish, and Canary Island – carbon dioxide, and nitrous oxide. One might add many others of like kind to this category – such as nutmeg and perhaps even smoked banana skins – though only marijuana in this grouping is of real significance as a widely used mind-altering drug. Yet certainly it is appropriate that marijuana should be treated separately from the substances which have been included in the 'major' grouping as both the behavioural and pharmacological evidence suggests that they should be kept discrete.

Indeed, it is becoming quite usual to deal with cannabis together with, but as being quite distinct from, the major 'hallucinogens'. For example, Bergel and Davies (1970), Blum *et al.* (1970 a and b), Laurie (1967) and de Ropp (1958) have all made such distinctions and Cohen (1965) even wrote his text *Drugs of Hallucination* with scarcely a reference to it. And more surprisingly, Hoffer and Osmond (1967) in *The Hallucinogens* ignored it completely although it did find a place later in Aaronson and Osmond's 1971 edited work *Psychedelics: The Uses and Implications of Hallucinogenic Drugs*. It therefore seems particularly right to begin this section with a consideration of cannabis and its relationship to the other psychedelic drugs.

Cannabis

'Cannabis' is a rather more precise way of referring to what is also commonly called marijuana or marihuana, Indian hemp, hemp, grass, pot, tea, weed, hashish (hash), kif, etc. The number of terms used, colloquial and local, is vast but the referent is always simply the product of a single plant, *Cannabis sativa.* There are also local botanical differences such as *Cannabis indica* and *Cannabis americana* though both refer to local variations of *Cannabis sativa* and, although some local usages of the generic 'cannabis' refer only to the resin, *all* products of the female plant are included in the World Health Organisation's definition. The fact that the female plant is singled out is because the male contains too little of the active ingredients to be practically useful for psychedelic purposes.

Cannabis sativa is a plant found growing wild throughout many of the warm parts of the world and is undoubtedly the most widely used of the psychedelic drugs. But the wild product is very much less potent than that of the cultivated plant, as is that which comes from the more northerly latitudes: the most pure and potent material tending to come from India where it still has a considerable religious and social use.

The plant itself belongs to the genus *Moraceae* and is related to our own familiar hop. It is a tall shrub-like herb which may grow up to twenty feet in height, though it is more usually of about six to twelve feet. At one time it was of considerable industrial significance, as the male plant was the source of hemp fibre for rope-making, but nowadays it is almost exclusively grown for the drug qualities of the female. The main sources are India, North Africa, the Middle East, and Mexico where it is both cultivated and found wild for, in true weed-like manner, it easily escapes cultivation. Even in the south-western states of the USA, and despite constant hunting by narcotic agents, it still manages to grow – sometimes wild, but often cultivated in a camouflage of other greenery.

Whatever the origin though, there is a wide variation in the finished product and in the ways in which it is used. The plant yields a range of substances ranging from the dried and crushed leaves to the solidified resin which is exuded from the flowers and upper leaves. In the United States, the 'marijuana' smoking mixture is usually of the former variety and, because of its sources, composition, and because it is frequently diluted with the virtually inactive male plant, it tends to be of a relatively low potency. This same product is also extremely common in India and in the Middle East where, known as 'bhang', it is regarded as being very much a poor man's diet. Finer qualities, such as 'ganja', are prepared from resin derived from the cut tops of specially cultivated plants and used for smoking, infusions, and the preparation of sweetmeats or 'charas'. Such is the choice of the wealthy and the more discriminating.

Because of the *bulk* of the marijuana-type crushed leaf, resin has considerable advantages for smugglers and is therefore very much more common in Britain. However, the pattern of use in the United Kingdom is probably, in range at least, similar to that of anywhere else in the world, i.e. inhalation via cigarettes or pipes and ingestion by means of infused drinks or in confectionaries; more rarely some people are known to consume large quantities of raw resin. However, as in America, smoking is the most common method of use – despite the fact that many users are not tobacco smokers and therefore experience particular discomfort in inhaling the smoke – which is commonly mixed with tobacco anyway.

The *effects* of cannabis will depend to some extent upon the smoking experience of the user – it being apparent that the more experienced are more able to take smoke deeper into their lungs and to retain it there for the extended length of time which yields the greatest absorption and the most potent results. Inhalation is a very direct way of introducing chemicals into the body and absorption is very rapid and efficient, with drug effects commencing within a few minutes. Because there *is* such a rapid connection between the cause and the effect, it is possible for the experienced user to achieve and maintain his desired 'high' state for periods typically of between two and four hours.

The chemical aspects of this drug are still not completely understood and it is only in the last few years that the many basic constituents have begun to be identified. Of these, a range of tetrahydrocannabinols (THC) seems to be particularly important with compounds known as $\triangle_1$ and $\triangle_6$ THC appearing to have the greatest pharmacological potency. However, the biochemical action of these complex substances is still far from being fully understood and is not helped by our having to rely almost exclusively upon animal research to provide information about the properties of constituent chemicals. But such procedures as injecting mice, or even fumigating them, has a very limited value in studying the effects of psycho-active drugs on *man*.

In view of the very grave restrictions that have now been placed upon rigorous research in virtually every scientifically advanced country, there is an undeniable slowing-down in our knowledge of the drug's effects on human physiological and psychological processes. However, though there is a good deal of information which continues to accumulate from illegal users, the trouble with most of this non-experimental evidence is that dosage, potency, and degree of adulteration are virtually unknown. Further, because we know that the subjective effects of *all* the psychedelic drugs are dependent upon the personality of the user plus his 'set' and 'setting', we must accept that we are seldom in a position to evaluate properly these variables and outcomes in circumstances which cannot be controlled by the researcher.

As a consequence, we now have a situation where our knowledge is not only artificially circumscribed but is also subject to severe difficulties in interpretation. Even so, cannabis has been widely used for a long time now and it is possible to produce a fairly good *descriptive* account of the effects that it may produce.

The generally agreed effects of cannabis, and it should be stressed that these *are* only generalizations and not likely to be completely true for any given individual, include very many unpleasant somatic experiences such as pains in the throat and chest, dry mouth, giddiness, sickness, cold extremities, increased pulse and blood pressure, and some loss of bodily coordination. But these effects may be quite minimal or absent, especially with an experienced user, and are offset by such pleasurable effects as the enhancement of visual and musical perception – with colours and rhythms taking on much richer qualities. Then, of course, there is the euphoria – the sense of relaxation, intuitive insights, happiness and the bouts of hilarity and laughter which make the drug so popular. Naturally, as with the negative reactions, the positive ones do not always occur either. Sometimes with high doses, or in people with low thresholds, these bodily and perceptual effects may be *extreme* and result in real distress, creating delusions or hallucinations, and really terrifying psychological experiences.

However, most cannabis used in the West appears to be of the 'weekend' variety; a pattern of occasional use of small quantities in order to achieve the 'high' or euphoria. This pattern has often been compared with social drinking, as opposed to the excesses of the alcoholic or the drug addict. Whether such usage constitutes a serious 'problem' will be dealt with later but the general point which should be made at the outset is that cannabis, like all of the other psychedelic drugs, does *not* create physical dependence, nor does it result in 'tolerance' such that progressively higher doses are required to achieve the same psychological results. Quite extraordinarily, the opposite is true; the experienced user requires *less* than the novice to achieve a 'high' – probably due in part to a lower initial anxiety about the drug effect, coupled with a greater technical proficiency in using it. Deep, relaxed, sleep usually comes after the 'high' and, unlike alcohol intoxication, waking is seldom accompanied by a 'hangover'.

Given that the later specialized chapters will deal with many of the more easily grouped and coherent aspects of drug action it remains only to outline the generalized psychic effects which also occur. At this stage though, we shall be at pains to avoid delving into the meanings which these experiences may be given – whether philosophical, social, or whatever – and avoiding, temporarily, questions concerning medical uses and the psychological and psychiatric hazards.

The unpleasant somatic experiences referred to, especially when they occur in a completely or relatively inexperienced user, very often set the pattern for the early part of the psychological experience. The respiratory system's intense discomfort, plus the nausea and general bodily feeling of distress, quite commonly result in considerable anxiety and fear that something may have gone wrong. However, this stage passes, though it may be exacerbated by the feeling that one is losing the capacity for purposeful and continuous thought

After this stage has passed, if indeed it occurs at all, come the much sought-after psychological rewards. High on the list of these are, of course, the perceptual changes – in which perceptions of such things as colour, form, texture and music become very much richer and more sensuous. Then there are the emotional pleasures: feelings of relief, happiness and euphoria – very often accompanied by periods of uncontrolled laughter which may or may not have any apparent cause. In between these periods, or in lieu of them, there may be spells of serenity in which philosophical, religious, and social ideas, and apparent insights may be preoccupying as topics for either contemplation or discussion.

It is also often claimed that the ability to communicate with others is much enhanced and a feeling of identification and togetherness generated. This is said to be a part of the drug's capacity to loosen up people's reserve and shyness by undermining the compulsion to project an *image* – that most corrosive strategy in social relationships. Trust and identification are held to replace the hostile watchfulness of being 'uptight'. Though whether these altogether desirable effects *actually* occur is another matter: it may be that the individual's drug-induced euphoria and reduced critical judgement make it *seem* that they do, but this would be something else again.

The same phenomenon, intoxicants being used to erode social reserve and engender feelings of togetherness, is, of course, also claimed as a major function of alcohol. And, though the subjective effects of the two drugs are undoubtedly very different in many respects, there are these similarities which may help to explain the popularity of 'pot' smoking. But for a really exhaustive account of the subjective states created by cannabis one might consult Tart (1971) who has undertaken an extensive questionnaire study with American students who use the drug and has summarized the variety of reactions in percentage form. Many of these results will be referred to later.

It has been argued that the perceptual changes which take place in the judgement of time, speeds, and distances may be marked enough to incapacitate the user in such complex co-ordinations as those involved in car driving. This point was made experimentally by Clark and Nakashima (1968) but they also drew attention to the very wide *individual differences* which occurred on all tests and which make any generalization extremely difficult even when research is conducted in controlled laboratory conditions with measured doses. Indeed, Snyder (1971), summarizing some of the existing research on driving skills, points out how difficult it is to interpret the results – especially where one is making comparisons on the relative effects of alcohol and cannabis. However, despite the variability of results and the differences in interpretation and experimental subjects used, it is surprising how *little* impairment of basic skills actually takes place with moderate cannabis use. Nevertheless, one cannot discount the possibility that changes in emotional state may well influence actual driving performance in the real conditions of aggression and competition on the road.

One aspect of experimental control which needs to be taken into account in the selection of subjects for such studies, as well as in the interpretation of results, derives from the fact that the inexperienced user requires a *higher* dose of the drug to achieve the same subjective effects as the experienced user. This is a point which is not always considered, as it is contrary to the usual course of drug abuse – that is, the user becomes 'tolerant' to the drug effects and requires progressively more to achieve the same state. Of course, this *reverse tolerance* of cannabis is a very puzzling phenomenon but Snyder, quoting the pharmacological evidence, suggests that although the THC rapidly disappears from the blood, one of the metabolites created in the process of degradation is itself highly psychoactive and remains in the body tissues for a much longer period and causes a reduced threshold for subsequent doses of THC.

As with all the psychedelic drugs, though, the reactions provoked depend not only upon dosage but also upon 'set' and 'setting'. The effects of taking cannabis by oneself may very well be to experience no pleasant effects at all whereas the same dosage taken in a social situation among friends may well produce a full range of perceptual, intellectual, and mood changes. Once again, there is a parallel here with alcohol: moderate drinking alone seldom leads to euphoria. However, *very large doses* of either alcohol or cannabis will – whatever the context – have powerful effects but, though the effects of high doses of alcohol are well enough known to everyone, those of cannabis are often unknown even to the average user.

Perhaps the flavour of the more florid 'high dose' experience, though elaborated in literary fashion, appears most agreeably in the writings of Gautier and Baudelaire – some examples of which are recorded in Solomon (1969). The preparation used by both writers was hashish (cannabis resin), taken in the form of sweetmeat, and in very·large amounts. The experiences recorded are comparable with those of the major psychedelics and include gross distortions of the perception of time, things, and people – including oneself; also there was euphoria, terror, grotesque hallucinations, and paranoid delusions. Although these literary accounts are undoubtedly composites of many experiences and enhanced by rich imaginations, they are certainly based on the very real happenings at Le Club des Hachichins, and all of the effects described continue to have their counterparts in the less readable clinical and experimental literature.

However, though the *major* psychedelics have many contemporary and highly literate commentators on their effects, cannabis is less celebrated as a 'mind-expanding' drug as it tends nowadays to be used mainly as a euphoriant. In other words, the currently most favoured effects come from a combination of relatively low doses and a method of use (smoking) which allows a great deal of control in achieving, and maintaining, particular states. At the present time very few of the users seem to want to employ this drug to its full psychedelic potential. But, given the effects of high doses when they *are* used, it is quite apparent that cannabis is not only properly grouped with the psychedelics, but that the division of 'minor' and 'major' drugs is very relative indeed.

Nutmeg

That the familiar kitchen spice, nutmeg, should turn out to be a powerful psychoactive drug comes as a complete surprise to many a home-baked cake or rice-pudding fancier, yet it undeniably does have these properties too.

Nutmeg is actually the dried seed-kernel of *Myristica fragrans*, an East Indian evergreen tree of the *Myristicaceae* family. Other psychedelically important members of this group include, according to Schultes (1969a), three types of virola tree which are to be found in the South American jungle and whose bark resin, when dried and pulverized, yields a snuff which is known as yakee, parica, epena, and by many other names. These snuffs are widely used amongst the Indians of several countries for religious, ceremonial, and pleasure purposes, the psychedelically active alkaloid common to both the snuffs and to nutmeg being thought to be myristicin – sometimes also called elemicen.

The effects of this drug in the epena snuff used by the Waiká Indians of Brazil include a tremendously distorted scale-perception which makes everything seem to be of giant size, including their own bodies – which seem to tower into the clouds where, conveniently, they can talk with their deities. There are other effects too; more mundane ones like euphoria and nausea, which are much more prominent in our own domestic commodity than are the exotic subjective experiences. Thus nutmeg appears to be much less of a major psychedelic than some of its close relations.

Why the effects of such similar drugs should be so different is far from being properly understood but it is no doubt a combination of such factors as dosage, the presence of other drugs, and cultural settings. But, whatever the reasons, there is little doubt that nutmeg is not in the same class of mind-altering drugs as those we shall consider as the 'major' psychedelics. Such effects as there are, though mild in the psychedelic sense, are very often exceedingly potent in their more somatic aspects. The amounts needed are large by comparison with almost any drug except alcohol: of the order of ten grams (or one-third of an ounce) to achieve even relatively mild effects. Beyond this amount, more profound effects can be produced but the risk of self-poisoning increases also. Hoffer and Osmond (1967) have summarized some cases of patients coming to the attention of clinicians and have also presented an account of the subjective experiences of nutmeg intoxication. What emerges is that nutmeg gives a rather unpredictable and, in many ways, somewhat unpleasant experience.

The disagreeable features begin with the very act of taking the substance: the process of swallowing upwards of a third to a half ounce of powdered nutmeg. This is generally achieved by stirring it into a glass of hot water or fruit juice, but the potion still tends to be emetic and users often fail to keep it down. Having swallowed the concoction, the ensuing results naturally depend upon how much was taken but, typically, the earlier part of the experience tends to be mainly related to fighting back the waves of nausea which sweep over the body until the sense of well-being and euphoria supervenes. This stage, reportedly very similar to the cannabis effects previously described, gives way after half an hour or so to a much greater impairment of the ability to think and concentrate. Instead comes attention to either the exotic visions and beautiful experiences which often accompany the major psychedelics or, as seems more usual with the users that I have spoken to, an engulfing feeling of being very unwell. These adverse effects, which include cold and clamminess, a very dry mouth, and disturbing and frightening perceptual effects, tend to accompany a typical 'bad trip' – and this may be rather long-lasting if the user has miscalculated and overdosed. Yet, despite the fact that bad trips seem so relatively common with nutmeg, its positive aspects must also be highly valued by users in order to make its continued use seem worthwhile.

But, having said this, it should also be noted that the use of this substance is said to be very much a prisoner's drug – presumably because of its easy availability and the fact that possession is not a crime. Yet the 'set' and 'setting' in which it is thus used might well be expected to colour the psychological effects created and account in part for its very bad reputation. But, bad reputation or not, it undoubtedly continues to be used also by young people who are experimenting with states of consciousness, or just looking for 'kicks'. However, the impression that one forms is that most of these young people will have had more than enough after one trip and that they tend to leave it alone after that. Unfortunately though, lacking the epidemiological studies, one really has no way of knowing at all precisely what the pattern of use is. The same is, of course, just as true for all other drugs but such evidence as does exist strongly suggests that nutmeg is not extensively used nor, given its known effects, would one expect it to become so unless other, more preferred, materials become much more difficult to obtain. Even so, Unwin (1968) has reported a spread in the abuse of nutmeg within North American high-school and college campuses, though the reasons why this should have occurred remain unclear.

Banana skins
This is yet another common material to have been exploited for psychedelic properties. And, though it may be astonishing that *any*

such sources should have been found amongst the familiar things in our homes, those mentioned in this book are by no means the only ones. Unlike the case of nutmeg, the drug effects of banana are not produced simply by consuming an excessively large quantity: rather, they require a special preparation. The method is to take the skins of a number of bananas and scrape out the inner layers. The scrapings are dried-out in a slow oven and then smoked in pipes or cigarettes.

Whether the effects created are psychedelic at all, or rather whether the stuff has any intrinsic hallucinogenic properties, has been a matter of some dispute. Bozzetti, Goldsmith and Ungerleider (1967), having looked at the chemical components, have described it as 'the great banana hoax', and agencies concerned with drug abuse and control have also tended to deny that there are any effective chemical attributes – though this line has often been interpreted as a pragmatic policy of reducing interest in a material which could not conceivably be controlled. On the other hand, Lingeman (1970) claims that there *is* evidence to show that constituents of the skin can, through the process of combustion, be converted into known psychedelic chemicals. But, in any case, the reported subjective effects are so mild, even compared with cannabis, that there seems very little likelihood of any widespread or intensive usage.

The search for psychedelic substances goes on and on. Whether one would classify some of the more obscure ones as 'minor' is a moot point for, though they are no doubt minor in the sense of being currently unimportant members of a larger grouping, this situation could change rapidly, and they often have rather major potentials. In fact, the chemistry of many of these substances is such that, if one's classificatory system was to be based on what high doses and widespread use *could* cause, then there is no doubt that most so-called 'minor psychedelics' would have to be regrouped.

A case in point has recently been provided by Kramer and Pierpaoli (1971) in their report on the effect of misusing certain aerosol deodorants. In their paper, they refer to the discovery by two of their patients that recurrence or 'flashback' of previous hallucinogenic trips can be achieved by inhaling deodorant sprays. One girl, a teenager, who since the age of thirteen has been a regular user of a range of drugs from heroin and barbiturates to LSD, and who has supported her drug-taking with prostitution, contrived to discover yet another way of putting her life into jeopardy by inhaling these sprays. At the time the report was written, she was fortunate enough to be still alive and had suffered no more than panic attacks by way of complications but the Freon propellants which accounted for the psychedelic effects have also been known to have lethal outcomes in cases of acute or chronic misuse. The products referred to in this case are not the only types of aerosol which carry these potentials and, no doubt, the quest for psychoactive materials will continue to lead the incautious on into the use of what may appear to them as relatively minor and commonplace domestic materials, only to find that the outcomes may be very much more powerful and dangerous than they had ever imagined.

3 Major Psychedelics

If we still provisionally accept the convention that psychedelics may be grouped into the category of either major or minor, then the principal members of the major group would undoubtedly be mescaline, psilocybin and LSD-25. These three chemicals, though originally deriving from very different sources, are all alkaloids and all create very similar psychological, pharmacological and physiological effects. Indeed, according to Hollister and Hartman (1962), the consequence of injecting any one of these drugs is, clinically speaking, almost identical and so it would seem to make sense to discuss the general aspects of these three drugs first and then distinguish between them.

One might expect that, as their effects on users are so very similar, these drugs would also be chemically very much alike. In reality though, despite the similarity of their action, they do not form part of a single chemical taxonomic group as there are considerable differences in their molecular structures. Instead, they are grouped according to their psychological and somatic effects and thus mescaline, psilocybin, LSD-25, and their congeners and derivatives are commonly classed as 'sympathetomimetic hallucinogens' (Jacobsen, 1968). Of the three, mescaline differs most pronouncedly from the other two in that it alone does not have the indole-ring molecular structure which is characteristic of not only many of the psychedelics but also of serotonin – a naturally occurring neurohumor of considerable importance in mediating the brain's activity. Nevertheless, the chemical similarities between all three are still quite clear and the structure of mescaline itself is closely related to two other important body amines which influence nervous activity – epinephrine and norepinephrine. Schema of these various chemical structures have been conveniently outlined and set beside one another for comparison in Barron, Jarvik, and Bunnell (1964), Cohen (1965) and de Ropp (1958).

And so, right at the outset, it begins to be apparent that despite many obvious similarities which bind different substances together there are also features which divide them. Even in relation to the subjective effects there is a great range in outcomes, not only between the different drugs, but also within the use of a single one. The common characteristics of which we speak are actually very variable and should be thought of as no more than tendencies or frequently reported outcomes. That this should be the case with subjective effects is really not surprising for, if one accepts the uniqueness of an individual's ordinary consciousness, one might also expect there to be a unique quality to his non-normal states of consciousness.

The variability of response at every level, somatic and psychological, seems to be very much related not only to the normal consciousness of the taker and to his personality but, most importantly, to the user's 'set' and 'setting'. This latter point became a key issue in the use of psychedelics for Timothy Leary (1965). From a very early stage in the use of these drugs, Leary was much concerned with publicizing the fact that the entire experience, and the hazards involved, were very much dependent upon the circumstances of use – particularly the perceived motivation of the giver, the personalities and behaviour of the other people present, and the state and expectations of the user.

In fact, it was in part due to Leary's acting-out of the derived principles of administration that he raised so many doubts, created so many enemies, and was finally driven from professional life. His belief was that psychedelic experiences are *always* disturbing and that they are almost always best arranged in a comforting and familiar domestic situation, and preferably in the presence of friends who can give reassurance when the verities on which people base their lives begin to dissolve. His opponents, though often agreeing that the environment affected the experience, held that a formal setting was to be preferred as they felt very unhappy at the informal, involved, and empathetic way in which Dr Leary used these drugs in his researches. But, whatever the pros and cons of that particular case, it is now generally accepted that setting *is* of critical importance in determining outcome.

The same conclusion is also true of 'set', referring as it does to attitudes, dispositions, and motivations brought by the subject to a session. The range of possibilities is, of course, infinite but might be typified by taking, at one extreme, cultivated and mystically minded people like Aldous Huxley who were looking for philosophical and religious inspiration and using psychedelics as a 'sacrament' and, at the other extreme, schoolboy gang-members swallowing assorted illegal tablets outside the local fish-and-chip shop in their search for 'kicks'. Somewhere in this range lies the more average situation but, as we shall see, there are many sub-groups of users and the range is so very great that it would not be wise to generalize about anything too confidently.

The overt and observable signs when a person has taken psychedelics are usually fairly minimal for although the user may early-on complain about nausea, giddiness, and being hot or cold, there is little to be observed at the gross somatic or behavioural level in either man or animal. Jacobsen (1968) reviews some of the research on animals – ranging from pigeons to elephants – but as this naturally reveals nothing about the subjective aspects, the observational findings tend to be of peripheral interest and add very little indeed beyond information on gross toxic or lethal doses. Thus, as human beings produce few observable changes in gross behaviour patterns, and as a death due to an overdose of these drugs has yet to be recorded, human research of a rather subjective type seems likely to remain the most illuminating approach to the study of social and psychological effects.

Studies of animal learning, discriminations, reactions, and emotional expression *are* valuable clues in coming to an understanding of the psychological and pharmacological action of these drugs. But, because they inevitably require a considerable amount of extrapolation and reasoning by analogy to fit the human case, they should not be over-valued as they are *extremely* crude tools for the study of what are essentially subjective, introspective and mental events. The approach certainly has its uses but, sad to say, *so far* analysis of the behavioural responses of a variety of animals under psychedelic drugs has yielded only idiosyncratic results which have little in common.

Certainly the response patterns of most animals can be obviously affected by the administration of these drugs – though generally only when relatively massive concentrations are involved: that is, when the conditions of body chemistry are very dissimilar from those of the 'normal' human usage in which we are interested. Also, in most of these studies, it is hard to avoid the uneasy feeling that the approach is so oblique as to miss the point entirely. Of much greater interest are those animal studies which have been undertaken to establish, not just the effect of a single drug administration, but the *long-term* effects of use on the individual, the foetus *in utero*, and on the genetic materials themselves. These are matters which we shall take up again in chapter 5, when considering the pathological side-effects which these drugs may create.

As has already been mentioned, the grossly observable effects of this group of 'sympathetomimetic hallucinogens' are rather slight, rather variable, and susceptible to wide individual differences. The main effects derive, as the generic classificatory term suggests, from stimulation of the peripheral sympathetic nervous system and typically include increased blood pressure and heart rate as well as pupil dilation and a range of less obvious physical signs such as slightly elevated temperature, changes in the thresholds of simple reflexes and in the electrical activity of the brain (Advisory Committee on Drug Dependence, 1970; Barron, Jarvik and Bunnell, 1964; Jacobsen, 1968). However, the specific mode and site of action of these drugs remains very little understood.

Behavioural and psychological research also has many serious gaps, many of which are due to the embargo on human research. But the deficiencies of the record are not entirely due to the prohibition of further work: some of them derive from the problem of *interpreting* many of the studies which were done. For example, Lienert (1966) gave L S D to sixty-five male and female student volunteers and found that, under the influence of the drug, the subjects performed significantly less well on a series of cognitive and intelligence tests. He concluded that the effect of the drug was to induce a 'mental age regression' – an anxiety-creating appellation for a phenomenon which really only signified what might be expected: that the subjects did less well on rather dull tests when they were also currently involved in profound, intriguing and novel psychological states and experiences. Not, you might think, very surprising!

The general picture is even more confused in that the *results* of this sort of behavioural research are also extremely variable. For example, Mogar (1969) cites three experimental studies which respectively report an enhancement, an impairment, and no change in instrumental learning capacities! As part of the explanation, Mogar refers to the insensitivity of many researchers to the situation and to the subject-determined variables. He particularly draws attention to the fact that there are great differences in outcomes which seem to depend upon whether the *orientation* of the reseach is towards investigating the stress and negative aspects of the experience or the positive and therapeutic ones. Such considerations bring us right back to 'set' and 'setting' and these are undoubtedly a potent source of variability in determining outcomes: so much so that no particular effects appear to be 'drug specific' – rather, all effects tend to be the result of a very general interaction of the drug, personality, set and setting.

The range and variety of the subjective psychedelic experience is, of course, extremely well known and has often been elegantly described in such volumes as those by Aaronson and Osmond (1971), Leary, Metzner, and Alpert (1964), and Masters and Houston (1966). In consequence, it would indeed be an invidious undertaking to try to compress this sort of rich material within the space of so brief a discussion, and especially so as Huxley's short essays *The Doors of Perception* and *Heaven and Hell*, which are published together in a slim paperback, give so excellent an account of experiences which range from the sublime to the nightmarish.

These reports of psychedelic 'trips' are particularly useful in that they underscore the fact that the same drug, under apparently similar conditions, with the same user, is capable of producing the 'transcendental experience', the 'bad trip', and the extreme panic reaction or 'freak-out'. However, determining what constitutes 'similar conditions' is virtually impossible as the psychological environment is never as much under our control, or as obvious, as is the physical. Yet there does seem to be a *fair* degree of stability of reaction within a given individual – with some people almost always having pleasurable and valued experiences whilst others encounter quite the opposite and have predominantly unpleasant reactions. Most regular users, though, seem to tend, over a period, towards some sort of personal balance or admixture of positive and negative effects.

The best known and most prevalent positive effect of the psychedelic drugs is that they radically affect visual perception. Colours, shapes, textures, light, and objects themselves become more arresting: they are transformed in beauty; they compel concentration and meditation and appear to have a reality which they normally lack. The natural creation itself, and even the most mundane of man-made artifacts, may seem possessed of qualities so heady that the individual is overcome by joy, peace and awe. The opposite, too, may be the case and the user may have a 'bad trip' or 'freak-out' – though, happily, this appears to be far less usual. But, whether the trip is good or bad, unusually powerful visual experiences are the rule. Whether the eyes are opened or closed, the effects may be much the same in quality – though closed eyes facilitate a freer range of subjects and more easily lead to visions of patterns, peoples, and places. As we shall see in later chapters, these particular properties are often highly valued by artists and people with developed artistic interests.

In Western culture at least, the experiences which occur are seldom hallucinations in the true sense, because the user is almost invariably aware of the nature of his perceptions; that is, that they are due to drug actions and that the world retains its own 'normality' and 'reality'. Indeed, some users are quite able to control their experiences to some degree and may be able, simply through the act of willing, to return to normal states of consciousness. For an example of this behaviour in a psilocybin session see Clark (1971). It may be possible to retain this control at certain dose levels but, for most people, at the higher doses, it seems that only other drugs like the phenothiazines will terminate the process once started.

The ecstasy often associated with perceptual enhancement frequently seems to be linked with other reactions such as a feeling of religious awareness – often expressed in terms of a sensitivity to the 'meaningfulness' and 'oneness' of all creation. This latter effect is probably also related to two other psychedelic effects – the first being a loss, or more often a loosening, of the perceived ego boundaries; an experience which has an analogue in the changed perception of one's own body. The 'body image' may change so that, for example, limbs may seem infinitely long and capable of embracing distant people, or even of stretching out to embrace the entire planet or heavens. Similarly, the individual may perceive himself as a giant, towering above the earth, or as a microscopic object on a minute planet. Often too there occur 'synesthesias' or experiences in which stimulation of one sense modality may result in a response in another modality also. For example, sounds made by a musical instrument may invoke their own distinctive visual patterns of shape or colour. This merging of perceptions, creating conditions which are so different from the processes of normal egocentric and utilitarian consciousness, is probably a most important element in creating the oceanic feeling which makes the experience so exhilarating.

However, the actual nature of this dissolution is of some interest in itself, with effects varying a great deal from person to person. At one extreme, it may imply an *enhanced* egocentricity because the individual comes to see the outside world as an extension of himself though, at the other, he may experience the more modest feeling of being simply a small facet of a greater whole. This distinction may well be relevant to the types of reaction which then follow: ranging from paranoid delusions of grandeur and omnipotence to total humility and the mystical 'loss of self'. The middle ground probably involves elements of both extremes, but we shall return again later for a closer look at the different types of reaction produced.

Personal will and the conventional rules of conduct are also temporarily suspended in some degree as being irrelevant and the user finds himself committed willy nilly to a series of events – a state which has often been compared with pushing off on a giant helter-skelter. By the same token, this loss of control can evoke terrible fears and anxieties, and quite horrible ideas and visions.

One of the other common effects which may help to potentiate this experience is a changed perception of time such that objectively measured moments may be converted into subjectively vast periods. People have said that, when consulting their watches, the second hand seemed scarcely to move at all and *knowledge* that the experience would terminate in an hour or two was meaningless as that length of objective time was almost unimaginable and unendurable. In fact, a psychiatrist colleague once told me that he experienced this feeling so strongly that he actually briefly considered the idea of suicide in order to end it – a reaction which he also later attributed very much to the dehumanizing laboratory conditions and to the lack of warmth and sympathy in the investigators. Conversely, the changed time perception may, in other cases, bring the user great tranquillity in this experience of 'eternity' due to time having stopped.

Psychedelic drugs are then all things to all men: they may produce terrifying psychotic-like experiences of depersonalization and unreality – feeling or seeing one's body rotting, seeing the skull behind the other person's face, and seeming to whirl downwards through one's own body tissue and molecular materials – or else they may produce beatific feelings and visions with subjectively meaningful, if ineffable, insights. In between these extremes are the mixed experiences; pleasant and unpleasant, of visual and time distortions, alogical and prelogical thought modes mixed in with normal awareness of events and relationships, the synesthesias, and visual pseudo-hallucinations. Whatever else may be said of the experiences resulting from effective amounts of psychedelics they are, as the term describes them, exceedingly 'mind-manifesting'.

The nature of the effects is naturally correlated to some degree with the dosage: relatively small amounts often producing only mild effects and relatively high doses often resulting in more powerful ones. The fact that much of the illegally available material is of unknown quality and potency makes the tracing of cause and effect more difficult but pharmacological analyses and experimental studies suggest that the 'normal dosages' given below are a fair average of what is used. Even so, there is no doubt that, due to ignorance or dishonesty, individuals sometimes take much more or much less of the substances than they realize.

Having looked at the general features of the major psychedelics, it now only remains to give a thumbnail sketch of the individual features of the particular drugs.

LSD-25

Of all the major psychedelic substances, LSD (d-lysergic acid diethylamide tartrate 25) is by far the best known, the most carefully researched, the most often used clinically, the most frequently written about, and the most widely used illegally. It is also the most pharmacologically potent of these substances – doses being calculated in millionth parts of a gram, with an effective amount being between fifty and one hundred of these micrograms (mcg). Almost incredibly, quantities as small as 1/700 millionth of a person's body weight are quite sufficient to project him into the psychedelic experience.

As with other drugs, the taking of larger amounts, or so called 'high doses', is quite common, 250 mcg being not unusual, and still greater amounts are not at all rare. The effect of the 'high dose' is usually to prolong the experience and to make it more intense. Leary (1965) regards the high dose as being necessary to get the direct subjective experience of one's own molecular constitution. Beyond a certain stage, though, the qualitative nature of the experience will change radically. A case is cited in the 1970 White Paper on amphetamines, barbiturates and cannabis of a man who on successive days doubled up his dosage until, on the fifth day, he was taking 4000 mcg and began to display such transient symptoms as slurred speech and general incoordination. However, this pattern is extremely rare as psychological tolerance builds up very rapidly and there is little incentive to perform such experiments. In itself, because the drug has so low a toxicity in man, such overdosing is not regarded as being particularly dangerous: it is just pointless and reckless.

The astonishing thing about LSD-25 is that such microscopic amounts of the chemical can so rapidly affect a person's entire relationship to the world and turn upside-down the learning and habits of a lifetime. Indeed, it is because the amounts involved are so minute that the properties of the drug were discovered at all. The drug itself, the twenty-fifth in a series of laboratory syntheses of chemicals derived from ergot, the rhizomorph of the fungus *Claviceps purpurea*, was first produced by Stoll and Hofmann in 1938 but it was not until Hofmann accidentally inhaled some of this material in his laboratory in 1943, and found himself caught up in a full-scale psychedelic experience, that the psychological effects of the drug were realized. Subsequently, because the nature of these mental changes suggested psychosis, the drug was widely evaluated both as a biochemical clue to the cause of schizophrenia and as a potentially powerful therapeutic drug for all types of mental disturbance. We shall be returning to the psychopathological and therapeutic implications in later chapters.

One of the most surprising things about LSD-25 is how it became the most easily available of all the major psychedelics and the principal material of the so-called psychedelic cult. It is though, despite its pre-eminence due to availability, only one of very many such chemicals and, as is pointed out in the 1970 White Paper on Amphetamines and LSD, there are at least another hundred similarly acting materials, many of which are capable of being manufactured with comparative ease. But LSD now has a powerful lead amongst the affectionados and the mass demand has, on occasion, even led to gluts: for example, recently the cost of LSD tablets fell in Glasgow and some other cities from an average of £1.50 to £2 to about 30p. This is amazing when compared with the prices quoted by Lingeman (1970) of $2.50 to $10 as pertaining in America in 1967. Most of our own supplies are usually held by the users to derive from America, though Lingeman, writing in America, cites Canada, England and other countries as their prime sources of illegal supplies! The point is however that the drug is widely manufactured illegally and becoming ever more available and, because of its minute size and relative ease of manufacture, is likely to become more so. To give some idea of the small bulk involved, it would only require 3 ozs of the drug to provide effective doses for every man woman, and child in a city the size of Glasgow!

The form of the drug is dependent upon its source. The usual laboratory form comes in 100 mcg ampoules ready for injection – generally into animals. The illegal variety is usually in pill form though very occasionally it may be in powder or liquid form. Injection appears to be very rare amongst users, though drug-addicts may prefer this method if they bother to use LSD at all. Treated sugar-cubes are also very rare, having given way to very professional looking tablets or capsules. The contents naturally vary with the supplier and his honesty: 250 and 500 mcg amounts are commonly stated but, because police seizures are rare and the chemical assays on the seized materials are seldom published, it is difficult to be certain about the actual potencies. Neverthe-less, they must generally equal or exceed the fully effective dose of about 100 mcg as there is little evidence from users of the circulation of ineffective or weakened materials.

The drug itself is colourless, tasteless, and odourless but comes in a variety of coloured and slightly flavoured tabloid forms suggestive of distinctions which, pharmacologically speaking, do not exist. Thus users speak warmly of 'purple haze', 'Amsterdam greens', 'orange flash', etc., as though they gave different, and more or less good, effects. If subjectively different effects *do* occur, this is presumably only due to suggestion, to the amount of LSD that is being put into the tablets, or else to a combination of the two.

The non-scientific and non-therapeutic methods of taking the drug are, of course, immensely variable, but one way is for a small number of people to gather in a dimly lit room with a background of music of their choice and to sit in a circle, perhaps with a candle or some other visually stimulating object in the middle, and to take their LSD together as a group. As any user will tell you, it is a much more hazardous and potentially unpleasant experience to take these drugs alone. Many groups also safe-guard themselves by having one member remain off the drug. This individual, who is called the 'guide' or 'ground control', can watch over and reassure people who might otherwise panic or take risks during a euphoric or unpleasant trip. And, if the group is fairly drug-sophisticated, the guide may even have a supply of one of the LSD inhibitors, perhaps a powerful tranquillizer such as chlorpromazine, in order to terminate a 'bad trip'.

The course of the LSD experience is much the same as that of the other psychedelics: often rather uncomfortable in the first place due to feelings of anxiety or nausea and a general sympathetic nervous system over-activity. This first stage lasts for perhaps anything up to an hour and is followed by a typically six- to twelve-hour period of the psychedelic experience proper. The duration of florid psychological effects is, as always with these drugs, quite variable but surprisingly long when one considers that only 0·01 per cent of the original tiny amount of drug passes the blood–brain barrier to come into direct contact with the brain. And even this microscopic quantity only remains in the brain tissues for a period of about twenty minutes and then is only detectable in the blood, using the most sensitive techniques, for a period of about two hours. It is therefore often assumed that LSD must act as a 'trigger' to activate more lasting effects in the body's own chemistry. Unfortunately though, there is little definite knowledge about the way in which LSD works, despite the excellent summary of research and derived hypotheses by Hoffer and Osmond (1967). Alas, even the most sensitive techniques of chemical detection cannot trace the progress of LSD and its metabolites in the body. The range of biochemical transformations involved is so complex that we shall probably have to wait a long time before a complete technical account can be compiled.

The latter part of the psychedelic experience typically comes in waves, between periods of more or less normal consciousness. The periods of normality grow progressively longer until the experience fades, leaving behind a feeling of tiredness and relaxation. But one further psychological hazard remains – the possibility of a spontaneous recurrence of the experience during any time up to a year or eighteen months later. In fact, a psychiatrist acquaintance, who had taken LSD some years previously as part of an experimental programme, and had enjoyed a particularly pleasant euphoric experience, told me that he can (and does) still sometimes voluntarily re-evoke this mode of perception even after nearly a decade. But it is the *involuntary* recurrence of frightening, grandiose, or paranoid feelings which is a matter of especial concern and this, together with other pathological conditions, will be the subject of much more detailed treatment in chapter 5.

Mescaline

In many respects, mescaline may be seen as the archetypal psychedelic substance of Western culture. Whether its use actually antedates that of the other major psychedelics will never be known because of the lack of written records before the Spaniards went to Mexico. But there they found well-established psychedelic drug usages amongst the Aztec with 'peyotl' employed as an important 'divine substance' (de Ropp, 1958). This was not though, as was for so long believed, the 'teonanactl' or 'flesh c̃ the gods' used so spectacularly at Montezuma's feasts and sacrifices. That has now, by a most fascinating process of linguistic and ethnobotanical research, been shown by Schultes (1940) to have been the mushroom *Paneolus campanulatus* L var. *sphinctrinus* – which is still in use amongst the remnants of the Aztec empire: in Mexican Indian tribes like the Mazatec, Chinantec, and Zapotec.

Peyotl was the name for a small desert cactus now known as the peyote cactus or, more technically, as *Lophophora williamsii*. This small member of the *Cactaceae* family grows in the arid northern regions of Mexico and, despite its astonishingly powerful effects on the human mind, rises only about three inches above the ground, is spineless, of a rather dull greyish-brown colour, and contrives to be completely insignificant. The cactus top is used for psychedelic purposes by slicing it into discs which are then dried and become peyote or mescal 'buttons' to be consumed later. The name 'mescaline' arose from its widespread use by the Mescalero Apaches, through whom it spread to very many other North American Indians (la Barre, 1938).

But, in fact, mescaline now also has a more restricted pharmacological meaning – referring to one only of the many (at least fifteen) active alkaloids derived from the cactus – and is nowadays most usually synthesized directly in the laboratory. The array of psychoactive substances contained in the peyote cactus itself results in a very complex and variable psychological experience and Schultes (1969a) has drawn attention to the unfortunate mistake, often made in the literature, of confusing the plant effects with those of the pure alkaloid. In fact, apart from the members of the Native American Church (see page 198), the use of both peyote and mescaline has not, in the past, been particularly common. But accounts of their effects by such gifted writers as Aldous Huxley, Havelock Ellis, and Carlos Castenada have done much to establish them as important substances in the lore of the psychedelic sub-culture.

Peyote is taken in the form of a number of 'buttons' which are either chewed and swallowed in dry form, or else infused to make tea. The taste and smell is apparently foul and vomiting and nausea is common. Williams (1967) describes, on the basis of American police experience, many other ways of taking it – most often in milk, tea, or coffee to neutralize the taste, though also as a brownish-grey liquid in ampoule form prepared for injection. By contrast, pure mescaline, in the form of a crystalline powder which is then either swallowed as a capsule or dissolved in a liquid, is a much more agreeable substance and is thus much more widely favoured.

About 500 milligrams (mg) of the pure chemical would constitute an average dose for an adult: that is to say, a quantity sufficient to produce the full psychedelic response. The onset of effects usually occurs within one to three hours and lasts for between four and twelve hours – sometimes longer, though this is unusual. The experience may be terminated chemically by the use of one of the major tranquillizers such as chlorpromazine though the effects may also be reduced by a very wide range of other transquillizing agents, sedatives, and anti-tension compounds (Hoffer and Osmond, 1967).

Despite the relative rarity of this drug, it does seem to be available in the larger cities of the United Kingdom and one has come across many young people who believe themselves to have used it. Unfortunately, there is no way of knowing for sure exactly what they have bought and used and the investigator obviously cannot compound the felony by asking the users to buy more just so that the material can be analysed for scientific purposes.

But, given the luxuriant visual effects which mescaline certainly creates, and the enthusiastic publicity it continues to receive from Huxley's still widely read *The Doors of Perception*, one might expect that supply will meet the demand and that the drug will become more common. This, of course, always presupposes that the users are knowledgeable enough to tell the difference between this and L S D on a basis other than the tablet's appearance, which is so easily varied.

Psilocybin

Like mescaline, psilocybin has also come to us from Mexico: this time in the form of an active alkaloid found occurring naturally in the mushroom *Psilocybe mexicana*. As with mescaline, psilocybin too was used by the Aztecs as part of their religious ceremonies. The parallel continues in that these 'sacred mushrooms' have also survived in a native tradition up until the present time in order to yield up the secrets of their chemical nature so that large quantities of pure materials could then be synthesized in the laboratory for a wider range of use. In 1958 Albert Hofmann, who had earlier synthesized L S D-25, isolated the active principle, psilocybin, from *P. mexicana*. This drug, chemically extremely similar to L S D-25, was also found to exist in several other members of the psilocybe species. However, synthetic forms manufactured in laboratories now account for most of the psilocybin used in technically advanced societies.

Weight for weight, psilocybin is more potent than mescaline: Hofmann's laboratory establishing that the effective dose for an adult is in the order of about 6 to 12 mg though doses of 25 to 50 mg are quite usual for both experimental use and for 'tripping'. Fortunately, though, psilocybin is relatively non-toxic for man and so higher doses of this substance, like most other psychedelics, are generally tolerated. But Hoffer and Osmond (1967) point out that the same may not be true of long-term users and they present some evidence which indicates that chronic use of psilocybin may be more hazardous than is apparently the case with L S D-25.

The experiences created under experimental conditions with psilocybin are, according to Isbell (1959), similar to those of

LSD-25, the first half-hour being rather unpleasant and typified by dizziness, nausea and anxiety; the second half-hour by further somatic effects such as sweating and ataxia, together with impaired cognitive control of thought and attention but with increased visual and auditory sensitivity. The following four to twelve hours contain the usual euphoric and psychedelic elements but these are followed by a quiescent period which is typified by feelings of lassitude, fatigue and headache – this 'hangover' element being unusual in LSD.

Some other major psychedelics

This grouping contains some still relatively rare substances which, though occasionally available, are still outside the experience of the average psychedelic drug-user. However, in our own researches into the epidemiology of drug abuse amongst young people, we have found that the scene can change with astonishing rapidity as consignments of drugs arrive in the market places, or as sources of supply become established or disappear. It would therefore be unwise to leave this section without at least a passing reference to some of the other interesting and potentially significant materials of tomorrow.

Of these, DMT – dimethyltriptamine – is probably one of the strongest contenders because it has such a short-term psychological effect. This drug, which has been dubbed 'the businessman's lunchtime high' (Lingeman, 1970) has an effective duration of only about half an hour and gives an experience similar to, but milder than, LSD (Unwin, 1968). It is a semi-synthetic chemical of similar structure to psilocin and psilocybin – of the indole-ring structure type – and also occurs naturally in certain plants. Apart from the attraction of its short duration, it can also be easily synthezised and is therefore doubly likely to find an increasing place in illegal use. It is usually prepared in liquid form – into which is dipped parsley, tobacco, or marijuana – and then the mixture is smoked in a pipe or cigarette. One drawback to this drug is that the rapid onset of both the autonomic and psychedelic effects may produce such a shock and feeling of loss of control as to produce a panic reaction.

Another potentially very disturbing material is STP – the

common name for 4-methyl-2, 5-dimethoxy-alpha-methylphen-ethylamine, a synthetic and naturally occurring chemical related to both mescaline and the amphetamines. One can understand the need for a shorter name, though its etymology is not exactly clear. One theory is that STP was a title given by some of the early users in motor-cycle gangs and that the initials derive from the favoured 'Scientifically Treated Petroleum'. Another theory links the initials with Timothy Leary and his injunction to seek 'Serenity, Tranquillity, and Peace'. Whatever the truth of the matter, the former explanation is nearer to the reality of the effects as the experience is usually far from serene and, according to users, most closely resembles the imagined effects of taking rocket fuel! The surge of uncontrolled psychic energy and the accompanying perceptual distortions are often terrifying – especially for those who attempt to resist rather than go with the experience. The chances of having a 'bad trip' with STP seem to be much greater than with any of the other more generally known psychedelics.

STP, or DOM as it is also called, is certainly a very potent hallucinogenic substance. Indeed, it has been dubbed a 'mega-hallucinogen' and, unfortunately, this very power is likely to be an attraction rather than a deterrent for many. But the risks are very real – at the least one might have to face four to five days of horror with a bad trip as STP is a very long-acting drug. There have also been reported fatalities due to respiratory failure and convulsions (Unwin, 1968), and the effect of well-meant medication, employing the usual psychedelic inhibitors such as the phenothiazines, has been known to be disastrous in the hands of both medical and untrained helpers. Several of the antidotes to LSD actually intensify the toxic symptoms of STP – a dangerous situation as it is often difficult to know just what drugs an illegal user has taken. The risks of severe psychotic reaction are also greater with this drug and it is very much to be hoped that this particular substance remains as one of the rarer varieties.

Another psychedelic substance which one would hope not to see being widely used is the mushroom fly agaric, scientifically known as *Amanita muscaria*, commonly named after its one-time use as a fly poison. Metzner (1971) has described it as still in use amongst certain Siberian tribes amongst whom it is traditional to ingest both the mushroom itself and also the urine passed by themselves and others who have taken it. This latter practice is not, as might be supposed, the result of aberrations following the use of the drug but so that the psychoactive ingredients which are excreted with little loss of potency can be re-ingested and the experience considerably extended or shared amongst many.

The mushroom itself is familiar enough in Europe as the white-spotted, red-topped, toadstool of children's illustrated books – though the American variations are lighter coloured. Amongst the active principles are muscarine, atropine, and bufotenine – the latter being chemically very similar to psilocybin and D M T and thus presumed to play some psychedelic role. It is interesting to note that bufotenine occurs in the skin of the toad – that ubiquitous materia medica of the witch, a circumstance which perhaps suggests a new perspective on accounts of flying, performing miracles, and seeing devils! However, bufotenine only occurs in amanita in very minute concentrations and it may be that the psychedelic results are due mainly to the presence of muscinole, certain amino acids, and the interaction of a host of other constituents, many of which have still to be determined (Schultes, 1969a).

The effect of this combination of drugs is to induce sweating, nausea, and much reduced cardiac rate, as well as a range of other unpleasant digestive and vegetative changes. In sufficient quantity, the heart will cease completely and the user will die (Wakefield, 1958). Mood changes include euphoria, feelings of omnipotence, and perhaps also powerful feelings of persecution and aggression. Visions and perceptual changes of the sort already discussed are usual and there is an interesting parallel between the subjective response to fly agaric amongst the Siberian Indians and to *Psilocybe mexicana* amongst the Mexican Indians: the relationship is particularly close with respect to the mystical and religious components (Wasson and Wasson, 1957).

At the present time modern re-discoverers of witchcraft are again also re-discovering this ancient component of magical brews, and traveller-writers like Jeremy Sandford (1972) are revealing more of the use and preparation of these materials.

Happily though, the use of fly agaric is currently very limited indeed but because it has played, or as we shall see later has been thought to play, so important a part in our cultural evolution, it will also receive further consideration in other chapters. However, the point should be very firmly underscored for anyone who may feel the impulse to experiment – this is a most dangerous drug, of very variable outcome, and should never be taken in any form.

The range of psychedelic drugs is infinitely greater than might be obvious from what has been said so far. Many of the materials described by such writers as Schultes (1969 a, b and c; 1970), though of considerable pharmacological and anthropological interest, cannot justify inclusion in this present work as they are not known within our own culture pattern – neither have they ever influenced it nor, so far as at present seems likely, does it appear that they ever will. There are also other psychedelic drugs which, though they are of contemporary interest, have been excluded because their usage is still very much restricted to the spheres of research or medicine. One is thinking here particularly of substances such as I T-290 or J B-329 (described by Hoffer and Osmond, 1967), or the range of belladonna alkaloids described by Leff and Bernstein (1968) which occur in certain proprietary medicines. Additionally, there are always the outlandish, and more or less potent, materials that have found high favour in some localities at one time or another – things like jimson-weed and rotting green peppers. But, despite the vast range of substances – from the exceedingly rare and exotic to the fairly common – it is still cannabis and LSD-25 which exert by far the greatest influence in psychedelic activities. Thus it is they that will inevitably bulk largest in our discussions.

4 Therapeutic Applications

One of the things which is often forgotten when discussing the psychedelics is that they have a therapeutic role as well as a social one and that, over the years, they have achieved a considerable reputation in some circles. That these properties should be overlooked is not particularly surprising as, in popular media terms, sober clinical use is so much less dramatic than drug abuse and cultic goings-on. There is also the fact that the psychedelics have often been referred to as 'psychotomimetic' or psychosis-mimicking, and are thus most closely identified with the *creation* of illness. Indeed, it may seem to be a paradox that the same drugs which can simulate major psychiatric disturbances may also be used to treat them.

But, paradox or not, psychedelic substances have been in the pharmacopoeia for a very long time now, stretching back through the milleniums to classical China. Unfortunately though, we know all too little of these medical practices of ancient times, and have few very complete accounts until the present – though we do know that cannabis has a venerable medical history in the Middle East and Far East, in India and Africa. Part of this history is chronicled by Shri Dwarakanath (1965), Indian Government Advisor on Indigenous Systems of Medicine, in his review of the place of cannabis (and opium) in the traditional systems of medicine in India. Both of the two prevalent systems, the Ayurveda and Unani Tibbi, have included cannabis as a therapeutic agent for many centuries: the authoritative eighth-century Ayurvedic work on materia medica, the *Dhanwantari Nighantu*, summarizing its properties, actions, and indications. Although the Unani Tibbi system did not arrive *in India* until the ninth century when it was imported by the Muslims, the use of cannabis in the system antedated that time. Indeed, it was derived from Greek sources, Dioscorides having summarized the therapeutic applications of cannabis as early as the first century AD In India itself, though, Dwarakanath traces back usage in folk medicine to a period somewhere between the third and fourth centuries B.C.

But the use of cannabis in the medicine of India is not just a matter of history: it is very much a part of the present scene. Dwarakanath points out that 80 per cent of the population of India live in villages – some 500,000 of them – and that most of these are served by at least one of the 116,865 Ayurvedic physicians or Unani hakims. Of this number, only 30,000 are institutionally qualified and permitted to prescribe the materia medica of scientific medicine and so, if one banned the use of cannabis and opium by these practitioners, a very serious vacuum in medical treatment would occur. As it is, cannabis continues to be used in the treatment of enteritis, dysentery, neuritis, rheumatism and neuralgia, as well as being used as a hypnotic and antispasmodic.

In the West, cannabis did not become widely used until the period 1840 to 1900 when more than a hundred articles were published on its therapeutic value. At this time, pioneers like W. B. O'Shaugnessy and R. R. M'meens tested and experimented with tinctures of cannabis and reported that they found it an excellent medicament for muscular tensions, spasms, and pain – in fact, a whole range of analgesic uses, as well as for such respiratory conditions as chronic bronchitis and asthma.

Others, too, reported similar successes and some of these also referred to its value in the treatment of a range of psychological conditions – including insomnia, migraine, and withdrawal from drug addiction. Despite its successes in medicine, its popularity began to wane in the face of competition from other drugs and the newly introduced hypodermic syringe. Unlike cannabis, the opiates are suitable for injection and thus their effect is more immediate and potent. And, though it was quite early realized that the newer drugs were potentially much more dangerous than cannabis, their more powerful and predictable effect made them more attractive for medicinal use. Declining clinical application, coupled with growing anxieties about its misuse in the form of marijuana, resulted, in 1941, in cannabis being removed from the American Pharmacopoeia and its becoming a prime target in narcotics control.

Grinspoon (1971) is somewhat cynical about many contemporary assessments of the therapeutic value of cannabis and points out that conclusions to the effect that the drug has no *known* medical use are made by a generation which has had no experience of its medical usage and which has chosen, arbitrarily, to ignore the work of previous generations. Yet such evidence as does exist suggests that the therapeutic qualities are well worth investigating and recent work indicates that it may have considerable value as an adjunct to psychotherapy in relieving anxiety and depression, and as an analgesic and specific for hypertension. In spite of all its popular associations, it seems that some of its many derivatives may still have a worthwhile therapeutic potential.

Taking the historical and ethnological viewpoint with the major psychedelics unfortunately leads to the omission of our most prevalent form – LSD-25 – which, being a product of the research laboratory, has a story that has hardly yet begun. However, this perspective *was* taken by Schultes (1940) with LSD's close cousin when he reviewed the aboriginal therapeutic uses of the peyote cactus and its active principle, mescaline.

According to Schultes, the prime importance of peyote in the culture of the North American Indian actually relates to its curative properties – both spiritual and bodily: its reputation as a medicine being so powerful as to replace many of the earlier herbal remedies. He wrote, 'Peyote is, without any doubt, the most important medicine used among the North American Indians at the present time.' The list of tribes and peoples, from the Aztecs on, who have found mescaline to be a valuable therapeutic is vast – but then so is the list of uses for which it is specified.

The conditions for which it is used vary from tribe to tribe but the full tally compares favourably with even the most lavishly promoted panacea or nostrum. The list includes tuberculosis, venereal diseases, influenza, diabetes, skin complaints, scarlet fever, rheumatism, wounds, bites, spasms, childbirth, etc. Some Mexican Indians attribute their robust health and long life to its regular use and it is also valued as a prophylactic against the effect of spells. As Schultes himself remarked, even with its extremely complex chemical structure, peyote could hardly have the therapeutic range claimed for it – though there is no doubt that great numbers of Indians have absolute faith in its powers. Their faith is not without some degree of scientific verification however; some of the constituent alkaloids do enjoy a modest degree of use in modern medicine in the treatment of angina and asthma, and as an analgesic. As in the case of cannabis, though the original claims may well be very much exaggerated, there is still room to argue that the derivatives of peyote may have some potential in contemporary therapeutics.

Use with alcoholics

One of the spheres in which the psychedelics have for some time been thought to be an important therapeutic agent is that of alcoholism. Students of the affairs of the North American Indian have often commented on how the use of peyote (mescaline) appears to be inimical to the excessive use of alcohol. Slotkin (1956) observes that, taking the evidence on this over many decades, peyote may be an effective aid to solving the problems which are responsible for leading people to excessive drinking in the first place. He also observes that many former alcoholics have been profoundly and positively changed by the use of peyote and, in many cases, have risen to become community leaders.

Of course, peyote is used by the Indians within a religious context and, as William James (1902) noted long ago, 'the cure of dipsomania is religiomania' – a point which Savage (1964) takes up to show how significant the religious motive, as opposed to the pharmaceutical agent, may be. In other words, the excessive use of alcohol is often caused by a terrible feeling of alienation and the emptiness of existence. Alcohol may help for a while but it is a weak medium and any advantages may be more than offset by the intoxication, social failure, addiction, and the consequent loss of self-respect. People who abuse alcohol are often seeking a meaning to life and, as James notes, even alcohol sometimes has the capacity to stimulate mystical faculties and thus form the basis for a more satisfying philosophy. But, given another substance which much more adequately helps to fulfil the visions and to give some sense of unity and meaning, the stimulus to using alcohol may be discarded and new adjustments made. This is one line of interpretation.

Another was developed in 1952 by Hoffer and Osmond (Hoffer, 1971; Osmond 1957), two psychiatrists working in Saskatchewan, who became particularly interested in the notion of using LSD in the treatment of alcoholism. They were especially interested in the observation that when the alcoholic 'hits bottom' with delirium tremens he seems most ready to come back up. The psychedelic drugs, with their intense hallucinogenic qualities, seemed an excellent way of simulating some of the properties of the DTs and thus of bringing the alcoholic rapidly to the stage where he might be ready for reconstructive therapy. In fact, by no means all patients did have a hallucinatory reaction, though experiences were profound in other ways. Nevertheless, of the nearly one thousand patients so treated in Saskatchewan, about 50 per cent recovered or evidenced a very much reduced drinking – a recovery rate which Hoffer says 'seems to be a universal statistic for LSD therapy'.

But Hoffer and Osmond do stress that LSD therapy is not just a matter of creating a reaction: rather it is a preparation for further supportive therapy – especially of the sort provided by Alcoholics Anonymous. As Hoffer summarized it, the aims of LSD treatment are particularly to liberate repressed memories and to create a new learning situation in which the newly discovered strengths and capacities can be harnessed to the development of personal responsibility. This point is emphasized by Savage (1964) who, whilst distinguishing LSD therapy from conventional psychotherapy in that it concentrates upon the individual's inner reserves and assets rather than his weaknesses, stresses that the patient's insights must be coupled with *strength* to adjust – energy deriving either from within, or from the therapist or group. As personal reserves are generally low, lack of external support may result in failure of the therapy and perhaps an intensified sense of guilt and alienation.

The problem of alcoholism is without doubt a very major one in psychopathology: Cohen (1965) puts the figure for the United States alone at a staggering five million. Of these, only 4 per cent will recover without treatment and although Alcoholics Anonymous exceed a 50 per cent recovery rate, they are drawing from a selected population with a necessarily limited catchment: most people receive no such support. The scale of the personal and social problems involved is vast and so *any* hopeful avenue of therapy is eagerly to be sought. In his review Cohen finds that, despite the problems of inadequate follow-up evaluations, the results of using LSD seem to be quite good over longish periods.

In fact, amongst therapists who have had experience of LSD, the one condition which seems to be universally accepted as a positive indication for use is alcoholism. Indeed, Freedman (1968) felt that 'the egocentric problems of the alcoholic may be specifically tailored for this ego-dissolving, ego-building, technique'. And, curiously enough, even given fundamentally different regimes of treatment, the outcomes still manage to be surprisingly favourable. Of course, some reports are less encouraging than others, but as Hoffer (1971) points out, some of the investigative studies supply less than optimal resources for solving the alcoholic's problem. As an example he cites a study by Smart *et al.* (1966) in which it appeared that no psychotherapy or support was provided and that the ten alcoholic subjects were strapped to the bed and given massive drug doses. Even so, the patients so treated did not differ in outcome from another group given more conventional drug therapy. This study is sometimes quoted as showing that LSD is not an exceptionally useful medicine for the treatment of alcoholism yet it could equally be argued that, given the conditions of the study, it worked remarkably well.

In another rather melancholy set of circumstances, Dally (1967) describes the treatment of a forty-two-year-old alcoholic businessman who was given, over a four-day period, increasing doses of LSD coupled with the emetic apomorphine. He responded not only with sickness, but also with considerable anxiety, tearfulness, and paranoid feeling. Four years after this he was still teetotal! Yet purely experimental work, like that of Cheek and Holstein (1971) which was simply concerned with assessing the effect of LSD on social interaction, may produce therapeutic results. In this case, five of their eight alcoholic subjects were still sober one year later – which would be very encouraging even if they had been receiving intensive therapy. Such cases certainly underline the robustness of LSD as an antidote to alcoholism and, if it can be successful in contexts such as these, it makes one wonder about its upper potential when used in optimal conditions.

Modes of use

As Hoffer observes, there is a distinction to be made between psychedelic *treatment* and simply inducing a psychedelic *reaction* – even if this also may sometimes have beneficial results. Most therapists who favour the use of psychedelic drugs place enormous stress upon producing an appropriately supportive preparation, setting, and follow-up but some, like Dally, take a very different line and recommend that amphetamine be given on the night before an LSD session – to ensure that the patient has a sleepless night in order to ruminate over his problems and then comes to the treatment session in an anxious and suggestible state of mind. Dally underlines the hazards of the treatment as being depression or precipitated suicide, and gives information on means of terminating the sessions themselves, though nowhere is there any guidance as to the psychological safeguards required.

In view of the many different ways in which the drug is used it is obvious that any assessment of value should be made within the context of the circumstances of use: it would be absurd to try to evaluate it as some sort of wonder-drug which at a swallow could permanently cure long-standing sources of maladjustment. There have been some dramatic results, but most people are not misled by these into seeing LSD as anything more than one element in a complex pattern – however important this element might be. As Savage *et al.* (1969) comment, drugs like LSD are not specific agents: they simply open up the patient for therapy and the results obtained will depend upon whether the therapy was good or bad. Only by bearing this in mind can the literature be properly approached.

The basic rationale behind using psychedelic drugs in psychiatric treatment is now fairly widely agreed. It is accepted that the effect of psychedelics like LSD is, so to speak, temporarily to put the individual back into the crucible – to melt down existing forms and allow much that is otherwise contained deep in the interior to float to the surface, to reveal new possibilities, and to render the patient malleable enough for restructuring. Not only psychoanalysts of various persuasions but also psychologists and psychiatrists of very wide ranging orientation are agreed about the importance of the unconscious in determining one's mode, and one's success, in adjusting to the world. One of the properties of LSD seems to be that it reduces tension and dissolves the defences and reserves which are normally concerned with maintaining the social face which we present.

Many of our most powerful memories and sources of guilt and fear are locked away deep within us, corroding the very fabric of our social and psychological lives. Many forms of psychotherapy are theoretically very concerned with penetrating these defences to reveal the sources of malfunction but this is an extremely time consuming, and therefore often an impractical, undertaking. LSD is felt by many therapists to achieve these ends not only with great economy but also very effectively.

In the state of psychological flux which is created by LSD, it is possible to evoke even the earliest memories: Johnsen (1964) refers to being able to return to the first six months of life, and opening the way back through childhood to allow one to search for the sources of damaging conflicts and psychological maladjustments. At this stage, conflicts and the facing of repressed material may be resolved through the patient abreacting, or dissipating his emotional tension, in the face of the original causes. Furthermore, this opening up of the individual's psyche is also held to be associated with a plasticity during which the learning of more healthy or realistic reactions, attitudes, and values may take place.

Which of these aspects are the therapeutically more important is a matter of opinion: some therapists place the greater emphasis on the dissipation of anxiety through abreaction whilst others stress the patient's new vision, or else his increased potential for re-learning through the therapist or the therapeutic group. Consequently, the precise course of the therapy will depend upon the therapist and upon his orientation and aims – as well as the way in which he chooses to use L S D. Broadly speaking, it is possible to distinguish at least three main ways in which the drugs may be used at the tactical level: these having been admirably summarized by Levine (1969), using the fairly standard terminology of *psycholytic*, *psychedelic*, and *hypnodelic* therapy.

Psycholytic therapy is typified by the use of a number of sessions using fairly low doses of L S D – in the range of perhaps 100 to 150 mcg and used with either individuals or groups. Its use dates back to the very earliest therapeutic work with Busch and Johnson (1950) and has as its main objective the dissolving of defences and opening up of the individual as a preliminary to conventional psychotherapeutic methods. The more intense phase of the drug effects would normally take place privately, though under supervision, and give the patient the opportunity to abreact to, and exorcise, repressed material. Then, as the effects wane, the patients would typically be brought together with their therapist, and perhaps also with other patients, in sessions where the experiences are evaluated and new modes of adjustment are worked out.

Psychedelic therapy, in its more technical sense, refers to the formulation pioneered and described by Osmond and Hoffer (1967). It is a high-dose treatment, of the range 300 to 600 mcg, which is specifically aimed at attaining rapid personality change by means of an extremely powerful transcendental experience. This sort of treatment is typified by either a single treatment, or else a very few, coming at the mid-point in intensive psychotherapy. Alcoholics are well suited to this type of treatment which, as already discussed, may simulate for them 'hitting bottom' – with all its consequent frightening insights and stimulus to change.

Hypnodelic therapy, introduced by Levine *et al.* (1963, 1967), is a most interesting further technical development. It differs from the other forms in that, as its name makes obvious, it involves hypnosis as well as drug use. The method involves hypnotizing the patient before the L S D session in order to be able to guide the course of events in such a way as to maximize the therapeutic effects. One can see that, apart from taking advantage of the heightened suggestibility and plasticity created by the psychedelic effects, much time can be saved by leading the patient in a purposeful way through associations and memories in the direction of his problems and conflicts.

However, hypnodelic therapy is not a form which has been widely used: no doubt the combination of two such unorthodox elements would make all but the most independent-minded feel rather vulnerable. Yet orthodoxy is the last thing one would expect to find in the treatment methods of most of the practitioners who use psychedelic drugs, the very process involved in the creation of appropriate set and setting tending to affect conventions radically. For example, the typical non-psychedelic individual psychiatric session tends to be conducted rather like a business transaction – something like an anxious customer being summoned to the bank manager's office. In both the therapeutic and commercial situations the designated individual is brought before an authority figure to explain his behaviour and to give assurances of cooperation and change. The one person sits, on home ground, behind a large desk covered with the symbols of authority – whether these are as humble as a telephone or stethoscope – and almost certainly with portentious notes referring to the resources and inadequacies of the individual seated before him. This latter person, in alien circumstances, must try to make the best impression he can and try to comply with the suggestions that are made to him. The two individuals, though unequally matched, meet like gladiators in a confrontation devised so that the stronger may dominate the other and restore regularity to the system.

By contrast, psychedelic sessions tend to be arranged in most carefully considered settings, it being regarded as axiomatic that environmental context will play an important part in the powerful experiences which are evoked by this type of psychological intervention. This ideal was expressed by Sherwood, Stolaroff, and Harman (1962) who recommended the use of tasteful rooms with music and works of art as aids to creating an optimally impressive new view of the world and as a guide to establishing more satisfying value systems. Alnaes (1964) goes beyond this in additionally recommending pictures, flowers, and candles as powerful symbols of Jung's postulated archetypal and universal forms – realities which are held to be the common substrate of all human thoughts and feelings. The symbols and the setting are then, in this instance, conceived of as parts of a bridge which will link the previous conception of the ego with the transformed one which replaces it after the ego-loss experience of the psychedelic session. In addition, symbols like candles, flowers and images may be recognized as being no more than *symbols* of a deeper reality and the patient may thus be led to apprehend a world which is more significant than the individual objects which compose it.

Not all therapists would agree with Alnaes's conceptualization of the process, but a great number of them have discovered the practical value of attractive and relaxing surroundings. This whole question of 'set' and 'setting' has been discussed elsewhere and it seems true to say that the importance of these conditions is at least as great for the mentally disturbed as for those who are not. But the whole notion carries with it rather radical implications for the treatment relationship: doctors may no longer remain the institutional figure behind a desk, directing medication and lecturing the patient. Instead, they are called upon to participate in the creation of non-institutional roles and environments which stress the uniqueness and integrity of the person being treated. Of course, this involves not only more time than many therapists feel they can spare but also the setting aside of status roles and the subject–object relationship which pertains in most medical situations. Such treatment is therefore, quite naturally, seen as being intensely threatening by those with well-established orthodox views.

Use by the therapist
Even more threatening is that many, if not most, of the proponents of the psychedelics have themselves taken these drugs – sometimes in company with their patients. That most of the therapists who have used L S D on their patients have also taken it themselves has long been a source of considerable criticism as it has been argued that, having been exposed to the psychedelic experience, one can no longer be an *objective* observer and so any subsequent conclusions about its therapeutic values must be contaminated. This line of criticism is not worth countering as it so

obviously covers other motives, but the case of the therapist who takes LSD with his patients is quite another matter. Blewett (1971) discusses this issue at some length and notes that, in low doses, it may help the therapist–patient relationship in the same way as it does the patient–patient one in group therapy by dissolving the defensive screening of the individuals involved and greatly augmenting their capacity for empathetic contact.

On this latter issue, Blewett asserts that, although schizophrenics are not a group that one would normally tend to treat with psychedelics, they may sometimes be most effectively contacted at an empathetic level by a therapist who has taken the drug himself. As he observes, when someone is lost deep in a forest simply calling them to come out is not very effective: one must sometimes go into the woods oneself to bring them out. Naturally, this is a highly controversial viewpoint and strategy, even if one accepts that there are certain empathetic advantages.

At the practical level alone, it can be seen how exhausting repeated usage of psychedelics would be for the therapist – as well as involving the unproven but possible dangers which may attend very regular use. But the greatest hazard foreseen is that the therapist himself may lose reality contact and that he may come to share, and thus to reinforce, the delusory systems of the patient – a situation which has happened many times before, even without the involvement of any powerful mind-manifesting chemicals. More realistic, and more in keeping with the thinking of most professional users of the psychedelic drugs, is his conclusion that they should form part of the therapist's background training in sensitivity and empathy.

The point that people who are concerned with the treatment of schizophrenics may profit a great deal from taking LSD on at least one occasion is one which actually enjoys a considerable measure of support, even amongst people who would not, themselves, use psychedelics therapeutically with schizophrenic patients. This position is well stated by Claridge (1970) who, though he is on the whole rather cool about LSD, feels that, even if it makes no further contribution to our understanding of human behaviour, the mischief that it has sometimes caused is justified by the insight and tolerance that it can bring to the understanding of schizophrenia.

Naturally enough though, anyone proposing to use these substances therapeutically certainly needs some sort of specific training before enthusiastically administering them. It would be unthinkable to let the young practitioner loose on someone with a scalpel before he had demonstrated an acceptable degree of knowledge and skill. The instrument that heals may also harm: the outcome will depend on the skill of the user, not just the instrument. Apart from the strategic expertise of knowing when the drug should and should not be used, there is also the need for rather unusual tactical measures and a particularly high degree of trust between the patient and his therapist or 'guide'. In addition to all other treatment considerations, it remains the therapist's most basic duty to act as a firm anchor: reassuring the patient that the old levels of reality continue to exist and that the 'psychenaut' is being carefully watched over until his 're-entry'. Without this trusting and empathetic relationship, the dangers of panic reactions are very great.

In preparing the patient, the therapist must himself know what to expect and in what ways he must help his patient to react. Clark (1969) reports that, in Czechoslovakia, doctors must have an acceptable degree of training before they may administer LSD in research or practice: they must first have observed at least thirty administrations and taken the drug themselves on at least five occasions. The experience is incontrovertibly powerful and difficult to control but the therapist must establish some sort of influence if he is to be more than a spectator and, it is felt, one of the greatest aids to being able to exercise this control is having first-hand experience of the processes involved. Though it is essential that the therapist has a thorough knowledge of the drugs used and of the ways of enhancing and inhibiting their effects, plus an ability to handle disturbed patients, this is not enough. Guidance also involves helping the individual to tread a path through the bewildering new world opened up to him. For the therapist, too, there is a need to establish a framework within which the patient's experiences can be understood and interpreted. One such aid may be first-hand psychedelic experience, but the other should be a coherent theoretical standpoint.

Theoretical orientations

The nature of the therapist's standpoint tends to be extremely variable, and this no doubt contributes in no small measure to the treatment outcomes. For example, the range extends from the direct empirical position of people like Osmond and Hoffer in their treatment of alcoholics, through usage as an adjunct to otherwise conventional Freudian psychoanalysis, to the sort of approach typified by Alnaes (1964) where Jungian therapy is coupled with extremely esotoric and mysterical conceptualizations. In his preparation of patients, Alnaes has found *The Tibetan Book of the Dead*, as rewritten by Leary, Metzner, and Alpert (1964), to be of especial value. Jung himself regarded the original form of this book as being of great psychological significance though, according to Leary, he missed much of the point by taking it at face value as a manual of preparation for the physically dying. A more recent interpretation is that the *esoteric* meaning of the book relates to ego-death, spiritual growth and change, and to the rebirth of the ego; thus it is very definitely a text for the living and evolving. This is the viewpoint also adopted by Alnaes, who uses Leary's updated version as a manual for the guidance of his patients when he launches them into their drug-induced voyages of psychological discovery. The descriptions which appear in the Tibetan book seemingly correspond very closely with the psychedelic experience and with many Jungian conceptualizations. But *The Tibetan Book of the Dead* is also, both in its original and its revised form, concerned with the optimal ways of *dealing with* the experiences and, to this extent, is very much a treatment manual – though one equally to be understood by both the doctor and the patient.

For Alnaes, there are three particularly important sequential stages – the death or dissolution of the personally striving and defensive ego; communication with both the personal and racial unconscious; finally rebirth of a changed ego. The theoretical substrate is necessarily quite complex but it includes a commitment to the idea that the patient, having penetrated unconscious sources, will benefit from abreacting directly to some material and gaining insight from yet another, whilst also bringing much unconscious material back for conscious appraisal after the session. Energy for subsequent psychotherapeutic integration and reconstruction is held to be greatly supplemented from a source tapped by the ecstatic experience itself.

Alnaes, like any other therapist, feels that one can specify particularly favourable circumstances for the use of psychedelic drugs. His first indication is for people in the age range thirty-five to forty-five, a period of life which is generally thought by Jungians to be critical in the sense that, at about this age, people tend again to become much more aware of spiritual and religious forces and may mature away from the simplistic materialism which has such pragmatic value when making one's way in the world. The second indication for optimal use is often a corollary of the first; it relates to people who have lost confidence in their previous life-style and have got into what he calls the 'neurosis of emptiness' where anxiety, depression, or alcoholism may be the sign that the individual has lost his way and needs a new ideal to guide his life by.

The combination of an orientation towards non-materialistic ends and a current vacuum in conscious life-ideals is an excellent starting point for the 'therapy model' suggested by Downing (1969) in which the therapist reassures the patient that *his own* innermost feelings are to be trusted and that the therapist will cooperate in achieving these ends. In other words, it supposes that beyond the social games, beyond the symptoms of anxiety, alcoholism, etc., reside in all of us much more profound systems of value – ones which are much more human and immutable and much less individual and egocentric but which may be suppressed by our styles of living. Whether this is so or not, Mogar (1969) is typical of many psychiatrists who have drawn attention to the increasingly large numbers of psychiatric patients who appear to be suffering from feelings of isolation, from a loss of apparent meaning, faith, or purpose to structure their lives. They feel alienated from God, from nature, from other people, and from themselves: they do not even trust their own deepest feelings. In order to handle this type of situation, Mogar feels that the therapist must take a religious, spiritual, or philosophical role – a course well suited to the psychedelics in general and Jungian therapy in particular.

Further applications

Cohen (1965) picks out these 'lost people' as being amongst the most promising type of patient and Savage *et al.* (1966) concluded that LSD treatment was especially good for 'philosophical neurosis', cases of which are supplanting the traditional childhood conflict or sexual-trauma type as societies change and evolve. There is a reaching backwards and inwards to older verities, whether identified as archetypal, spiritual, or natural, to find constant landmarks in an evermore rapidly changing psychological terrain.

Other groups of patients with whom psychedelics have been satisfactorily used, and who the majority of therapists using these drugs tend to agree are most likely to benefit, include those who are suffering with anxiety or depression from over-strict consciences; reactive depressions due to traumatic events such as bereavement, loss of confidence and self esteem, and sexual abnormalities or perversions. The general agreement that the psychedelics may be valuable in most personality disorder and neurotic conditions, even with very long-standing and demonstrably intractable cases, is paralleled by a similar degree of agreement that the psychoses are *not* a suitable area of use.

Of course there are exceptions, including the use of LSD with children. The distinguished child psychiatrist, Lauretta Bender (1970), has reported what she considers to be valuable results in the case of autistic children who exhibited typical schizophrenic-type behaviour, and claimed that they became more insightful, objective, and realistic. But the numbers involved, and the degree of recovery indicated in the research reports, might lead most people to agree with the 1970 HMSO *Report on Public Health and Medical Subjects* – that the outcomes hardly seem to justify the continued use of such a potentially dangerous drug with young children. Certainly, few workers would use LSD with either children or adults suffering from psychosis; the results have generally been extremely poor, and most agree with Hoffer and Osmond (1967) that all evidences of schizophrenic illness are absolutely contra-indicated for treatment.

One circumstance in which L S D has been held to be of positive use in the treatment of psychotics lies, not in the field of treatment so much, but in establishing an early diagnosis. Johnsen (1964) and Masters and Houston (1971) each found that the effect of LSD is to exacerbate the condition of an early or developing psychosis and thus to make diagonosis more certain. The advantages deriving from this procedure are that, in helping to distinguish whether the individual is suffering from, say, schizophrenia, endogenous psychosis, or severe neurosis, the most appropriate line of treatment will emerge at an early stage and this temporary condensation of the pathological condition will also be of value in predicting the course of its development, and thus also the best strategies for handling it. However, it appears that this procedure is widely held to be rather extreme and hazardous in outcome and, in consequence, it has not found very wide favour.

Another rather unusual clinical spin-off has been claimed for the use of L S D though, this time, when administered to a perfectly normal man. The man was Kiyo Izumi who between 1954 and 1958 worked as the architect member of a team concerned with the improvements of Saskatchewan mental hospital buildings (Izumi, 1971). The experiences which followed the ingestion of L S D, and which appear to have been almost exclusively at the sensory level, resulted in a host of design solutions. For example, the space–time distortions which are common in schizophrenia and are so faithfully mimicked by the psychedelics produced some extremely disturbing responses within existing hospital premises. Long and narrow corridors, doors which disturbingly opened into the centre of rooms, clocks or signs on the wall which appeared to defy the laws of gravity, etc. all resulted in corrective designs. Doors were placed so as to make entrances and exits more unobtrusive, ill-defined detailing of walls and windows was made less ambiguous, passages were restructured, acoustics made more soft, and so on. The effect of all this was to produce environments which were not so frightening and were positively reassuring to psychotic patients. Though Izumi had no way of knowing *how far* the LSD had helped him with his solutions, nevertheless he felt that the insights gained from his direct personal experiences came much more quickly than is usual from conventional investigations and that the quality of his knowledge was much more immediate.

This, then, is a case in which a psychedelic drug has been used to enhance the treatment conditions of those who would themselves never be given it. But the flaw in this study is that, as Izumi himself points out, it lacks the follow-through: he himself having never returned to the psychedelically inspired surroundings whilst again under the influence of LSD in order to check his design solutions. Of course, it is a tremendously subjective study anyway in that it depends so heavily on the experience of a single individual and, as it lacks any systematic follow-up or comparisons involving patients, it must only be regarded as an anecdote – an interesting example or clue as to what might be a potentially valuable application.

Dying and analgesic uses

Another unusual clinical application of LSD is the way in which it has been used with the terminally ill. The potential value of using this drug in these circumstances is suggested by the association, already noted, between the psychedelic experience of ego-death and the account of physically dying as presented in *The Tibetan Book of the Dead*. If the psychedelic experience can be so constructively used in the face of ego-dissolution, then it is argued, it may also be of help to those who are actually dying. The history of this idea is not very clear but certainly, if not the first to grasp the connection, then Aldous Huxley was certainly amongst the first. In 1962 he published his last novel, *Island*, a story about an island people and the gracious and humane society which they managed to create with the help of their own psychedelic – 'moksha-medicine'. The critical section here relates to the death of an old woman who, with the dignity and clarity she had been helped to achieve by the drug, accepted her own dissolution as a poignant but pregnant stage in her life.

The following year, Huxley himself followed in the steps of his fictional character – though his own cancer, the use of psychedelic drugs, and his death were real enough. The account of his dying, recorded by L. A. Huxley (1968), is a monument to much more than this event but it is also a moving testament to his ideal of integrating death into life: and leaving the world in psychedelically stimulated awareness and understanding, rather than being dulled and stupified with morphine.

Naturally, the problems of controlling intolerable pain are omnipresent in the case of the terminally ill and thus must plainly be an important consideration in determining the appropriate treatment. But, if it should prove that LSD, or one of the related drugs, also has powerful analgesic qualities, then the conflicts relating to the use of psychedelics rather than the more orthodox medications would be resolved. Kast and Collins (1964) decided to explore this possibility as they felt that two features about LSD augured well. In the first place, a common effect of the drug is to influence people's 'body image' – our mental representation of the position and the extent of our bodies in space. Also ego-boundaries, the conception of what is and is not part of ourselves, is very much affected by all psychedelic drugs. Secondly, one's ability to concentrate on a particular sensory source is very much affected: attention even to pain, which normally exerts a tremendous focusing capacity because of its importance to biological survival, might be expected to lose its primacy in the face of so much alternative stimulation.

In setting up their study, Kast and Collins made a comparison of the effects of LSD with two established and potent analgesics, dihydromorphinone and meperidine. As subjects, they used fifty gravely ill patients, mainly suffering with cancer and gangrene and who were also complaining of severe intolerable pain. The effects of the various drugs were estimated from data based on reports by the patients themselves and observation of such behaviours as wincing, thrashing and crying, as reported by both hospital staff and other patients. On these criteria, the experimenters found that LSD was a better analgesic than either of the other two for, though it had a slower onset, it was both more profound and longer acting.

In another series, Kast (1964) also studied the effects of LSD when used with non-terminal patients. The work was only done with very small numbers – by way of a pilot study – and involved four cases of amputees suffering from 'phantom limb' pains and ten women who were to have a hysterectomy. The phantom limb cases derived no relief or advantages from the drug either during or after the treatment but the women, who had received LSD as a pre-anaesthetic agent, recorded good results with a positive effect and no reluctance to be given it again. But the *main* part of this study was once again principally concerned with the terminally ill and related to the experiences of 128 people, all of whom were affected by malignant tumours and for whom death was foreseen within one to two months.

Unusually, the patients were *not* told about the LSD before their treatment had begun; being reassured only when the effects made themselves felt. Once again the relief from pain was pronounced and long lasting. However, many did experience panic and anxiety reactions which, though not judged to be severe enough to require a pharmacological termination of the session, resulted in 30 per cent of patients later saying that they would be unwilling to repeat the experience. How far the adverse reactions were connected with the method of administration is difficult to say but most subsequent work would suggest that a great deal might be avoided by more lengthy preparation. On the credit side, the patients achieved a remarkable unconcern with oppressive fears of death during the session and showed a marked reduction in sleep disturbances for up to ten nights afterwards. As in his paper with Collins, Kast again reports that there were no adverse medical reactions, despite the critical conditions pertaining – a fact which has led him to describe the use of LSD as an innocuous medical procedure, though one with great practical potential.

In yet another series, Kast (1971) treated eighty terminal cancer patients – all of whom had been told of their diagnosis and prognosis. There was no attempt at a 'research approach' with measured variables and controls; all patients were given an intravenous dose of 100 mcg of LSD and their moods, attitudes, and condition were followed up daily for three weeks. It is particularly interesting that only ten of these patients went for more than ten hours before the session had to be terminated because of fear or anxiety reactions. And, perhaps as a result of this, only 10 per cent of the patients did not wish for a repeat of the experience – compared with a third of those in the Kast and Collins study where sessions were not terminated. Again, the results showed a reduction of pain, and an improvement in mood and sleeping for a period of about ten days. As Kast himself commented, the psychedelic experiences seemed to go beyond simple anaesthetic effects by offsetting the monotony and isolation of the dying. Thus, enriching experiences may support the dreary round of those lying on their bed just waiting for it all to be over.

Walter Pahnke's approach to the same problem appears to be much more mystically orientated, his 1969 Ingersoll Lecture at Harvard being specifically concerned with showing the relationship of science and medicine to theology. The study which he described relates to seventeen terminally ill cancer patients who, sometimes with their families, were drawn into psychotherapy to face the coming events. After eight to ten intensive psychotherapy sessions – in which the patients were also given a sober evaluation of the ways in which LSD might effect their pain mood, and outlook – the patient was taken by the therapist to a private room where, amongst stereo classical music, flowers, and meaningful objects, the LSD session was to take place.

The results showed that a third of the patients were not helped at all by the session, one-third being somewhat helped, and the remaining third being dramatically so. There were no control subjects involved and it might be argued that the results are perhaps mainly due to the effects of the psychotherapy, but Pahnke himself designates the mystical experiences of the psychedelic session as the prime therapeutic agent. His conclusion was that all human beings contain vast, often little-tapped resources of love, joy, and peace and that these become accessible to the person who is able to let go of his defences and accept ego-surrender. The joy that comes from renouncing egocentricity through accepting a psychological ego-death makes the acceptance of actual death so much easier. For many of Pahnke's patients their experiences led them to a greater serenity and peace, a greater pleasure in the present, and a 'sense of security that transcends even death'.

The same theme is taken up by Savage *et al.* (1969) who also refer to the quasi-anaesthetic effect of L S D and cite the case of a terminally ill cancer patient who, though he had been heavily dependent upon pain-killing drugs, gave them up for the last six months of his life in favour of bi-monthly sessions with L S D. The pain continued but the patient had come to terms with it. But much more poignant is an account of the emotional and philosophical blossoming of one of their colleagues who was dying of cancer. This story, like so many of the others, is a record of courage, serenity, and dignity and, though the pathological condition of the body is quite unaffected by all of this, the balm to the whole person makes it seem that L S D may often in these circumstances be a very potent restorative or therapy.

Therapeutic evaluation

But, returning to the more central issue of treating those who are in distress but see no end to it, the question remains as to how effective psychedelic drugs are in psychiatric practice. Unfortunately the question is far more easily put than the answer, or rather answers, for the range of opinion on this subject is vast. Savage *et al.* (1966) felt that the whole issue was being allowed to turn on polemic rather than on data, though they observed that one of the weaknesses of the existing data is due to the fact that it is extremely difficult to assess psychiatric change and thus there is ample scope for argument about results which one particularly likes or dislikes. The same problem exists for all therapeutic techniques but few, if any, have aroused such emotional involvement and partisan polarization. The nearest contemporary situation to this one is probably the case of 'behaviour therapy' which, the analytically and humanistically orientated argue, is simply crude conditioning that deals only with *symptoms*, not the underlying illness. In the case of both psychedelic and behaviour therapies, the argument runs, spectacular changes may be quite transitory and followed by a relapse to the previous situation or, at best, the adoption of a new set of symptoms.

The relapse and substitution arguments are very important issues and draw attention to the need to fill a hiatus in our knowledge through long-term follow-up studies. Aware of the problems, people like Savage and his co-workers have been at pains to arrange for regular follow-up assessments and tests. Their results with neurotic out-patients who had been treated with single 'peak experience' psychedelic sessions, supplemented with conventional psychotherapy, led them to conclude that the results were effective, that they did not result in symptom substitution and that they were stable. They found that their patients evidenced a reduction in material and status strivings and a consequent sense of belonging and meaningfulness. An across-the-board long-term improvement in working, interpersonal, and sexual relationships was also observed – as well as a reduction in anxiety and fears.

There is certainly no shortage of reported studies: the English-language literature relating to the therapeutic value of LSD, beginning with the first such publication by Busch and Johnson in 1950, has been summarized by Unger (1964) – and Masters and Houston (1971) point out that there now exists more than two thousand published reports referring to treatment outcomes for between thirty and forty thousand patients. Not all of the literature is favourable, though most if it is – a fact which has led Masters and Houston to speculate as to why so many 'Establishment figures' of American psychiatry continue to deny the value of a treatment which on the weight of evidence would be regarded as well established in most other circumstances.

No doubt there are many reasons for caution in accepting these new drugs but one of them, stated as early as 1964 by Cole and Katz, is that there still remains some doubt as to the intrinsic value of LSD, even though they themselves had had very good results using it. Their own conclusion was a 'not proven' one because it was not possible to disentangle the relative contribution of the drug and the very powerful effects of enthusiasm, suggestion, and the associated intensive therapy. They remark that Alcoholics Anonymous also produce remarkable results with that class of patient which responds so well to psychedelic treatment – whilst using no drugs whatsoever. This same objection continues to be argued, amongst others by Barber (1970), Mogar (1969), and the two British Government reports dealing with LSD. In each of these publications, reservations about the causal chain of proof linking the drug to therapeutic outcomes is questioned. The scientific requirements for establishing this nexus are held to demand that patients should be randomly assigned to experimental and control groups and that the conditions of administration should ideally be of a 'double-blind' type – in which without knowing which patient has taken what drug, it is impossible for the investigator to unwittingly influence the results. Follow-up evaluation should then be made by independent parties.

Unfortunately, the classical double-blind drug trial is virtually impossible with LSD as the effects would be all too obvious to trained personnel, but it is clear that some attempt should be made to improve on the scientific precision under which most studies have taken place. A distinguished medical pharmacologist, Jacobsen (1968), observed rather darkly that one cannot judge the outcomes of LSD therapy by the usual pharmacological yardstick and, though he is perhaps quite right in this, he is amongst the most anxious to fashion other objective criteria. The question of the part played by drugs used in psychedelic treatment was suggestively made by Downing (1965) when he recounted how the Mexican training centre of Leary and his colleagues was gatecrashed by a psychotic woman who demanded LSD. She was given none, and despite being extremely disruptive, was treated with the tolerance and care which typified the group. Downing, a psychiatrist who was there as an observer, wanted to have her committed to a hospital but the group refused and, after three days, she was showing marked improvement. Of course, this is no more than an anecdote but one wonders whether the outcome would have been added to the list of drug successes had she been permitted to take LSD. Most workers in this field would probably reply with an emphatic negative – and say that, had she been given LSD, she would probably have needed hospitalization.

And this is where it is important to re-state some of the many qualifications which must be made before dealing with any generalizations about the therapeutic value of the drugs: outcomes relate to an unusually large range of antecedent conditions, events, and procedures in the case of psychedelic treatments.

Generalization is not always as valuable as particularization – even though overviews like this one do rather commit us to the attempt. But, if we are to deal in generalizations, as we remarked earlier, neurotics with over-strict consciences, those who have lost confidence in themselves or have lost their purpose in life, all *tend* to be accepted as good material for the various types of therapy which employ psychedelic drugs.

Most workers would also probably agree with Hoffer and Osmond (1967) that active psychotics should always be excluded and that pseudoneurotics and pre-psychotics, if they can be identified in time, should on no account be treated with these drugs which appear to intensify their biochemical abnormalities. But there are no *accepted* conditions for use. For example, Masters and Houston (1971) feel that psychedelic therapy may be indicated in circumstances where the patient seems likely to commit suicide as, they argue, the symbolic death of the psychedelic experience itself may satisfy the patient's wish to die. Needless to say, these conditions are not generally regarded as being favourable, or even acceptable, ones.

And so the debate continues about the effectiveness of L S D and its chemical kin in the treatment of psychological distress. The criticism has undoubtedly been much more severe than might have been expected on the basis of such a widely favourable literature but, as Masters and Houston observe, the spearhead of the attack has been ideological and polemical rather than scientific and based on evidence. Psychoanalytic factions, who themselves have often been accused of the very same methodological shortcomings that attach to psychedelic treatments, have been amongst the foremost critics since the drugs have been promoted as the central feature of a new type of therapy rather than an adjunct to traditional analytic procedures. Inevitably, developments such as these pose very severe threats to such closed and doctrinaire systems as psychoanalysis.

The scientific community, too, has been rather hostile, but for the same reason that they were hostile towards psychoanalysis – lack of properly controlled and evaluated studies. Yet, as Mogar (1969) reminds us, all unproved therapies have to begin somewhere, and even the most orthodox contemporary treatments were once only experimental. However, the question of where and how these new treatments should be proved is the real stumbling block. In America, with its great apprehensions about drug abuse, the Food and Drug Administration has designated LSD an 'experimental drug' which may only be used in research settings, never as a part of medical practice; and so, as Levine (1969) points out, therapeutic research in the United States has virtually ceased and consequently so too have the conditions under which the drug might realistically demonstrate its clinical potential.

In the United Kingdom a slightly more tolerant view prevails and, in fact, the 1970 Advisory Committee on the Amphetamines and LSD reported that, whilst not feeling that LSD has been *proved* to be an effective agent in psychiatry, they saw no reason to recommend that its existing miniscular use should be prevented in research or treatment by 'approved and responsible practitioners'. In coming to their conclusions, the Advisory Committee were also guided by the evidence about side-effects and the potential pathogenic effects of the drug. These are matters which we have not, as yet, raised but which will be dealt with at length in the next chapter.

5 Pathogenic Aspects

The great controversy over whether psychedelic drugs have any useful part to play in either clinical medicine or society generally turns, at least ostensibly, upon our estimates of their potential hazards to health. There is no doubt that people are very concerned over the medical and psychiatric risks but, even so, the discussion almost invariably takes place in an atmosphere, and in a spirit, in which prejudice is noticeably prominent. This is true not only of the enthusiasts but also of scientists and practitioners who should know better. But, of course, it is one of the charms of the psychedelics, from a psychologist's point of view, that they should create such intellectual and emotional mayhem and thus make such a rich field for study.

However, as has already been mentioned elsewhere, the partiality and prejudice involved in this field also makes it one in which, above all others, it is wise to refer to as many sources as possible. But, in doing so, one should be particularly wary of the confident viewpoint presented on the basis of the ubiquitous 'example'. The trouble with this sort of evidence is that one has no way of knowing how far the writer's own beliefs and prejudices are blinding him to other, equally likely, causal explanations of abnormal behaviour. The typical case presented is of the patient who is admitted to hospital with a pyschotic illness and who has taken, or claims that he has been administered, one of these drugs. But the question in such cases often seems more a matter of whether a discussion of the effects of psychedelic drugs is even *relevant*, let alone causal.

If such a caution seems to suggest that one should ignore the reported clinical cases, or that psychedelics are not potentially very dangerous drugs, then it has been put badly. What I am trying to encourage is a certain coolness in the face of a very heated argument in which 'proof' of causality is often based on simple *association* and presented in a form which would not be acceptable in any other area of scientific discourse. This by no means excludes the possibility that correct conclusions may have been drawn from weak evidence, but it does serve to make the point that anecdotes and a feeling of certainty are not of the same value as broadly based research and a due analysis of all the causal possibilities.

Unfortunately though, the former type of report is much more prevalent than the latter because of the problems of doing controlled scientific research in an area which might involve serious health hazards to participants. In consequence, apart from reports deriving from therapeutic situations where the subjects were by definition unstable personalities to begin with, most of our evidence must come from descriptions of people who were seen as psychiatric casualties and in whose cases there was some evidence of their having used psychedelic drugs. But, alas, it is often virtually impossible to work out an unequivocal causal argument in these scientifically uncontrolled situations as there is seldom any certain information about the drugs involved, the doses taken, or the circumstances of use or the user. Even if the user was in a perfectly clear state of mind on admission, it is not to be assumed that he knows what he has taken. For example, Marshman and Gibbins (1970) performed chemical assays on 621 samples of illicit drugs gathered in Ontario and recorded the considerable variations which occurred in both composition and toxicity. Thus, what the user thought he was buying was by no means a good guide as to what he actually took: of the fifty-eight alleged samples of mescaline, for example, not one of them was this drug. LSD was frequently adulterated with strychnine, cocaine, and amphetamine and one can clearly see how, in such cases, 'freak-outs' or 'bad trips' and other muscular and somatic effects may have a good deal to do with the inclusion of these additional drugs. The potency of (say) LSD, expressed perhaps as 100, 300, or 500 mcg by the seller, could not possibly be checked without the aid of sophisticated laboratory procedures and so the size of a dose is therefore a matter of faith, or the lack of it.

Perhaps, though, the most celebrated case of the label being no guide to the contents occurred during the 1967 'Summer of

Love' at the Californian Monterey Folk Rock Festival. At some stage in the proceedings there started the rumour that THC (purified extract of cannabis) was to be made available. Users had heard of THC as a recently refined laboratory chemical which they dubbed the 'New Marihuana Super Kick', but even they could have been expected to show a little more caution when it arrived in a truck and was distributed in handfuls to the crowd. The results were indeed a 'super kick' as many of the users collapsed unconscious and were exceedingly poorly with vomiting, panic, and so on (Berg, 1969). Later analysis of the drug showed that it was not THC but PCP – a medicine used by vets to anaesthetize large animals!

Forensic laboratories of all countries, working on the seizures of police and customs authorities, are quite used to finding these great discrepancies between what drugs are supposed to be and what they actually are. But still much of the clinical literature proceeds as though the word of the user is an accurate guide to what he has taken. The evidence shows that this is very far from the truth, and yet all too few studies accept Marshman and Gibbins' conclusions that it is extremely unwise to base any theoretical explanations of specific drug effects on the experience of people who have taken unidentified substances bought in the street.

Fortunately, not all of the evidence available is of this sort; therapeutic experience is an exception, though one which is limited because of the already abnormal state of the patient and thus the difficulty of predicting the hazards to normal people from the apparently untoward drug reactions of mental patients. But, having stressed some of the difficulties in interpreting the mass of empirical observations which have accrued, and bearing these theoretical objections in mind, we can now turn to the literature to tell its own story.

Transient effects

Our evidence concerning transient effects is perhaps the least contaminated by the variables to which we have referred. In this area at least, there is a mass of evidence based on laboratory studies using healthy subjects and pharmaceutically pure chemicals of known potency. An excellent example of this type of research is that of Ames (1958) in which ten medically qualified volunteers took a single oral dose of between four and seven grains of cannabis (depending on body weight) and were carefully monitored for both subjective and objective effects. We are already quite familiar with most of the subjective effects which followed but the doctors were particularly acute in their detailed recording of minor physical symptoms like coldness, nausea, and dryness of the mouth, and additionally checked for changes in muscular activity, brain activity (E E G), pulse-rate, conjunctival suffusion, blood-sugar, and so on. One subject was given an overdose (forty-eight grains) and 'behaved very like a manic' whereas the other subjects showed 'more of a schizophrenic picture' with their perceptual and other cognitive aberrations. Yet none of the subjects became psychotic in any sense – they simply exhibited certain changes which are common to mental patients. However, the study is a good example of a mass of experiments with all of the psychedelics which have in common the finding that they induce a state which is more or less *similar* to certain psychotic conditions.

But so far we have not, ourselves, specified what a 'pathological' outcome would be. If we partially define it to include either extended or long-term changes in mode of functioning to something similar to that which we call 'psychotic', then we should probably be in complete accord with all investigators: as should we if we also included genetic disorder. But, if we further include unpleasant, but brief, responses such as nausea, panic, and disorientation, we should find that these are treated differently by different writers. For myself, I should have thought that such transient deviations from normal functioning could not be classified in terms of illness and disease. If, however, we do accept these outcomes as being evidence of the pathogenic quality of these drugs, we may also be committed to including *all* the examples of non-normal states – presumably both pleasant and unpleasant, and quite certainly the 'bad trip'.

Now there is absolutely no disagreement that the 'bad trip' is a very familiar reality to drug users, and in *some* instances it is a very stark one, yet the term is also used to cover what amounts only to rather painful subjective experiences of a very brief duration. How *frequent* these unpleasant reactions are is difficult to say and can only be guessed at because, as the Canadian Government Commission of Inquiry observed in their interim report (1970), we have no way of gauging the proportion which receive no treatment or else are treated with tranquillizers in the home. Freedman (1968) gave his estimate as being about 10 per cent in any given batch of trips, whether initial experiences or not; becoming far fewer with 'skilled guides' present, and dropping to less than 1 per cent when supervised by skilled therapists. This is only an informed estimate of course and may be very wide of the mark, particularly in relation to illicit users, but few if any would deny that 'bad trips' are to be expected in some proportion of all use.

However, it is a matter of deciding what constitutes a 'bad trip': the literature is quite confusing in that the term is often used indiscriminately to cover both disagreeable and unpleasant experiences and cases of acute psychotic breakdown. For many, the 'bad trip' may be the whole, or only a part, of a session in which the individual experiences fear and anxiety – fear of going mad or of the content of their hallucinatory experiences, or perhaps panic due to their suspicions of others. Stafford and Golightly (1967) have cautioned of the particular dangers in LSD 'tripping' of sexual paranoia – a reaction which may occur in subjects with insecure sexual orientations. They therefore recommend that guides of both sexes be present so that the presence and comfortings of individuals of a given sex shall not trigger powerful sources of insecurity.

In the therapeutic context, Hoffer and Osmond (1967) have also stressed the point that complications in LSD sessions with patients can usually be traced to the inexperience, incompetence, or lack of sensitivity of the physician, psychologist, or nurse supervising the therapy. The complications that they list as most common are panic and short-lived depression and, though suicides occurred, the rate was held to be rather low considering the type of patients being treated. Severe somatic complications did not occur in their experience.

Kast and Collins (1964) who were administering LSD to

patients, all of whom were gravely ill and some pre-terminal, found that *no* medical complications occurred in the course of their study – despite the very vulnerable physical condition of their subjects. Similarly, Denson (1969) presented a review of 237 psychiatric cases – covering L S D treatment outcomes over a ten-year period – and showed that 87 per cent of these were entirely uncomplicated; 96 per cent were free of any major complication; and none suffered any permanent harm. However, he did note that the condition of two or three patients showed a temporary worsening.

This generally favourable situation in therapeutic use has, of course, already been referred to in the previous chapter but bears mentioning again as it is extremely relevant to the question of whether such drugs as L S D are the *cause* of mental disorder. The clinical experience, as one has seen, does not support the notion that this group of drugs regularly produces adverse reactions – even with the already ill.

This same conclusion was also arrived at by Cohen (1960) on the basis of the information he had collected in a survey of the experience of forty-four of the sixty-two American and European investigators who had published work on L S D or mescaline, and who had replied to his questionnaire. The data thus collected referred to use by about 5000 people, taking the drugs between one and eight times, and represented more than twenty-five thousand such sessions. The results revealed many minor side-effects such as vomiting, aches and pains, and transient panic or paranoid feelings but the worst effect with normal investigational users was one case of prolonged hallucination, lasting between twenty-four and forty-eight hours, and this was treated with tranquillizers. There were no serious physical complications with these healthy persons.

The results with mentally disturbed patients showed that there occurred a prolonged psychotic reaction in one out of every 550 patients – though management was implicated in some of these. Serious depression, leading to subsequent suicide attempts, was noted in one in every 830 cases, and one in every 2500 of these was successful. Cohen concluded that the effect of drug use was 'far from clear in most cases' and that such untoward reactions as occurred are a risk with *any type* of therapy with people suffering from severe emotional disturbances. The evidence suggested to Cohen that psychedelic treatment was not a particularly risky business and that these drugs were not, by themselves, normally pathogenic, in short-term use at least. Denson, too, concluded that his own experience had shown that LSD therapy, when carried out in the correct setting, was a procedure which carries 'minimal hazard' to the patient, probably less than that which accompanies routine medical treatment.

One further point might be made in connection with the transient 'bad trip', as opposed to a short-term psychotic break, and this is that it *may* have a positive value. The treatment of alcoholics by inducing the 'hitting bottom' experience of DTs before the patient is too deteriorated to affect an efficient recovery is an example which has already been given in the previous chapter. But Freedman (1968) has made the interesting point that a really frightening drug experience may be just what is needed in many cases to turn the individual away from the use of all drugs. Certainly I have known a number of LSD users giving up this particular drug, or of much reducing its use, after a bad trip – though I have never actually known them to give up cannabis as well – a drug which users generally consider to be completely benign in its effects.

Cannabis and psychosis
However, the idea that cannabis may be the sufficient cause of serious psychotic breaks is one which has long been firmly embedded in the literature deriving from India and the Middle East where this drug is abused particularly heavily. Indeed, the Indian Hemp Drugs Commission Report of 1894, which is frequently cited as a source which repudiated all such pathogenic claims, did in fact record that 'the effect of hemp drugs in this respect has hitherto been greatly exaggerated, but that they do sometimes produce insanity seems beyond question'. In their investigation they found that, of the 1344 diagnosed cases of 'cannabis psychosis' which they reviewed, cannabis could only reasonably be implicated as a factor in ninety-eight cases and, of these, thirty-seven involved other known pathogenic factors.

They concluded that, despite the evident lack of diagnostic skill in distinguishing hemp drug insanity from ordinary mania, there remained some cases which led them to accept that insanity may result from excessive use 'especially where there is any weakness or hereditary disposition'.

Another of these early reports which has so often been represented as being favourable to the use of cannabis is that of Warnock (1903) in Egypt. But, although Warnock was well aware that it was not possible to make a differential diagnosis in all cases and that 'incipient insanity' is often a cause rather than the effect of heavy hashish use, he nevertheless goes on to disagree with the Indian Report and states that the experience in Egypt shows that the drug does not *sometimes* result in insanity, it does so *frequently*. Warnock speculates that it may only be excessive use that results in mental illness but leaves open the question of whether moderate use also has ill effects.

Dhunjibhoy (1930) also expressed his grave feelings about the seriousness of cannabis, describing it as a 'direct cerebral poison' and placing the hazards of 'hemp drug psychosis' above even those of alcohol, opium, and cocaine. His clinical description of the condition, involving as it does intense excitement, tendency to violence, grandiose ideas, amnesias, and conjunctival congestion, seems like a fairly typical toxic reaction – not unlike alcohol intoxication – to which he adds the further diagnostic criteria of history of cannabis use and no previous psychiatric history. He reports this as a very prevalent clinical condition – particularly in the provinces of Punjab, Bengal (where it was mainly cultivated), Bihar and Orissa and gives a most full, and fascinating, account of the ways in which the drug is prepared. Interestingly, too, he observes that the cannabis preparations involved frequently contain a number of additional ingredients, aromatics and presumed aphrodisiacs like nux vomica as well as that most powerful and dangerous drug, to which we shall elsewhere refer, datura.

Precision in defining the actual drug being used was the starting point for another early report by Watt and Breyer-Brandwijk (1936) in which they set out to distinguish the South African usage of the term 'dagga' as referring to both the products of

Cannabis sativa and leonotis, a relatively innocuous plant. From this starting point, the writers reviewed the incidence of 'dagga psychosis' as reflected in the experience of the Pretoria Mental Hospital during the years 1908–23. The hospital records revealed that, in the years 1908–12, 'dagga psychosis' accounted for 17·8 per cent of all native male admissions, and that this figure was 14·35 per cent between 1913–23. The change in incidence was said to be somewhat related to the diagnostic criteria used – which was broadly a picture of a toxic psychosis associated with *dagga addiction*, but with no evidence of alcohol being implicated. At this time, up until 1936 certainly, there was no doubt in their minds that cannabis was a major cause of serious psychosis in which, though the recovery rate was held to be very good, the average length of hospitalization was nine months.

Chopra and Chopra (1939), reporting an eight-year study in India of 1238 cannabis users, found a range of reactions from the relatively benign ones of moderate users to very serious ones amongst the heavy users. And although the Chopras were quite clear about the fact that many of the psychiatric casualties had pre-existing adjustment problems, their study nevertheless implicated cannabis as a very potent cause of psychotic break-down. But, as McGlothlin and West (1968) point out, the sort of heavy doses referred to are of an enormously greater magnitude than are met with in Western countries and we should not therefore extrapolate too confidently from these extreme situations to our own patterns of use, but should bear in mind, that even in many Eastern countries, their experience leads them to believe that *moderate* use is not a health hazard.

However, writers like Kaplan (1971) would not accept such a conclusion and argue instead that, although moderate marijuana use may be perfectly harmless in most cases, it carries real dangers for some people who may be precipitated into an acute toxic psychosis. Kaplan terms such episodes as 'toxic brain syndromes' which are recognizable by being similar to schizophrenia but distinguished from it by its favourable outcome, by sometimes occurring in people with no previous psychiatric problems, and by the evidence of marijuana use just prior to developing the symptoms of malfunction. His five case histories reveal that three of the individuals had pre-existing psychiatric problems and that the psychotic aspects of all such reactions were very transitory – one lasted less than twenty-four hours. The overall picture is of rather mild disorder: no very clear causal picture emerges.

Kaplan obviously feels justified in describing his cases of 'marijuana psychosis' and, though he accepts that a causal link has not been scientifically demonstrated, he concludes that 'compelling clinical evidence suggests marijuana may induce acute and serious psychosis in some persons'. But, whilst sympathizing with the subjective feeling of conviction which this clinician has developed, and accepting that clinical practice is the front-line of medical knowledge, one must be extremely careful in relation to this very numerous type of report which, though added to the scientific literature, ignores the essence of scientific work in disregarding objectivity in favour of frank subjectivity.

It has often been said that the literature on the psychiatric effects of cannabis is extremely confused and contradictory, but running through it is a fair degree of agreement which might be taken as a consensus. Confusion seems to turn on the use of definitions and diagnoses: some doctors tend to record cases of 'transient psychosis' where others would say that the patient was 'stoned' or 'high' and reacting with fears or anxiety. Few people would be prepared to use the label 'transient alcoholic psychosis' for the noisy, weeping, staggering, incoherent drunk but are tempted to infer more from a behaviourally similar situation where *drugs* are involved.

In consequence, some clinicians see grave epidemics whereas others see only simple cases of intoxication. Smith (1968), the physician who ran the Haight-Ashbury Free Clinic throughout the period of the psychedelic explosion in San Francisco, reported that he had never in the course of dealing with 35,000 marijuana users come across a single case of 'cannabis psychosis' – intoxication was, of course, a very different matter!

But, on the other hand, Ungerleider *et al.* (1968), conducting a statistical survey of adverse reactions to a variety of psychedelic drugs, and also operating in California – though in the Los Angeles area – reported 1887 'adverse reactions' to marijuana. This data was based on a survey of the work of 2700 professionals and thus the casualty rate is estimated at 0·7 of a case per therapist but, as the definition of what constituted an 'adverse reaction' was left entirely to the respondent and may well include simple toxic and panic responses, the initial rather impressive number of cases looks less convincing as evidence of a serious epidemic.

Unwin (1969), working in Canada, reported that he had seen only three adverse reactions in two years' experience, each of which followed the smoking of large quantities of cannabis resin, and all occurring in individuals with pre-existing problems. This point is taken up by Bialos (1970) who uses the literature to argue that the evidence shows it to be naïve to suppose that there is any simple one-to-one relationship between drug and effects – whether adverse or not. As with the 'normal' use of the drug, outcomes are the result of a complex interaction between set, setting, dosage, drug type, and personal adjustment. But the values for this formula also allow for seriously adverse results: the greatest risk being to the hysterical, maladjusted, or compensated psychotic – in other words, the person whose adjustment is delicately poised and can be knocked disastrously off balance by the cannabis experience. However, Bialos, in one academic year's experience of the Department of Student Mental Hygiene at Yale, only came across one case in which marijuana was part of the aetiology leading to severe breakdown.

Grinspoon (1969, 1971) is probably one of the very best and most knowledgeable contemporary students of marijuana and, in his book *Marihuana Reconsidered*, he exercises his skills as a psychiatrist to particularly good effect in examining the question of whether the drug may precipitate serious mental breakdown. The evidence for acute reactions such as panic and anxiety are not in dispute but he is forced to reject the argument that cannabis may produce, *de novo*, a psychotic reaction in an otherwise healthy person. All the evidence is that, where psychosis has followed use, it is only in cases of *previously* sick people. The precipitation of serious reactions in the already vulnerable is accepted but, it is argued, sources of psychological crisis are a probability for such individuals – whether or not they use any sort of drug.

Actually this conclusion is by no means novel: the same general conclusion had already been drawn in 1944 by the Mayor of New York's Committee on marijuana – when the effects of the drug were uniquely evaluated by specialists in sociology, medicine, psychology, and pharmaceutical chemistry. Even in cases of comparatively high doses sustained over many years, the committee were unable to find any evidence of either mental or physical decline as a result of such usage: the sort of finding which provoked the vociferous antis to howls of rage, charges of irresponsibility and incompetence levelled at the specialists, and an even more vigorous repetition of their own beliefs. Thus the matter is too emotionally and politically charged to be settled by a single report, and so the process of review and reporting goes on – despite the similarity of the results – and the predictability of the response.

The 'Wootton Report' (Advisory Committee on Drug Dependence, 1968) has again come to conclusions broadly similar to those of previous reports, as has the 'Le Dain Report' (Canadian Government's Interim Report on *The Non-Medical Use of Drugs*, 1970). The consensus opinion, then, based on the analysis by critical minds of both the existing literature and the written and oral testimony of interested parties, is that there is little scientific evidence that cannabis is a major or sufficient cause of any form of psychosis. The *moderate* use of cannabis has been seen, since at least the time of the Indian Hemp Commission in 1894, as a fairly safe procedure – though excessive usage has been thought to be a source of danger to the psychiatrically vulnerable for as long. At present though there appears to be absolutely no scientific justification for referring to 'cannabis psychosis'.

LSD and psychosis
The question of whether L S D is capable of inducing a prolonged psychotic reaction or even a very short-term one which is hazardous to either the user or to society is one which has many

features in common with the cannabis question. The logical problems of ascribing causality are the same, the sources and nature of the data are very similar, but where the greatest difference occurs is that there is much greater unanimity of opinion – a consensus which even includes most of the users. Certainly there can be no question that LSD has been closely implicated in a very large number of psychiatric breakdowns but, as with the case of cannabis, the question of causality is not just a matter of establishing association.

Unfortunately, much of the reporting of LSD disasters is such that it engages our emotions and may dull our analytic capacity. Our very natural human reaction to a tragic event is a feeling that it should never have happened and that immediate steps should be taken to make sure that it cannot happen again. In the face of someone's death or maiming we can hardly be blamed for thinking that the requirement of scientific *proof* is a luxury not to be set against the stark reality of possible human suffering – and so we, too, may be tempted to suspend reason in favour of feeling.

Regretfully though, it seems that it is only a short step from unsupported opinion and righteous indignation to the manu-facturing of 'facts'. A good example of the fabricated dramatic case is that of LSD users going blind through staring at the sun. Louria (1970) re-tells one of these incidents, with all the circum-stantial details, as happening to four students in California. But, as the Canadian Government Commission (1970) points out, though variations of this story were widely circulated in the mass media, the reality is that it was a 'hoax' perpetrated by an American state official. This latter fact is, of course, less well known. However, cases like this, though complete fabrication is probably rare, do make the point that it is important to check such good stories very carefully before getting heated about them.

Louria makes this very point for us elsewhere in his book when he refers to the clash between himself and Allen Ginsberg, the psychedelic-using poet, over the case of five-year-old Donna Wingenroth who ate a sugar cube of LSD which she found in the refrigerator at home. Ginsberg had ridiculed much of the newspaper reporting as hysterical rubbish – especially that which described the girl as going 'wild', being 'critical', and 'fighting for her life'. Instead, he regarded it as a predictable 'bad trip' and accepted the reporting which described her release from hospital a few days later in an apparently normal condition. But, as Louria observes, the detailed medical follow-up revealed that it was five months before EEG and psychological tests showed Donna to have returned to normal. Subsequent visual-motor tests were additionally said to continue to show unco-ordination and impairment even beyond this time – though one's capacity to accept such results in relation to a child whose capacities were not *previously* known do start to become a little strained at this point. However, the thing is that a committed viewpoint – whether at one extreme or the other – can be a very treacherous guide to the truth.

Another dramatic example that leaves us wondering is reported by Bruyn (1970). He describes the case of a twenty-one-year-old student who has taken LSD on thirty-one occasions but who, on her thirty-second 'trip', declared that she was a swan and dived to her death from a fifth floor window. The only psychiatric evidence given with this case is that the girl's friend said after-wards, 'I don't know how it happened. She never had any trouble before.' Now this is a very news-worthy sort of happen-ing but it is, scientifically speaking, a perfectly useless piece of reporting – and one which is only likely to shape opinion without informing it. The popular mythology of LSD is replete with such incidents, but what is very often lacking is a full previous history though, where this exists, it is usual to discover that the individual concerned was already known to be psychiatrically unstable.

For example, Blumenfield and Glickman (1967) reported one of their own series of admissions with untoward reactions associated with LSD. Fourteen of their twenty-three cases were admitted within one day of ingestion and, amongst this fourteen, seven of the patients accounted for a range of quite dramatic behaviours – including four suicide attempts, two attempted murders, one smashed parental home, and one sexual offence. Dramatic enough results, but the analysis of the histories disclosed that the patients in this series were far from psychologically normal – 40 per cent of them were heroin users and a typical pattern of psychiatric treatment, arrests, overt homosexuality, and the use of other drugs almost always antedated the use of LSD. Analysis of this series indicated to the researchers that the use of LSD was certainly a *factor*, though the majority were clear psychotics or borderline cases who had been hospitalized not solely, or even principally, because of the effect of using the drug but as a result of 'the interaction of chronic psychiatric conflicts and current environmental pressures'.

In another series of fifteen patients, Glickman and Blumenfield (1967) found that each one of them had commenced using LSD at a time of sexual, social, or professional crisis – in stressful circumstances that they felt unable to cope with. The LSD appeared to be used as a way of dealing with a pre-existing problem and, Glickman and Blumenfield inferred, the psychiatric decompensations observed would probably have occurred anyway and it is only the *underlying* pathology which is clinically relevant to treatment.

Frosch, Robbins, and Stern (1965) were also interested in the part played by LSD in the creation of extended psychosis. On the basis of twelve such patients selected for intensive study, they found that all of them 'clearly had long-standing schizophrenia'. The place of LSD in accounting for their present acute episode appeared to be that it had upset their precarious adjustment by undermining their existing view of themselves and producing a new one to which they were unable to adjust.

It would be much more difficult than in the case of cannabis to arrive at a consensus as to whether LSD is capable of inducing a *long-term* psychotic reaction in an otherwise healthy individual. The 1970 Department of Health and Social Security *Report on Public Health and Medical Subjects* (no. 124) tends to take a conservative view of the evidence and, as with Smart and Jones's 1970 review, came to the conclusion that a previous history of psychiatric disorder was the norm – whilst leaving open the question of whether it is also the rule. Other influential clinicians and students of LSD, people like Louria (1968, 1970), are much closer to the 1970 Advisory Committee on Drug Dependence in their conclusion that psychosis may be induced in otherwise normal and well-adjusted individuals. Louria's own clinical experience led him to believe that chronic illness is a not uncommon sequel in many cases. Authorities are clearly divided over this issue; thus the conclusion must be, for the moment, that there is no consensus.

Recurrence phenomena

An interesting side-line to the question of the clinical effects of psychedelics is that of 'flashbacks' or spontaneous recurrences of previous drug-induced states. It seemed to Smart and Bateman (1967), reviewing eleven cases reported in the literature, that persistent use of LSD was a pre-condition to the phenomenon and that the mode of action, though quite obscure, is probably something to do with the cumulative effect of the drug. The problem is that the pharmacological activity of LSD appears to be extremely transient – disappearing from the organism in a matter of hours – and this fact presents considerable theoretical difficulties.

Favazza and Domino (1969) suggest some of the possible mechanisms, but show how any explanation would be made more complex by a case of their own in which a *single* LSD experience was later re-evoked by cannabis. As they point out, the evidence is that cannabis and LSD act through entirely different pharmacological mechanisms and thus the explanation of the phenomenon will probably have to be primarily psychological.

Favazza and Domino's case is interesting, not only because it introduces additional complications into the problem, but because the incident is otherwise atypical in some respects – the case history being unusually complete and referring to an individual who came from a normal home and was himself otherwise well-adjusted. The patient concerned was an eighteen-year-old college student who had used cannabis satisfactorily for some time but who, on a single occasion, used LSD and had a very frightening experience. Although it began pleasantly enough, the 'trip' gradually became more threatening: his friends appeared to be lunatics and he was transformed into a terrifying 'Day of Judgement' scene in which the room became a boiling hell and he one of the dead. Three months later he smoked some marijuana and was back into the very same scene: fear haunted him for some time after and, for the next three weeks, he was too frightened to go to sleep. Fortunately, he responded to treatment and ceased to exhibit any other symptoms.

Recurrence is a phenomonen which, though most usually connected with the use of LSD and its more closely related compounds, has also been many times recorded in relation to the use of cannabis alone. Keeler, Reifler, and Liptzin (1968) cite four such cases – three of which involved disabling anxiety though, in the fourth, the individual looked forward to the perceptual changes which occurred, and very much enjoyed them! On the subject of prevalence, the authors went on to make the interesting point that, as it is clearly naïve to suppose that the 'flashback' experience is always unpleasant or needful of treatment, psychiatrists are not necessarily in a strong position to provide information about more than a limited quantity and type of reaction.

Whether the flashback phenomenon can always be classed as a pathological outcome might, therefore, seem to depend upon the nature of the experiences and the way in which the individual reacts to them. Nevertheless, it is also clear that the *context* of the recurrence is another important consideration – whether it is benign or not – for one can imagine the disastrous results which might follow when someone is driving or engaged in any other potentially dangerous activity. Scott (1971) observes that, in his own experience, the occurrence of the phenomenon usually takes place only in the pre-psychotic and otherwise mentally maladjusted. But, if we take the point that there may occur many other cases of flashback which do not cause panic and thus bring the user to psychiatric attention, then the danger in daily situations may be greater than is supposed.

A classic case of the tragic effect of such 'echoes' is recorded by Cohen (1965) in which a young man, three weeks after having a very anxiety-provoking experience due to chewing 300 morning-glory seeds, went out in a state of considerable agitation and killed himself in a 100 m.p.h. crash into a house at the bottom of a near-by hill. Whether this was due to a recrudescence of the drug effect is a matter of opinion rather than fact, though it is usually presumed that this must have been the cause.

Addiction and dependence

Another source of considerable anxiety about any drug, though one on which there *is* a great measure of agreement this time, is whether the psychedelics lead to addiction or dependence. Properly speaking, the term 'addiction' is now obsolete and, since the 1965 report of the World Health Organisation's expert committee (see Eddy *et al.*, 1965) the more usual terminology refers to either physical or psychic dependence (or both) in relation to a particular type of drug. The impetus for this change in terminology proved necessary as the range of important drugs of abuse increased. Definitions which had served admirably in specifying the effects of opiate addiction began to run into considerable difficulties when they were applied to the very diverse substances which are now of concern.

Physical dependence, of whatever drug type, has reasonably straightforward and assessable characteristics and the concept is therefore not too difficult to grasp and apply to any particular drug. One of its main defining characteristics lies in the development of tolerance to the drug, such that increasingly larger quantities are needed to produce a given level of effect. As we have already seen, the reverse of this seems to be the case with cannabis as regular users come to require less in order to achieve the same effects. Thus, *one* of the criteria for designating physical dependence is absent in the case of cannabis.

Neither is the user of major psychedelics such as L S D likely to become involved in the *same sort* of repetitive use as typifies, say, heroin or alcohol. The reason is that his body will rapidly develop a reaction such that the drugs cease to produce their psychological effects after somewhere between four and seven days of repeated use and it takes another three days after such a series before the individual is again sensitive to the effects (Jacobsen, 1968). The estimate of this period varies; for example, in the government White Paper, *The Amphetamines and L S D* (1970), the Advisory Committee on Drug Dependence concluded that a fairly substantial loss in sensitivity to the drug occurs for a period of one to two days after a *single* dose. The principle is the same in both cases, though the government report limits itself to LSD whereas Jacobsen generalized in order to take in other members of this drug group.

But the real crux of physical dependence, the sort of thing we see with such drugs as the opiates, is that withholding these substances from established users results in the physical trauma of the 'withdrawal syndrome'. The suggestion that physical dependence of this sort may accompany the use of any psychedelic drug has seldom been proposed in scientific circles, although there have been occasional reports of considerable behavioural reaction to withdrawal of cannabis. For example, Fraser (1949) described the violent and difficult behaviour which came over 'addicted' Indian soldiers whose supplies were suddenly terminated. But whether the noted reaction was due to biochemical effects or a very understandable aggravation and annoyance at the cutting off of a valued source of relaxation is another matter.

Chapple (1966), in a retrospective study of eighty heroin and cocaine addicts, found that, though these patients were prepared to give up 'heavy' drugs, they remained very positive about cannabis and claimed that it was something they could use and leave alone as they pleased. However, Chapple, in the course of a curiously rambling argument in which he appears to reject the accepted criteria of drug dependence, concludes of cannabis that 'they would go to any lengths to get it'. The emphasis with which this sort of statement is made seems, consciously or unconsciously, to imply the sort of desperate determination motivated by physical dependence of the opiate type. However, despite some accounts which *imply* what we used to mean by the old term 'addiction', it is unlikely that anyone would now assert that the psychedelics may create a physically based state of dependence.

But, on the subject of whether the psychedelics may result in psychic (or psychological) dependence, there is a good deal of disagreement. One reason why expert opinion should be so variable on this subject is undoubtedly because the term itself is so difficult to apply. The criteria suggested by the World Health Organisation to distinguish it from physical dependence, as evidenced by the presence of a characteristic abstinence syndrome, embody two main concepts. Firstly, there should be periodic or continuous use of the drug for the purpose of achieving desired subjective effects and, secondly, there should be little tendency to increase the dose because of increasing tolerance to the substance.

This psychological dependence may vary in intensity from a mild desire to a strong compulsion and the mental discomfort which the frustration of this drive may cause will, naturally, be equally variable. But the definition which has been suggested is, as the Canadian Government Commission of Inquiry (1970) points out, one which describes a perfectly normal psychological state which, though it certainly refers to much psychedelic usage, might equally occur in relation to a whole host of situations and things – including television, music, religion, sex, and so on. As they then go on to say, the question is therefore not whether such a dependency occurs – we have abundant evidence of repetitive usage – but whether this dependency is physically, socially, or psychologically harmful. Thus, this particular issue cannot be dealt with simply as a facet of clinical medicine but must also be judged against the background of the entire discussion of psychedelic effects.

Escalation

'Escalation', or progress to the use of more obviously dangerous drugs, like heroin, is yet another area in which the pathological picture is not clear. The argument runs that, though people may begin by taking relatively innocuous substances like cannabis, one of three things is likely to happen to them.

1. They may 'graduate' to more powerful drugs like heroin, in order to obtain the thrills which the psychedelics no longer give after a period of use.

2. They may conclude that, as the psychedelics proved to be much less dangerous than they had been led to believe, the dangers of opiate and other 'heavy' drugs are probably overstated also.

3. Association with those people who are the sources of illegal drugs makes the individual psychedelic user more vulnerable as a result of the ready availability of other drugs.

However, as West (1970) observes, the statistics which relate the rate of increase in heroin use to that of cannabis do not support the view that use of the one leads on to use of the other.

The evidence that any of these processes happens in any significant degree is, as the two British and the one Canadian Government reports show, very contradictory and elusive. The basis of such causal arguments is, as most critical scientists have realized, the classical logical fallacy of *post hoc ergo propter hoc*, literally, 'after this, therefore on account of this' – or assuming that just because one thing regularly follows another in sequence they must be related as cause and effect. However, despite the fact that things which *are* causally related do exhibit this temporal sequence, the sequence itself is not a guarantee of causality. If it was, we might for example conclude that coffee was a causal factor in murder as one of the few features common to each event might be that nearly all murderers had drunk coffee at some time or other – and most of them not long before the crime! There would be no point in labouring the absurdities of this argument; they jump out and hit us in a way which may not be so when the conclusion fits our preconceptions. Yet, even allowing for the logical weakness of the argument and the poverty of the acceptable scientific proof, the possibility that some people may progress to more dangerous drugs for the reasons given continues to make considerable intuitive sense to many researchers and practitioners in the drugs field.

On the other side of the coin, the counter-arguments to 'escalation theory' include the claim that the users of psychedelics and opiates or barbiturates are basically different types and that escalation is therefore not a likelihood. This again is a difficult point to prove. As Schofield (1971) points out, heroin is *not* just a more powerful form of cannabis to which people turn when they cease to get satisfying effects: opiate drugs are of a quite different nature and meet totally different psychological needs. Moreover, the cannabis users are generally held to look down on, or at least pity, heroin users and would not therefore be likely to emulate them. Interestingly enough, Klein and Phillips (1968) uncovered some oblique support for this conclusion in their study of American street gangs where they found that some gangs, having observed the effect of heroin abuse on others, consciously rejected 'heavy' drugs in favour of the 'softer' ones – including marijuana. In other words, the availability, proximity, and example of opiate users proved, in this case, to be a deterrent rather than an invitation.

Cheek, Newell, and Sarett (1969) have added to this theme of the basic difference between psychedelic and opiate users through their intensive study of a group of heroin addicts, all of whom had also taken L S D. The conclusion of this study was very much against the escalation hypothesis as they found that such people were either neutral or negative to the L S D experience and gave every indication of being distinctively different types from the psychedelic users – with whom the group has worked very intensively. The addicts appeared to be using opiate drugs for quite different reasons and were seeking different psychological effects.

But cannabis is perhaps a little different again, and one is tempted to think that many of the feelings of euphoria, confidence and relaxation which the teenager seeks in cannabis can equally be found in the amphetamine, barbiturate and opiate groups and that, given their availability, the likelihood of an 'escalation' may be much greater than it has, as yet, been possible to demonstrate unequivocally.

Chromosomal and teratogenic effects

Since 1967 there has been a new source of controversy, though this time focused upon the possible pathogenic effects of the arch-psychedelic, L S D-25. At about this time, reports began to appear in which chromosomal damage was shown to be associated with the use of L S D – both when taken illegally and as part of a therapeutic programme. Irwin and Egozcue (1967), in a study of eight illicit users, found that six of these showed considerable chromosomal damage in the case of their lymphocytes. White blood cells were also studied by Cohen, Marinello, and Back (1967) in the case of a patient undergoing L S D treatment and they confirmed chromosomal damage in this case also. Loughman, Sargent, and Israelstam (1967), looking at similar cells in eight subjects who had recent exposure to large doses of L S D, also reported the presence of chromosome abnormalities in significantly greater degree than existed in the control subjects. Thus the evidence continued to amass.

However, not all reports told the same story. Sparkes, Melnyk, and Bozzetti (1968), for example, cultured the cells of both subjects who had taken L S D in a therapeutic situation and those who had used it privately and were currently in treatment for psychoneurotic reactions. They also took control subjects who had *not* used L S D and then, as an experimental check, sent duplicate samples to two separate laboratories for analysis. The results showed no significant difference between the groups, between users and non-users, it being the case that a percentage of aberrations in such chromosomal material is quite normal. This work was subsequently criticized by Kruskal and Haberman (1968) on the grounds of the statistical treatment used but the authors still concluded that their findings gave neither statistical nor substantive evidence of chromosomal damage due to L S D.

In the meantime, studies with animals were regularly producing evidence of genetic change. For example, in that old favourite of genetic researchers, the fruit-fly, *drosophila*, Browning (1968) was demonstrating that the injection of massive doses of L S D significantly increased recessive lethal mutations in the X-chromosomes whilst Skakkebaek, Philip, and Rafaelsen (1968), also injecting vast doses – but this time into mice – revealed that meiotic chromosomes in his treated group showed substantial breakage whereas this was exceptional in his untreated animals. And, at a rather fundamental level, Yielding and Sterglanz (1968) demonstrated with calf thymus that L S D can bind to D N A – the basic genetic material – though, being careful scientists, they curbed the impulse to draw any inferences about biological effects in living animals as being only a matter of conjecture at this point. Nevertheless, an interesting and congruent piece of information.

Hungerford *et al*. (1968) produced further very interesting evidence when they demonstrated a temporary genetic effect, by examining cells from four patients before and after they underwent three L S D therapy sessions (during which they consumed 200 mcg of material on each occasion) and comparing their chromosomal materials with those of non-treated controls. The results showed that the LSD-using group did, in fact, evidence an increase in chromosomal aberrations but that this effect subsided and had disappeared in a time scale ranging from one to six months. The researchers concluded that, though such a result would not strongly contra-indicate the use of LSD in therapy, it did suggest the need for greater caution and for more research.

Lauretta Bender, who had for some time been using LSD in the treatment of psychotic children, also decided to check on the possible ill-effects on seven of her patients, each of whom had received 100 to 150 mcg of LSD twice daily for a period of weeks or months. Cytogenetic results showed that there were no differences between such children and a group of non-user controls (Bender and Siva-Sankar, 1968). However, the point is that this study was not made until between twenty to forty-eight months after the administration of the last dose and, as Hungerford *et al.* observed, their own results would indicate that no effect would still be apparent after that time – and that it did not preclude the possibility that there *had been* chromosomal damage.

The fact is though, as the Canadian Government Inquiry (1970) reported, chromosome breakage in white blood cells is a response which may occur in the presence of many other substances such as radioactivity, certain virus infections, and even aspirin and caffeine in certain cases, and that this type of 'chromosome damage *per se* does not necessarily affect either the individual or his offspring, although the possibility must be considered'. The British 1970 Advisory Committee on Drug Dependence also came to a very open verdict when they judged that the existing evidence for LSD causing genetic abnormalities which might be transmitted on to future generations was very incomplete and that the genetic evidence was, in any case, very one-sided – only presenting the alarming cases and opinions. This has not, of course, prevented such evidence as does exist from being presented rather confidently as 'proof' that genetic damage does result from using LSD.

One paradoxical outcome of this sort of hasty judgement and propagandizing has been, as Cheek, Newell, and Joffe (1970) showed when they assayed supplies of illicit drugs, that it is now less possible to identify the product and thus to take appropriate precautions. Since the chromosome scare, much L S D has been marketed as mescaline or psilocybin and this creates three unfortunate effects. Firstly, the deception encourages the individual to take what he might otherwise judge to be an unacceptable risk. Secondly, the new exotic brands, like 'magic pumpkin seeds' and 'strawberry mescaline', cannot be relied upon even to be L S D in disguise: sometimes they cover other known dangerous substances like S T P – and this becomes even more dangerous if one has been misled about the drug taken and uses phenothiazines to treat casualties. Thirdly, the effect of this new terminological deceit is to make it much more difficult to draw causal inferences from street-user sources.

The present position regarding chromosomal damage in humans as a result of using L S D is much as it was when summarized by Smart and Bateman in 1968. The evidence which we have, though still incomplete, does seem to suggest that further investigations may well produce scientific confirmation of such effects – but work is very much hampered by the ethical problems of doing controlled research with a potentially dangerous substance, even in countries where there is no absolute ban on using the drug.

The same problems also surround the question of whether L S D is a teratogen, or cause of congenital malformation in the unborn child. In 1967 Zellweger, McDonald, and Abbo published a very celebrated case history which has created a good deal of interest and controversy. The case was of a child with a deformed leg born to parents, both of whom were users of L S D, the mother having taken it as late as the ninety-eighth day of her pregnancy. Chromosomal examination of white cells revealed that the child and both of the parents all exhibited some degree of breakage.

However, Jacobson and Magyar (1968), who had studied fifty cases of L S D use prior to pregnancy, were inclined to think that chromosome breakage in neonates was probably due to humoral toxicity caused by the drug and that *in surviving children* exposed during pregnancy, it would have little consequence and might be expected to disappear with time. Moreover, the 1970 Advisory Committee Report on *The Amphetamines and LSD*, like the Canadian Commission, felt that the few cases of deformity reported bore little, if any, correlation with the great amount of LSD use and that such cases as do occur might be expected as part of the risk which attends any pregnancy.

Even so, few people who have surveyed the evidence have discounted the possibility of teratogenic effects as, apart from the occasional human case, some of the numerous animal studies have proved positive. One of these, that of Alexander *et al.* (1967), has been particularly significant in shaping opinion. This study showed that mice, injected with LSD on the fourth day of their pregnancy, produced litters of decreased size and with a high proportion of still-born, stunted, and young who showed a poor subsequent development. Injection later in pregnancy did not create these effects. Geber and Schramm (1969) also demonstrated marked teratogenic effects as a result of injecting cannabis derivatives into pregnant hamsters. But, in both of these studies, the doses used were vast by human standards and so are generally regarded as no more than suggestive at the present time, but not to be ignored.

Obviously, a better guide to the effects on humans is experience with human beings but, before it is possible to arrive at any final conclusions, it will clearly be necessary to assemble a great deal more information on prevalence and circumstances of use and to find ways of collecting and collating other relevant data on the polluted drugs, unknown doses, nutritional deficiencies and diseases to which many drug users are susceptible. The possibility of achieving so much control of variables is now, especially given the illegal nature of the behaviour, extremely remote.

Yet the members of the Native American Church do offer one such exception: their use of mescaline is very carefully regulated, and takes place within an ordered society. Watts (1971) comments that none of the anthropologists or other students of the peyote groups have ever noted any particularly unusual sorts or incidences of deformity, malformation or any other special sorts of pathology amongst such people. But, if we are here dealing with occurrences which, though not common, are real enough, this should be revealed by an intensive study of the reproductive and general medical history of this group when set beside that of a comparable group of non-users. The conducting of such medical studies is not, as Aberle (1966) comments, a rare occurrence but so far the literature has revealed no specific mentally or physically harmful effects of using mescaline in the sort of doses which the church members take. However, it is as well to remember that LSD is pharmacologically very distinct from mescaline and so one would be very wrong to extrapolate from the one to the other.

Organic injury

Cases of *physical* ill-effects due to the use of LSD have scarcely ever been reported – except for cases where people act in response to a fantasy and injure or kill themselves by believing that they can fly, stop traffic with a gesture, or influence traffic lights by their thoughts. STP is another matter: it, according to Unwin (1968), produces symptoms similar to atropine poisoning and has been responsible for a number of deaths following respiratory failure or convulsions. Also, where an adverse response has been treated with phenothiazines, an appropriate antidote to LSD, the effect has been to intensify the toxic symptoms and this has been known to cause deaths.

But, rather surprisingly and STP aside, it is cannabis which is currently under the gravest suspicion. It has always provoked the most reckless of charges, but recently there has been an accumulating literature on cases where cannabis is held to have resulted in brain damage. Some of these reports, like that of Keeler and Reifler (1967) might tend to carry little conviction as they concern only a single case and depend upon pure *post hoc* reasoning. The case in point concerns a twenty-year-old student who, though an epileptic, had successfully given up the use of his medication for six months; then, after using marijuana seven times in three weeks, he had three grand mal seizures. Yet, though Keeler and Reifler find themselves unable to explain why the seizures did not occur *during* the marijuana reactions, they argue for an association amounting to a 'precipitating circumstance' which they only just stop short of pronouncing 'causal'.

Unfortunately, this case study has since frequently been used by the unsophisticated as evidence that 'cannabis causes epilepsy' – though to many people it perhaps looks more like a perfectly ordinary case of the symptoms returning in the absence of continued medication. There have been other unsatisfying reports since – like that of Hekimian and Gershon (1968) who, when reviewing the course of a series of drug-provoked hospital admissions, claimed to have found 'one acute brain syndrome due to marihuana'. Like most of this type of information, it comes as an assertion by a clinician who gives very little information, and does less to dispel our doubts about whether he has fully considered all of the other possible causal alternatives, and indeed whether an *organic* syndrome has been clearly identified at all.

In 1970, West crystallized an impression popular with people having the opportunity to observe long-term cannabis users at close quarters. On the basis of his own observations of users, sometimes made over a period of up to three or four years, he felt that the subtle personality changes which he observed taking place – particularly lessened drive and ambition, reduced attention span, magical thinking, deepening introversion, feelings of unreality, habit deterioration, loss of planning ability and foresight – all pointed to organic deterioration as the most credible explanation. But West's report, like many others we have criticized for their lack of scientific control, suffers from great subjectivity.

However, in 1971, objective neurological evidence was put forward by Campbell and his colleagues when they claimed that air encephalographic investigations with ten cannabis-using patients had revealed clear signs of cerebral atrophy. Their results showed that there was substantial enlargement of the cavities formed by the lateral and third ventricles, and that this distinguished them from thirteen controls of a similar age group (i.e. early twenties). Not everyone has been equally impressed by these results – some have pointed out that all of the subjects were either neurological or serious psychiatric cases anyway and that the controls were not a random sample of the normal population but were *selected* on a predetermined criterion of normalcy, not of representativeness.

Plainly, this new line of inquiry opened up by Campbell and his associates will take some time to evaluate properly; particularly as air encephalography is not the sort of technique which may readily be justified for use in surveys with otherwise normal individuals. But, though no conclusive results may yet be claimed, this work remains as the most striking evidence so far that cannabis may hold very considerable dangers.

And so, curiously enough, in concluding this review of the potential hazards of using psychedelic drugs it transpires that what we had, at the outset, classed as a 'minor' psychedelic might have the most serious consequences. Only time will tell but, for the moment, this new research may at least act as a cautionary tale for anyone who is tempted to think that the present lack of acceptable scientific proof of pathogenic characteristics in most psychedelic substances is equivalent to a conclusion that they are not dangerous.

6 Psychedelic Philosophy

On the face of it, it may seem preposterous that chemicals can generate philosophies, but there is no doubt at all that the use of psychedelic drugs is very much associated with certain philosophical outlooks and aims. Whether this association is causal or not, and the degree to which a philosophical position or positions may be discerned, will be the main subject-matter of this chapter.

The very idea that illegal drug-taking can be causally linked with philosophical explorations in ethics, epistemology and metaphysics is certainly not one which commends itself to most people. That this is so is suggested by many conversations with intelligent friends, colleagues, and acquaintances – most of whom prefer to dismiss the ideals as woolly rationalizations or the camouflage of irresponsibility and psychological disturbance. The philosophy, like the use of the drugs themselves, tends to be seen as disreputable, dangerous, and better suppressed than considered.

It seems a pity for many reasons that so little critical interest should be shown in the philosophical statements of the psychedelic movement for, even if they are not entirely new, and if they are often confused, conflicting, and unusually presented, there is evidence that they also express potent beliefs and values which have an increasing meaning and truth for young people all over the world. Whether these beliefs and values seem to be basically good, bad, or neutral is beside the point – they are intrinsically interesting and potentially agents of considerable social change. It would therefore be both intellectually and socially unwise to ignore them or to underestimate their influence.

The very fact that, in English-speaking countries alone, the number of people who have used psychedelic drugs already runs into millions suggests that new ways of looking at things are actively being sought after. So, whether or not the new visions reported by the spokesmen for psychedelic philosophy turn out to have any sort of real meaning and value, one has to accept that they reflect a very prevalent need to experience the world differently. This point is an important one in that there is a tendency in society to treat all classes of drug use as a 'bad habit' like masturbating and to attempt to stamp them out without due regard to their meaning and their value to the users. To undervalue or fail to understand the positive qualities is, even at the practical level, to court failure as the young are just as sensitive to ignorance and bigotry as is the older generation. Moreover, members of the older generation must recognize that, when they attack the use of psychedelic drugs, they also come into conflict with strongly and sincerely held philosophies and ideologies of which drugs are currently an integral part. I say 'currently' because many feel that chemical means may be superseded as instruments for 'turning-on' or that the philosophies which have been generated may develop their own autonomy in the same way that many mystical religions have done.

Indeed, as we shall see later, there are very many points of similarity between the psychedelic scene and mystical religion and it is interesting that the prime philosopher of the movement, Timothy Leary, has commonly been described as the 'High Priest' and has chosen this title for his autobiography (Leary, 1968). But this is no mystery cult: Leary has used every channel of communication open to him in his attempts to expound the aims of the psychedelic movement – and perhaps one of the best collections of this multimedia attempt to communicate is contained in his *The Politics of Ecstacy* (1964). In this book, through a series of articles, reported speeches, and interviews, Dr Leary explains why he believes people should turn to psychedelic drugs in order to achieve a more humane and satisfying relationship with the universe and everyone and everything in it. In so doing, he is undeniably proselytizing for converts and agitating for change, yet he is quite specific in that he does not wish to encourage anyone to break laws but rather to work for their repeal. The tone is moderate and opposed to any sort of aggressive revolt against the established order – though he does believe that revolutionary changes will occur anyway. Yet the exposition of these ideas is construed by many people, and particularly his own countrymen, as subversive attacks on all that they hold dear.

But what exactly *is* being advocated by the philosophizers of the psychedelic movement? Of course there are many variations but the most coherent answer would seem to begin, and perhaps also to end, with Leary's injunction 'Drop-out, turn-on, tune-in'. 'Dropping-out' is already a somewhat overworked and degenerate cliché used to describe almost any state of negativeness, failure, or avoiding responsibility. The layabout nowadays solemnly assures one that he has 'dropped-out of mass/capitalist society' when he really means that he finds drawing unemployment benefits better than working. But in Leary's sense, it refers to a positive action: to the sacrifice of familiar, comfortable things and to a painful renunciation of the sort that Jesus demanded when he asked the rich man to sell all that he had and to give away the proceeds before attempting to live the spiritual life. And so it is with the psychedelics: most of the young people looking for this spiritual way are not poor, nor are they from deprived homes, rather they tend to be well educated and come from good material backgrounds.

The specific mode of 'dropping-out' is usually left to the individual to work out. The most extreme advice suggests the giving up of education, occupation, and any sort of political participation but the less drastic measures simply advise *detachment* from these things without literally giving them up. Each person is expected to decide just what steps are necessary in order to be able to step aside from the enslaving bonds of habit, routine, and convention which Leary describes with the metaphor of a TV studio in which individuals must play out unnatural and bogus roles against a backdrop of contrived props and fakery. The essential thing is to cease playing the 'games' to which society is addicted – the struggle for power, status, and wealth, and the tragi-comic way in which the profound identity of ourselves and others is constantly being submerged by roles, whether we are acting, or responding to, the stereotype of 'socialist', 'old age pensioner', 'housewife', 'doctor', 'spastic', 'Negro', 'priest', or whatever.

Dropping-out means giving up ambitions and the symbolic

rewards of society in order to pursue the aim of developing inner wisdom and philosophical satisfaction. But there is no necessary expectation that people will remain outside of their normal 'tribal games' forever, or even for a very extended period. It is concerned with a period of philosophical exploration and growth which will prove enriching to the individual returning to involvement in the preoccupations of organized society. Thus dropping-out is neither revolutionary nor iconoclastic in its intent, nor is it a permanent state unless, as with the case of Leary himself, society enforces and reinforces the alienation.

The route to dropping-out is generally, but not always, the result of previously 'turning-on' or coming to a new awareness of one's own internal processes. But the technique is not the intellectual one of introspection and self-dialogue; it is through responding to those abnormal states of consciousness which are produced by the psychedelic drugs. Leary identifies several levels of awareness varying from those which affect our perceptions or enhance the ways in which we experience the external world, to those which seem to whirl the user down into the cellular and atomic structures of his body. Levels vary with the drugs used and with the amounts taken. It is claimed that the information and experiences gained in them also have their parallels in scientific disciplines – like neurology and astrophysics–though the main gains are held to be of a more personal and humanitarian kind. However, it is accepted that these various levels of consciousness involved in 'turning-on' may also be achieved by means ranging from rhythmic forms like music and dance, through sensory deprivation and fasting, to yoga or spontaneous insight. Thus drugs are not a necessary condition though they are held to be extremely effective and time-saving in most cases.

The concept of 'tuning-in' is no less elusive than the others and is used to refer to a state which may occur before or after 'dropping-out'. However, becoming 'tuned-in', in the psychedelic sense, is usually the sequel to having been 'turned-on' with drugs. It is typified by a more or less rapid shift in values which is generally, though not always, due to revelatory experiences in drug-induced states of consciousness. Being 'tuned-in'

implies a range of aesthetic, emotional, and intellectual responses which are held to lead the individual on to a greater,
and more philosophical, concern with beauty, peacefulness, and
with the more fundamental questions of cosmic design. His life
is thus adjusted to a more detached and abstract view of the
world than is usual for people who participate fully in the
'tribal games'.

There are many reasons given for using the psychedelics but a
particularly important one is the neurological/psychological
argument that the language required for the logical processing
and analysis of experience normally results in a necessary
restriction of consciousness – a filtering which dilutes and dis-
torts reality (Leary, Alpert, and Metzner, 1965). The capacity
of the brain, exceeding that of the greatest computer imaginable
by many magnitudes, is socially conditioned to operate only at
the speed of a single output channel. The putative effect of the
psychedelic drugs is to override this programming and to let
the brain operate at full capacity and energy levels. In this way,
it is claimed, an understanding of the illusory nature of most
of the socially conditioned values and response patterns may
be grasped and the individual becomes capable of a more
profound re-structuring of the world: old mental habits may be
unlearned and new ones, based on more complete data, and less
social convention, may be learned (Downing, 1965). The condi-
tional tense is relevant here because it is accepted that most
people will not wish to, nor be capable of, such radical re-
structuring and that, for most, the experiences will simply be
enriching and modifying without having much permanent effect
on life adjustments beyond creating more insight into their real
nature.

That most people soon returned to 'straight society', quite
happy to revert to playing 'personal-cultural games', was
Leary's own experience. He concluded that a longer preparation
and training with skilled guides, plus the motivation for radical
change, is necessary to achieve lasting effects in most cases.
Thus the outline forms of a philosophy of life may be roughly
delineated by the psychedelic effects but a good deal of effort is
still required to bring it to life. What *is* created by the drug

effects may be better thought of as an activity, a changed reaction to the world, than as a topographically formulated verbal map. This being the case, one should also look at the behaviour generated by 'psychedelic philosophy' and see what generic characteristics, if any, exist and how they compare with idealistic accounts.

The first point that is often made is to comment on how much the psychedelic viewpoint seems to be a *reaction* to other forms and values which already exist in society. Much of its motive power seems to derive from this source – being not just an alternative philosophy but an opposite one to present social organizations, instruments of government, and aspirations. For this reason, many people have become concerned about the apparent negativism and threat to established order and civilized living which it seems to imply. Alan Watts (1962), for example, in his *The Joyous Cosmology*, does seem to present a very nihilistic viewpoint which would appear to sap any impulse to improve the quality of life. And, though he denies that there is any need to abandon our present form of culture and return to some pre-civilized way of living, his philosophy certainly suggests very little in the way of helping other people to lead better lives. Or rather, nothing beyond a doctrine of non-interference and encouragement of others to develop their mental awareness.

Yet the very processes involved in 'turning-on' and 'tuning-in' are held to lead to spontaneous values and experiences of a positive kind developing within the individual. The 'Joyous' part of Watts' Cosmology is the result of ceasing to see the spirit as something 'imprisoned in incompatible flesh' and set within an incomprehensible and hostile universe composed of irreconcilable differences. The psychedelic experience is held to reconcile the apparent differences between mind, body, other people, and the rest of the universe – freeing the individual from the burdensome feelings of alienation and aloneness which are the products of the socially created conscious self. The psychedelic insight appears to be an important aspect of this liberation as *intellectually* motivated rejections of the conventions of social conformity tend to lead only to another sort of painful alienation. This experience of unity with all things and the consequent rejection of the world of definitions and disjunctions is held to be the key source of joy.

Even 'love' is a concept which, through the operation of restrictive conceptual boxes, has come to be governed largely by stereotypes. We currently use such categories as spiritual, brotherly, and sexual love but, Watts argues, such groupings leave out the sort of loving-kindness and affectionate contact which most people yearn to experience and be able to express, yet are unable to do so. That one cannot achieve this is because the use of categories and a conditioned focus on *differences* makes universal thinking virtually impossible. Thus there is alienation and disharmony amongst people, groups, and nations.

Watts, like most of the psychedelic philosophers, is tremendously enthusiastic about the value of psychedelic drugs yet does not see them as either the source of new perceptions or the only means of achieving them. It is Watts' thesis that drugs cannot create from what does not exist – his own case being a perfect example of the psychedelics being incorporated into a pre-existing philosophy. For example, one of his accounts of Zen Buddhism which was written a quarter of a century ago contains just the same characteristic involvement and forcefulness to express much of what he is now trying to explain of his psychedelic insights, e.g., 'we have to get away from this abstract and dead realm of concepts and come face to face with reality' (Watts, 1947). The more things change, the more they are the same!

In fact, there is a very considerable area of common ground between the philosophies of the psychedelic movement and oriental ones such as Zen, with its emphasis on non-verbal intuitions, and Taoism, with its emphasis on harmony, nature, and a cosmic order which also cannot be expressed in words. Both Zen and Taoism are deeply rooted in religious thought and, following both convenience and convention, it is proposed to deal with these ideas in chapter 10. However some of the more practical observances of these systems are relevant in a discussion of philosophies of life. Ranking very highly amongst these observances are practices concerned with developing non-attachment to material things and the relinquishing of all forms of striving, competition, and assertiveness. Also, closely related to these, are the principles of ceasing to judge, rank, regard, or respond to other people in terms of their wealth, status, cultural values or anything else. A working philosophy of this sort, though acceptable as a religious idealism, is obviously at variance with the requirements of an organized, industrial, and commercial society. This is especially so as broader psychedelic philosophy lays great emphasis in the individual 'doing his own thing' in the company of other people with similar 'vibrations'.

The whole ideal is therefore one which tends to create individuals, and ultimately a sub-culture, unfitted to our present society. In this sense, the critics of the psychedelic movement are perfectly correct in describing it as 'subversive'. The apologists would deny this and say that the intention was not to overthrow or change present forms; they do not believe this would be possible for them, but they do aim to create an alternative – a *parallel* society – for those who wish to opt out of mass industrial/commercial culture. However, though this was certainly true of the aims of the early phase of the movement, and probably still is for by far the greater part, more of the young people influenced by the movement are now trying to move mass society their way rather than to set up a parallel form.

In Amsterdam for instance, a town which has been called 'the psychedelic centre of Europe' (Bloomberg, 1971), cannabis-smoking young councillors – 'Kabouters' or 'Gnomes/Pixies/Dwarfs/Elves' – form part of the city administration. Their party, representing the 'Orange Free State', was reported as having won five seats with their 11 per cent of the election poll and acts as a force for change in established society as well as providing a platform and diplomatic representation for their (invisible) dissenting state. The philosophies that they promote have their psychedelic components but there is also a coalition with other groups more concerned with positive political and social aims such as pacifism, women's lib, sexual freedom, and so on. This is a long way from the philosophies generated at the core of the psychedelic movement but it is hardly surprising that popular interpretations and outcomes should be very different from those outlined by the basically scholarly, aesthetic, and religious founders of the movement. But then theory and practice are usually very much at variance.

Drawing attention to the gap between word and deed, critics of the psychedelic movement have often pointed to such places as the Haight-Ashbury district of San Francisco and argued that, far from being Utopian places of love, they are often both depressing and violent. Haight-Ashbury is a particularly fascinating example and it has the advantage of having been very carefully observed and documented. One of the best, and most readable, accounts is that of Helen Perry (1970) who was a participant observer during the period of its rise and fall. In her book she describes most vividly how the psychedelic movement came to life amongst the students and intellectuals of the area and how its outward signs, like hair-styles and dress, began to make it more visible to the outside world until, as a rich source of colourful copy for the mass media, it became a magnet to the country's alienated, footloose and delinquent young. The publicity killed it. There were too few facilities: crowding, poverty and disease were inevitable, and the gentle 'flower people' became the prey of every sort of pressure from civic ones to the motor-cycle gangs who beat them up on the street.

Smith, Luce, and Dernburg (1970) in their article 'Love needs care: Haight-Ashbury dies' have also presented a vivid, though depressing, account of the disease, robbery, rape and gratuitous violence which has typified 'Psychedelphia' ever since the publicity which followed the 1967 'Summer of Love'. A very similar evolution and devolution was also observed by Gopala Alampur in the Yorkville area of Toronto (Smart and Jackson, 1969). The presented evidence appears, in both cases, to suggest that it would be as wrong to blame hippies for the woes which befell them as it would be to blame the citizens of Warsaw for the German 'blitzkrieg'. Yet, if they were not the cause, it could be argued that the hippies were the *catalyst* of social disasters which society has a perfect right, and indeed a duty, to prevent happening. Whatever one's views on this, the psychedelic movement has been saddled with a deplorable image as a result of disasters like Haight-Ashbury and Yorkville, and continues to suffer from it.

'Hippie' has now become synonymous with dirt, disease,

apathy, and intoxication – no doubt a perfectly just picture of a proportion of those who are interpreting psychedelic philosophy in their own way. Yet it would be wrong to judge any movement by the behaviour of some of its members – many Christians for example would feel it wrong to judge their faith entirely by the behaviour of people who claim adherence – especially if these members were picked out by the press from the most extreme, disturbed, or eccentric. And particularly in the case of Haight-Ashbury, by the time that public attention had focused on the original hippie community, their place was being taken by other young people who moved in, adopted the garb and some of the other more obvious outward signs of hippiedom, and were taken for the original thing. This is not unlike going to Rome and mistaking the later church for the early one: despite the stated similarities, there is a world of difference between them.

Whilst the new residents of Haight-Ashbury drifted away from the superheated atmosphere of the city, their place was taken by people of very different values – some of them, as Helen Perry remarked, only too pleased to get press and TV interviews in order to spout grandiose, egocentric gibberish. Of the old group who remained, most lived as recluses, afraid to go onto the streets because of the violence there. The new order, though looking much like the earlier one, and also extolling 'love' as the core of their philosophy, were, alas, mostly bad imitations of the genuine hippies and cared more about using one another sexually and economically than about enlarging their capacities for loving-kindness. Meanwhile, the original members of the community quietly slipped away – leaving their battered and misunderstood 'image' to be projected by others.

What happened to some of these exiled hippies, and to others who shared their ideals, is richly related by William Hedgepeth and Dennis Stock (1970) in their photographic and literary essay *The Alternative*. Here, they trace the course of expatriates finding their way to remote settlements in Northern California, New Mexico, and indeed wherever they could find space and peace. Their aim, as before, was not to drop-out of industrial society in a negative sense of going on to unemployment benefit and spending their days drinking, lazing, and gambling: rather they were concerned with seeking an alternative way of making their own living. Mostly they set up agricultural communes, generally on land scarcely fitted for farming, and worked to make themselves independent. This way of life is not without considerable rigours, as was quite befitting for such communities, which were *intended* to be testing places for the individual and for new types of social organizations.

The tangible results of the 'return to the land' phase vary from the creation of well-run farms to tented temporary encampments but, unlike the Israeli Kibbutzim, very few appear to be motivated by any wish to be efficient in either social or economic terms. Rather, the primary value of such places lies in the fact that they are environments in which individuals can do things *in their own way* and, in the company of other people, seek their personal ideal of harmony and fulfilment. In pursuit of this aim, some communities have evolved quite complex forms: some have established their own schools and developed cultural activities whereas others have remained at the level of drab tinkers' camps – litter-strewn eyesores, which serve mainly as temporary stopping places for the shiftless. Yet, in this great diversity, there is a common element – a yearning for the simple and obviously meaningful as an alternative to the urban package-deal of a life organized by unions and big companies in a noisy, polluted, and incomprehensible city.

As always, generalizations are all too easy to make and all too likely to mislead. The psychedelic movement is different things to different people. Even systems as tightly defined and controlled as Marxism encompass a vast range of beliefs and practices so, given the non-dogmatic and non-organized nature of the psychedelic movement, one might expect more differences than points of agreement. However, it is the points of agreement which tend to be of greatest importance, and most representative of the crucial issues: diversity, though often so apparent and disruptive, is frequently mainly about minor points of belief and procedure. The same is true of the Christian Church and, like the Christians, the movement professes the values of love, peace, wonderment, and a reverent approach to the creation. Unlike the Christians, though, they may not have any religious beliefs or need for a personal god or mediator and, though many are also religious, many more are mystically and magically minded.

But alas, psychenauts, Christians, and the magically minded alike all have their good and their bad. The outcomes speak for themselves. Just as the Christians had their inquisitions and murderers of 'heretics' and 'witches', so too the psychedelic scene and hippiedom has to live with the memory of its own vicious degenerates. And, if this present chapter appears to emphasize only the admirable, or at least the non-negative, aspects of the psychedelic scene, it is not that they are overlooked but simply that the darker aspects are specifically treated elsewhere. For the moment we are simply looking at the implied philosophy – whilst accepting that philosophies may or may not be lived and that words are not always accompanied by congruous behaviour.

The fascinating thing about psychedelic philosophy is the way in which it seems to fit the value systems of so many different sorts of people. For example, on the face of it, it appears to represent values absolutely at variance with those of middle-aged parents and thus to be an ideal vehicle for youthful rebellion. But essentially the philosophy is not extremist: there is no advocacy of violent change in society or modes of living for those who do not feel the need. Actually, the prospect of relinquishing the social role of always being responsible and circumspect is often rather attractive to the middle-aged. But, most of all, the philosophy may offer a second chance to achieve a wide circle of close friends of both sexes and the opportunity to spend time with them developing a sense of community interdependence, mutual affection and support.

Again, one is speaking of *ideals* but it is certainly true that very many people in the middle-aged bracket have this basic yearning to break out of the isolation that the realities of setting up a home, playing the competitive 'games', and raising a family have imposed. The middle-aged are not a different species from the young; neither are the old. And the old, too, can find much for them in the philosophies of the psychedelic movement; after all, their sense of dependency on others is particularly well developed through having experienced at first hand the inevitable, and inescapable, cycle of dependence – relative independence – and then back to dependence. Moreover older people, like the young, are also deeply concerned with the same ontological and eschatological problems of the nature of being, and of death and life beyond its bodily correlates. They, too, may find great understanding and peace in the oriental philosophies and religions which are an integral part of the psychedelic movement proper.

However, the young do have two qualities which are much diminished in later life and which do tend to make psychedelic philosophy more acceptable to them. In the first place they have a greater sense of adventure and are more likely to accept the risks, both psychological and legal, which the use of psychedelic drugs involves. And, secondly, they are less bound by habit and the tendencies towards achieving broad social conformity and orthodoxy. Also they have probably been less exposed to the forming values of Christianity than has any generation in the last thousand years. Thus, although the psychedelic movement may contain much that would be acceptable to older generations, it will probably have little effect on most of us already in these categories. But, given a younger generation which evolves from a different psychological matrix, and there is evidence that the psychedelics are already reaching a large and growing proportion, then one might expect to see a more general diffusion of many of the psychedelic tenets as the younger generations move through life.

Already the philosophies have many adherents and practitioners. At the most extreme, some of the more committed users of psychedelics have 'dropped-out' of existing society to become 'hippies' but a much greater number remain within the social system, often in influential occupations, and their philosophies naturally have important social implications. Where these occupations are concerned with, or promulgated by, the mass media, a great potential for influencing social beliefs, attitudes, and behaviour plainly exists (see Halloran, 1970). Pop-stars, many of whom are widely known to use psychedelic drugs, have wide-open communication channels with virtually all young people and a great deal of prestige and time to communicate their values. Helen Perry (1970) gives a very interesting example of the way in which one pop song, the Beatles' 'Yellow Submarine', has been used in the hip scene to provide ideals, symbols, and a rallying call to the like-minded. Of course the whole folk-music revival is related to Utopian yearnings but many contemporary songs are much more directly concerned with drugs themselves and comprise more or less obvious codes for the drug-using in-groups. Assessing their intent and meaning is as difficult as appraising their effect but the phenomenon does seem to suggest that some need to communicate exists; and a fairly substantial audience is tuned-in to these communications.

One of the focal points which, one suspects, has served to unify the users of psychedelic drugs into what is now commonly referred to as a 'movement' is the war in Vietnam. Real life atrocity has become commonplace viewing for most of us and is supplemented by the endless flow of vicious programmes about 'private eyes', gangsters, murderers, and cowboys. Add to this the trappings of prestige associated with thuggery – the flashy cars and women, the mystique of the gun, the casinos and high living – intersperse it with phoney commercials, and one has the mixture that has at last sickened its more idealistic audiences and driven them in search of an alternative.

The two main tenets of the new movement are simple: non-aggressiveness and non-acquisitiveness which, though here stated in their negative form, are actually the primary positive values of all the great religions and philosophies that civilized men admire. How then has the psychedelic movement come into such absolute conflict with the rest of society which, in the abstract at least, has a great regard for the philosophical principles? No doubt the answer to this question will occupy sociologists for a very long time to come but one might hazard one or two tentative hypotheses.

In the first place, there is obviously a good deal of unhappiness about the appearance of the young: their external trappings tend to proclaim a rejection of many of the attributes of cleanliness, smartness, propriety and respectability that have served their predominantly middle-class parents as ideals. Moreover, the youngsters choose to live away from home and parents are naturally disturbed when their own influence is supplanted by a milieu which, because it involves illegal drug use, is thought to be permanently close to crime, poverty, and all that goes with them. Then there is a conflict between the parental belief in work, security, and success as absolute goods in themselves.

The young, having relatively little experience of the effects of major economic depressions and the sort of poverty which cannot be escaped by deciding to change one's mode of life, are understandably less concerned than are their parents with working hard in order to protect themselves and secure the future of their dependents. Not surprisingly the older generation looks with some apprehension at this lightly-worn vulnerability and abrogation of responsibility, and is particularly concerned about the quality of life which will be available to the young after they have rejected their existing life-style. They see the diseases – hepatitis, venereal infections, and even bubonic plague – which have affected the Utopian communities (Hedgepeth and Stock, 1970) and they naturally fear for their own children. Most of all though, they are afraid of their young people becoming drug-addicts – moribund cripples, preyed on, and consorting with gangsters.

Indeed, it is probably not too much to say that the older generations tend to see all psychedelic drug usage as an ultimately self-destructive reaction of despair and inadequacy in the face of the difficult problems which any society must meet and solve. They see the committed hippies as egocentric weaklings – too concerned with their own problems and too feeble and backward-looking to be of any use to an evolving society.

But, rightly or wrongly, a considerable number of young people continue to look to the psychedelic movement for help in their search for a more harmonious way of living. Levy (1968), referring to teenagers and their use of various types of drugs, came to the conclusion that the users of psychedelics were those who were motivated to find a more meaningful existence than the one which they envisaged under normal circumstances. He contrasts such youngsters with those who use narcotic drugs to surmount their gross inability to relate to, or make meaningful contact with, people and society *but* he also notes the fundamental *similarity* of both types of drug-user in that they are both in need of help to find their points of contact.

Interestingly enough, though, the major psychedelics seem to have a paradoxical role to play in helping people find a way of coming to terms with others. The effect of these drugs is to dissolve the ego-boundaries and the boundaries between the self and other people and things, thus soothing what are often experienced as painful feelings of separateness and alienation. But the price of this relief is to turn over a large part of one's motivational autonomy to the group with whom one uses drugs. That the user achieves greater harmony with his fellows seems to be a generally acceptable conclusion but, as Freedman (1968) has pointed out, the drug-using group is quite likely to comprise only people who have been drawn together by the devised mutual despair of its members. Thus, though the individual may escape from personal feelings of alienation and achieve a sense of integration and community, it may be that he has only found companions in alienation and, because of the associated pressures of the group and its behaviour patterns, he may become ever less fitted to achieve his goal of becoming adapted to his culture. In other words, one succeeds by failing in the fellowship of others. As Young (1971) has pointed out, the very fact of illegally using drugs is a major new influence in the individual's life, adding to his sources of anxiety and very realistically making him one of society's outsiders and hunted deviants.

But, whether one feels that psychedelic philosophy comprises a positively derived set of attitudes towards living, or whether it is seen as the rationalizations of inadequate people unable to cope with life in the more usual manner, one has to ask whether society's reactions to the users of these drugs embody a more noble philosophy. Whichever way one sees it – as the need to express a more peaceful and passive way of life or to seek relief from alienation – surely a society must itself be near to moral bankruptcy if its solution to these things is suppression and imprisonment rather than help.

We all live by a system of necessary myths which guide our lives. In previous ages these myths and taboos concerning religion, morality, sexuality, economics and man's nature have always been in a state of flux but radical change has usually happened in one or two areas at a time, and at a pace which is much less drastic than it may sometimes seem when viewed later in the long-term historical perspective. But the present rate of political and technological change – coupled with easier travel, radio and television, and the explosive growth of all com- munication media – has changed all this. The cross-cultural comparisons of philosophies, religion and taboos which are now a part of our daily lives have made it easier for us to believe that all systems are more or less arbitrary and thus not the immutable things which they have often been taken for. Consequently, young people find it much easier than hitherto to form their own ideas of morality and to ditch those licensed by the strict rules of society. Paradoxically, though, these philosophical shifts are very much facilitated by, for example, the economic security and the birth-control methods provided by 'straight society': a debt which is not, of course, acknow- ledged.

But whatever the reason, the rate of change in our way of life is greater now than ever before and this, in itself, is cause enough to motivate younger people to continuous experimentation with a whole host of new social forms – including those which value drug-induced states. But, if these particular experimental forms are unwelcome, the *context* within which such thought takes place is more so. The wider philosophy argues that only when the rate of social evolution is slow can the older generations usefully instruct the younger ones from their greater experience: when the rate of change is very rapid, much knowledge and experience becomes redundant in preparing for a changed future and new principles must be worked out all the time. The outcome is the so-called 'generation gap' with the young claiming that they are not just rebellious but preparing themselves for a new and emerging world, not for the old world which is rapidly disappearing. Evaluating such conclusions is, thankfully, far beyond our present remit but the premise does seem ines- capable that the most basic values of Western society are cur- rently in the melting pot and that there is a need to re-fashion them.

Charles Reich (1970), in his celebrated and controversial book,

The Greening of America, writes of a coming revolution amongst young people which is as relevant to the rest of the West as it is to America. His analysis of the current scene leads him to foresee a non-violent revolution developing outwards from the individual's manifestly changing attitudes towards social justice, sex, dress, drugs, art and so on. Reich argues that the process is inevitable and gives examples of the ways in which it is proceeding. By its very nature, it cannot be halted by force as it is non-aggressive and therefore does not lead to direct confrontations but, it is argued, it will finally culminate in the radical change of all social and political institutions.

The use of psychedelic drugs, being a part of this revolution, is the one front on which direct counter-attacks can be made by 'Establishment' forces and, in this area, their opposition has been particularly bitter – though whether the fierce policies employed are provoked by a general disquiet about the rising problem of drug *addiction*, or whether this is a response to the typically unacceptable social values of psychedelic users, is a moot point.

What is less in doubt is that there is emerging this acid-using, pot-smoking, radically minded section of young people who are on the whole somewhat censorious, not only of the values of the older generations, but also of their traditional consciousness-modifying drug – alcohol! And, though it may be true that the majority of similarly radically minded youngsters have never themselves used any form of drug, evidence will later be presented to show how much they have been exposed to the influence of a large number of articulate and creative people who have.

Back in 1954, Maurice Carstairs made a most delicate empirical and intellectual analysis of the cultural reasons which lead people to prefer one drug to another – specifically, alcohol versus cannabis. His study took place in India but he concluded that Westerners are extremely unlikely to turn from alcohol to drugs such as cannabis as their *effects* do not accord with our own basic value systems. Cultural values seemed to be so decisive in determining the choice of drug that he could not imagine cannabis becoming widely popular unless there also occurred some unforeseen reversal of our basic values. In view of the now widespread use of drugs amongst the younger generation, if one accepts Carstairs' conclusions we should also look for what has indeed come to pass – a very marked shift in the value systems of the younger generation. Yet, even if it is true, that both cultural change and changes in drug-using behaviour have paralleled one another during the last twenty years, we should weigh most carefully any arguments which link them in any *causal* relationship.

Such inferential and observational evidence as there is does make it seem likely that psychedelic experiences do have some effect in modifying people's views and dispositions in the ways that have been discussed. However, it would be wrong to suppose that what we have been referring to as a 'philosophy' is something uniquely caused by the drugs: there are many other possibilities to account for this association. We might, for example, note that many people who have never taken psychedelic drugs share the same point of view. This being the case, the logical status of the drug itself could be a sufficient, though not necessary, cause. Then we might query whether the fact of taking these substances in the first place was not preceded by a particular disposition or readiness. And, if we accept a particular readiness for change, we are then beginning to think of the drugs as no more than 'causal factors'. But we may wish to go all the way and deny that the drugs have *any* causal role in shaping philosophical views and thus we should be asserting that the only connection was that of simple *association*. In other words, people of a certain type often *also* use psychedelic drugs. Finally, we may maintain quite the opposite – that the use of certain mind-altering drugs is the *result* of changing views, customs and values.

All of these alternative explanations are possible and all have their adherents but, without anticipating much of the content of this book, it would be extremely difficult to present the case for one or another. At this stage it is sufficient just to note the general trends which seem to be typical of the 'dropped-out, turned-on, and tuned-in' philosophy of the users of psychedelics. When we have considered more of the evidence about the effect of these drugs, particularly in relation to religious, aggressive, and sexual adjustments, it will then be a lot easier for us to return to the topic and make some assessment of the causal part played by these substances in shaping people's attitudes towards life.

7 Sex and Sexuality

Unlike most of the issues dealt with in this book, the effect of psychedelic drugs on human sexual behaviour is not one which has led to significant programmes of observation and research. On the whole, people keep quiet about the details of their own sexual activities (though not necessarily other people's) – however normal or unusual these may be. Evidence of the sexual activity of others, particularly where it derives from anonymous mass-media sources, has to be treated with a more than usual degree of caution.

In all branches of sex research the basic problem is always the same: to collect a wide and *representative* sample of data from the population about which we wish to generalize whilst avoiding an undue emphasis upon striking events or the contributions of 'volunteers'. The same is, of course, true of all psychological research, but nowhere is caution more important, nor implementing the principle more difficult. For example, the sources which would be by far the most acceptable – experiments and direct observation by uninvolved researchers – are not, as is obvious, readily possible with representative and non-volunteer subjects. Even in anthropological studies where the nature of sex taboos may be more favourable and the scientists hardened and unabashed observers, the data is often exceedingly inferential, the observations themselves oblique, and comparisons of situations with and without drug availability rarer still.

Yet, despite the difficulties of assembling real evidence on this topic, there is no shortage of opinion and strongly held belief – the users of psychedelic drugs being closely linked in most people's minds, and in much that is written, with notions of hypersexuality and 'free love'. The hippie communes themselves probably attract most of the attention that they receive because of the real or assumed sexual relationships of the men and women who compose them. The stereotype, and in many cases the reality, is of young people living together and rejecting notions not only of formal marriage, but even of stable common law contracts and indeed of any relationship implying special responsibilities to the other person. Polygamous and polyandrous arrangements are not unheard of, and accounts drawn from many types of observation suggest a very generalized degree of promiscuity amongst all regular users of the drugs with, in many cases, a tendency towards group sexual activities of the so-called 'orgy' type.

Given such associations, and one can certainly produce a great deal of evidence of the associational type, an analysis of the effects and causal status of the drugs becomes of some moral, social, and sociological importance. However, the question is not just whether an association between sexual behaviour and psychedelic drug use exists, but whether there is a *causal* relationship. For example, it may be the case that men who smoke corona cigars tend to be successfully involved in business, but this *association* is not likely to be taken for a causal one. Few people would assume that because many tycoons smoke big cigars their motivations and skills derive from them. We should most likely think of the cigars as part of a life-style which also includes large cars and houses, pretty secretaries, well-cut suits and other expensive tastes. So with the regular psychedelic users: it may be that their sexuality and drug usage are simply elements in another quite recognizable style which, by contrast, is often typified by crumpled clothes, beads, long hair, pop music, religious totems, vegetarian food fads, and so on. So we must continue to bear in mind the question of causality when reviewing the evidence which connects sexual behaviour with the use of psychedelic drugs.

Some of the associations, and ones where causality *has* been claimed, date back to quite ancient times. In this respect, John Allegro (1970) is a source of some fascinating, and controversial, facts and conclusions. Later, in the chapter on religious uses of psychedelics, we shall have occasion to look more closely at his account of fertility cults and at the great sexual content of these. Indeed, Allegro is primarily concerned with uncovering esoteric forms of the ancient worship of the 'Sacred Phallus' and how they relate to the Judeo-Christian tradition. As we shall see, his thesis is that the 'Sacred Phallus' actually refers to the psychedelic mushroom, *Amanita muscaria*, and that the sexual-religious impact of this fungus has been exceedingly powerful in many, and diverse, cultic practices.

For example, he argues that the Greek god Bacchus, whom he refers to as the 'Phallus God', was closely identified with *Amanita muscaria* and that the 'little children' which his female votaries, the Bacchantes, were supposed to have pulled apart and eaten were really mushrooms. Their identification as 'children', as in ancient Sumer, derived from their resemblance to small images of the phallus-god. The wild copulation and frenzied eroticism which typified the Bacchanalia, together with the violent and unnaturally prolonged sexual orgasms, were features which Allegro ascribes to the effect of the drug. As with much of the material with which he deals, he is attempting to piece together fragmentary clues to build up a picture of a mystery cult which, even in its time, would have been very difficult to penetrate by any but its more senior initiates. Accordingly, the evidence and inferences are abstruse and difficult to summarize briefly but should be consulted in the original by those interested.

Mystery also surrounds the use, and identity, of the ancient Indian 'Soma'. Andrews and Vinkenoog (1967) still identify it with cannabis though the mushroom *Amanita muscaria* seems a more convincing candidate, especially where it is poetically referred to as 'Soma's golden phallus' (*Rig-Veda*, IV, 58). But whatever its exact identification, Soma was undoubtedly a powerful psychedelic substance which, hundreds of years before the birth of Christ, was being praised in the Vedic Hymns of the Hindus and was playing its part in the erotic tradition of that most complex of religious forms. But neither cannabis nor amanita find any mention amongst the numerous recipes for exciting or enhancing sexual performance which are so carefully detailed in those venerable Indian guides to love making, *The Kama Sutra* of Vatsyayana and *The Ananga Ranga* of Kalyana Malla. One assumes that these particular materials were either not known, had somehow become taboo for secular use in the meantime, or else that they were not regarded as being particularly sex-specific.

The precise identification of these ancient potions, which are known to us only by archaic terms, their effects and, more rarely, by some descriptive clues, is a perpetual source of difficulty. For example de Ropp (1958) disagrees with Allegro about the substance used for creating the sexual excitement of the Bacchanalia. De Ropp confidently identifies it as *Datura stramonium*, a plant hallucinogen of the potato family which contains the alkaloids stramonium, hyoscyamine and atropine: a substance still known currently in the United States as jimson-weed, thorn apple, etc. *This* plant does appear in *The Ananga Ranga*, in the seventh prayoga – a recipe of 'sovereign virtue' – in hastening the paroxysms of a woman. But, whatever the correct identification of these drugs, it seems clear that psychedelic substances have found sexual uses since ancient times.

Other substances with great botanical and chemical similarities to datura, like belladonna and henbane, also have a rather long history of association with sexual orgies. These plants were prominent herbs in the recipes of 'The Old Religion' and of medieval witchcraft (Maple, 1965) and, as de Ropp observes, were no doubt responsible for the hallucinations, sexual frenzy, and terrible visions of the witch's world. As an example of a not untypical happening, de Ropp describes the case of Lise, the young daughter of a sixteenth-century Bavarian pastor. The girl, lured to a midnight meeting of witches in the mountains, drank some of the brew which was circulated then, stripping herself naked, was annointed with 'The Witch's Salve' – both substances presumably containing either belladonna or henbane as traditionally used psychedelic herbs. Her terrifying visions of hell and her supposed soaring on a broom-stick were also accompanied by wild sexual activity during which she believed herself to have had intercourse with the devil. The aftermath – the confession to her father, the torture and 'confessions' of the others, and the inevitable fiery deaths in the town square – completed the sequence. Perhaps she was simply a schizophrenic youngster, tormented with the sick images of a brutal church but, whether this particular girl was otherwise unhinged or not, the pattern is so common and the subjective responses would so well fit the known facts of using these powerful hallucinatory drugs, that one is tempted to believe that they were causally involved in many if not all such cases: sexual excesses and all.

Hashish, too, has ancient sexual associations, allegedly being given to young men in the paradisical gardens of Hasan-i-Sabba, the 'Old Man of the Mountain', leader of the Assassin sect during the eleventh century. Marco Polo richly chronicled the events which took place, though his account is based on tales told after the mountain fortress had been destroyed and the sect crushed. However, though the stories of houris and sensual delight are well enough supported, the evidence for hashish use is much more inferential and tangential. But if for sake of the argument we accept that something called 'hashish' was used, we should still have the problem of deciding what this something was. It may have been what is exclusively referred to by that name today but, as Blum (1969) points out, the term has several meanings and, according to a Moslem traveller in the fourteenth century, hashish might be either conventional hemp or else it might be that other potent psychedelic, henbane. Henbane hashish was apparently common in Turkey, Persia and India and may very well have been the drug of the Assassins, but then we have no proof or clear evidence that *any* psychedelic substance was used – despite later myths to that effect.

Almost as widely referred to was the self-publicized scandalous conduct of those bohemian literary gentlemen who formed the mid-ninteenth century 'Le Club des Hachichins'. Not surprisingly, writers like Gautier and Baudelaire found it very difficult to stick to temperate reporting, preferring to present all their experiences in the most dramatic and extravagant way: what is realistic and what poetic licence is very difficult to say. What *is* certain is that both these men had very erotic natures – indeed Gautier paid the ultimate price by dying of venereal disease. Yet, recounting his experience with hashish (in Solomon, 1969) he describes his erotic vision as unmoving and concluded that 'the prettiest girl in Verona, to a hashisheen, is not worth the bother of stirring'. From such a person one might be inclined to accept that hashish, cannabis in this case, really was not a sexual stimulant – but remember that this was in the early stage of experimentation and that the club was a male one, so perhaps the circumstances were not themselves as stimulating as they might have been!

But Gautier is not alone in claiming that cannabis has ana-phrodisiac qualities: Lindesmith (1969), too, basing his judge-ment upon reports of users, says that the effect of the drugs is actually to depress sexual activity. But McGlothlin (1969) is nearer to the consensus of opinion when he cites a range of other work which claims to show that cannabis causes everything from sexual inhibition and even impotence through to the enhancement of normal relations or the encouragement of perverted behaviour. The consensus opinion is then, so to speak, a matter of agreeing that no unequivocal conclusion can be drawn. The *main* problem is one of having no experimental evidence but it is also, at least in part, a semantic one too: a question of defining what we mean when we speak of 'aphrodisiac' qualities. Normal usage would tend to mean that a substance possessed particular qualities which would excite or arouse sexual impulses. However, there are at least two concepts em-bedded in even so simple a definition: there is the notion of enhancing sexual impulses which may already be manifest, and there is the meaning of triggering sexual impulses which may not have pre-existed.

The idea of a sexual 'trigger' has a very long history indeed and the search for such substances has been almost as vigorously pursued as the alchemist's quest for the secret of turning base metal into gold. Crow (1969) lists many of the ancient favourites including that most dangerous of substances, cantharides or 'Spanish fly', which still takes its toll of young women's lives when criminally administered by men seeking an advantage. But, Crow concludes, no drug has yet proved capable of be-having as a *specific* sex stimulant. Exceptions to this rule may, however, exist amongst the psychedelic drugs: Hoffer and Osmond (1967) cite an example of Meso-American Indians drinking a brew of Ololiuqui which was held to act as an aphro-disiac and Cohen (1965) observes that the brew derived by the Amazonian Indians from the vine *Banisteria caapi*, apart from its other uses in ecstasy, divination, and prophesy, is also valued as an aphrodisiac which, it is claimed, causes clitorial distension and penile engorgement. However, this direct form of sexual arousal by psychedelic substances appears to be an extremely rare quality.

Even so, Louria (1970) claims that L S D has been used in the same fashion as cantharides, that is, administered without the victim's knowledge, rendering her vulnerable to sexual or orgiastic activity as a result of confusion and suggestibility caused by the drug.

This sort of misgiving was earlier expressed by Kingman (1927) in relation to cannabis when he drew a contrast with the effects of hypnotically induced suggestibility. The comparison made was that, even under hypnosis, one would not commit theft, murder, or rape if this was contrary to one's principles but, in the suggestibility resulting from hashish intoxication, 'the last vestige of man's artificially acquired restraint is swept aside'.

The picture of innocent youngsters being set alight by the biological urges induced through such drugs as cannabis and thus being drawn into orgies is, according to Schofield (1971), who has made first-hand studies of both adolescent sexuality and cannabis use, pure fantasy. Yet few people working in the field would be likely to deny that there is some sort of relationship between psychedelic drug use and sexual behaviour or feelings. What does seem unlikely, though, is that the psychedelics will 'trigger' a sexual pattern of behaviour in the same sense that, say, digitalis will specifically boost heart activity. The evidence supporting the idea that psychedelics promote a specific behavioural response would seem to be exceedingly scanty, despite the subjective impressions of people using them.

Animal studies provide a certain type of objective evidence but their conclusions tend to be extremely difficult to evaluate in human terms. For example, Miras (1965), reported that cannabis administered to rats results in a 90 per cent decrease in their reproductive activity and thus the drug is clearly a potent anaphrodisiac. But mankind is much more complex than any other animal and his behaviour much less directly determined by biological states: for example, humans castrated after puberty may still continue to enjoy rich sexual relationships! Consequently, it would be naïve to accept uncritically that what is true for rats, or any other animal, is necessarily so for human beings.

Clinical evidence deriving from cases of chronic indulgence with cannabis seemed to the Chopras (1942) to follow the course of an *initial* sexual enhancement followed by a progressive deterioration in the quality of all interpersonal relationships – frequently culminating in sexual perversions of one sort or another. By contrast, Schofield's (1971) assessment of the evidence is that even overdoses of cannabis will not, in themselves, lead normal personalities into perversion, rape, or violent sex. Nevertheless, this contradiction of the Chopras' conclusions may be more apparent than real – the young people still flirting with 'pot', and who are the majority group discussed by Schofield, are a very different group from the hospitilized psychiatric cases referred to by the Chopras. As always, the value of any piece of evidence is governed by the circumstances in which it was derived: studies conducted solely upon psychiatric casualties, or indeed upon any selectively drawn group, run the risk of being quite unrepresentative. Therefore the best that can be done at this stage is to present the evidence from as many sources as possible and leave readers to draw their own conclusions.

Undoubtedly the 'evidence' which captures public appeal most strongly is that which refers to perversion, orgies, and situations where the morals of young girls are being affected. Taylor (1970), in his book *Satan's Slaves*, a racy paperback dealing largely with the murders of Sharon Tate and others by Charles Manson's 'family', is a good example of this type of writing. The evocation of crime and the firelight scenes of group sex and obscenity certainly seem to imply a causal relationship between the use of psychedelics and the behaviour reported. No doubt most of us find murder, sadism and sexual outrages so incomprehensible that we almost automatically look for an 'explanation' and, in the tiny minority of cases where drugs are also known to be present, we are often motivated to solve the problem by proposing a simplistic causal relationship. We may, or may not, be right in our conclusions: there is seldom any way of finding out.

In this vein of ascribing guilt by association, Louria (1970) also quotes a case of a young woman who, after taking L S D, lay out in the street with her clothes pulled up and her legs apart calling on God to have a sexual relationship with her. The trouble with this sort of anecdote is that one has no idea how to evaluate it. Are we to suppose that if one gave the drug to a group of healthy young women something of the sort would happen in a given percentage of cases or are we only describing the misfortune of a particular girl who was, or would have been, a psychiatric case anyway? Certainly I have also come across no less bizarre things in clinical situations where, because there was no suggestion of any drugs being involved, quite different 'causes' had to be invoked. Cases like the one mentioned are of no scientific value unless they occur within the context of a proper evaluation, though they do have considerable propaganda impact.

Schofield (1971), who has spent a considerable amount of time evaluating cannabis as a member of the British Government's Advisory Committee on Drug Dependence, concluded that the lurid stories of teenage drug and sex orgies which are so commonly believed are actually complete myths. The same conclusion had been reached many years earlier, in 1940, by Mayor la Guardia's Committee in New York (see Solomon, 1969). They found that, contrary to much contemporary speculation and agitation, marijuana was not a direct causal factor in stimulating debauchery, prostitution and hypersexuality – despite the fact that prostitution and marijuana smoking went together in some of the brothels or 'tea-pads'.

On the other hand, Charen and Perelman (1946) found that amongst the predominantly American Negro soldiers who were referred to them for psychological and psychiatric evaluation, attendance at 'tea-parties' was common and the association between sexuality and the use of marijuana was very close. Most of these soldiers had aberrant sexual problems – both hetero- and homosexual and, interestingly enough, many also professed heterosexual desires but claimed that they lacked this interest in women unless under the influence of the drug. The reason was not, apparently, due to any deficiency of libido but because they otherwise lacked the confidence to attempt seduction. At these 'tea-parties' loss of inhibition was the rule: public spectacles of perversions, so-called 'circuses', were common and many of the practices reported were more than usually obscene. The drug appeared to the investigators to be closely associated with a compulsion towards sexual gratification at the level of infantile behaviour – impulses which they felt to be released as a result of the suspension of all sense of shame and disgust.

Association there certainly is. Helen Perry (1970), in her observations of hippie life in the Haight-Ashbury district of Los Angeles, comments on the sexual 'liberation' of the girls, giving examples of their pleasure at watching dogs copulate and of their very unhibited hetero- and homosexual embracing in public. Unfortunately, we are again left to guess at the part played by drugs in this liberation: Haight-Ashbury was then the centre of psychedelic drug usage but no evidence is offered as to whether the girls so observed were, or had been, drug-users. Despite the very real sociological value of this account, it does leave some considerable causal gaps to be filled in by inference, often allowing a good deal of scope for the working of our own prejudices, expectations, and ignorance of the real situation.

David Smith, medical director of the Haight-Ashbury Free Medical Clinic, writing of a later stage in the history of 'Psychedelphia', refers to the way in which publicity attracted a new type of person to the area – typically alienated, psychotic, and violent young people who came for the promised intoxication and easy sex and who succeeded in destroying the original community and driving the 'flower people' away (Smith, Luce, and Dernburg, 1970). Thus the rising incidence of sexually transmitted disease which occurred, and which gives some measure of promiscuity, must nevertheless be linked both to the changing type of population and also the associated change in pattern of drug use – with heroin, alcohol, barbiturates and amphetamines replacing the psychedelics of the earlier phase.

Yet, even in its hippie heyday when psychedelics were the principal drugs in use, Haight-Ashbury was generally regarded as a considerable centre of promiscuity and general permissiveness. Still, even if one accepts that using psychedelic drugs was closely associated with such behaviour, the motivations would seem to be important. Helen Perry (1970) felt that the sexuality was part and parcel of a more general philosophy of life in which loving contact, most fully expressed in a sexual relationship, was simply a vehicle for achieving a sense of complete unity, and unreserved tenderness with others. The same philosophy apparently prevailed in Toronto's Yorkville where Alampur (see Smart and Jackson, 1969) observed that though sexual relationships were, by most definitions, promiscuous, they were not indiscriminate: it was just that sex was expected to follow on naturally from liking. Sex was not, in the hippie philosophy, the basis for their moral code; love was, and sex was *one* of the ways of expressing widespread love.

This, of course, was the ideal. The reality was often far less appealing for, though ideal expressions may have prevailed in many cases, the principle of 'free love' was difficult to manage in practice and sexual jealousies and hostilities frequently broke out. That most experienced psychedelic user and observer, Timothy Leary (1965), is very plain on the likely disruptive effect of sex unless very carefully managed and stresses the need for groups (or 'clans') to establish policies about its use. But caution and restraint are seldom the most characteristic qualities of young people away from home and, for example, Alampur observed a good deal of fairly conventional promiscuity between the hippie males, who formed a majority within Yorkville's resident community, and 'weekend hippies' – girls who came for the thrills, sex, and prestige of appearing to be 'with-it'.

An element of youthful rebellion also seemed to play a large part in determining Yorkville's prevailing sexual pattern. Courting and marriage were despised as middle-class conventions in which sex was the bait and so, for the hippies, it became an article of faith that no binding relationship was assumed before people entered a sexual relationship. In other words the adolescent ideal: free, unresponsible, sex with a variety of partners. Children were not wanted by these urban flat dwellers and abortion and adoption were common stratagems for avoiding long-term responsibilities. Again, though, it would be wrong to generalize on the basis of a limited sample only. For example, Hedgepeth and Stock (1970), on the basis of a much wider experience of American communes where psychedelic drug-taking was most usual, found that though promiscuity and group sex was standard practice in some, monogamy was preferred by the majority as the most practical and satisfying arrangement for both individuals and the society. In the groups visited, children were generally well loved and cared for. Yet, having said this, these stable and generally rural communes represent only a tiny proportion of the young people who regularly use psychedelics and they may well be much less representative of the body of users than are the urban ones.

As we have seen, the evidence regarding the aphrodisiac qualities of these substances is extremely patchy and difficult to generalize from. One reason is that we have been discussing the psychedelics in a very general sense and perhaps assuming a greater degree of psycho-pharmacological similarity than is justified. On the other hand, it is possible to express general propositions about certain particular, and exceptional, substances like nutmeg, which have been clearly reported as having very specific sexual effects. Hoffer and Osmond (1967), describing its use in a prison context, note that it can result in a very considerable and long-lasting effect, producing a more or less constant erection for between twenty-four and thirty-six hours with heightened pleasure in masturbating. So far as I know, no one has denied this effect though, because of its other unpleasant aspects, nutmeg-abuse has remained a very minor affair and its contribution to the lore is thus minimal also.

The case of LSD is perhaps the most intriguing because of the total disagreement between Timothy Leary and so many other writers. In view of Leary's great experience and knowledge, one can scarcely overlook his conclusions: especially as he has personally introduced hundreds, and possibly thousands, to the use of LSD. In the early 1960s Leary had been very reticent about the aphrodisiac qualities of the drug but, in one of the classic accounts of the psychedelic experience given in 1966 as an interview to *Playboy* magazine (see 1970 reprint of Leary, 1965), he made some very plain statements on the subject of sexual response. During the interview he confided that he had kept quiet about sexual effects in order to avoid provoking even more vehement attacks than had occurred but, as he was already under a thirty-year prison sentence for a minor marijuana offence – a sentence which represented an effective life (or death) sentence for a middle-aged man – there was nothing else society could do to him and he thus felt able to speak more freely. There is, in his view, no shadow of doubt that L S D is the most powerful aphrodisiac ever discovered.

He describes it, not as an irritant like cantharides, nor as a specific physiological stimulant or trigger, nor yet as a numbing disinhibitor like alcohol, but as a substance which is capable of tuning-up all our sensitivities, including the sexual ones, a thousandfold. Sexual intercourse is, he says, enormously extended without exhaustion, and even women who otherwise have difficulty in achieving orgasm at all, may experience literally hundreds during a single love-making. The comparison between L S D-supplemented intercourse and the normal state would be the difference between ecstasy and the experience of making love to a department-store dummy. Inherent in this comparison is not only the difference in physical sensuality but also the enormously enhanced communion of the people concerned. But far from this leading to the urge for many sexual partners, and disclaiming the knowledge to generalize about other people, Leary himself said that he found all women in the eyes of his own wife, and thus could see no point in promiscuous relationships. So, whilst not condemning or having any moral views about what other people should do, he personally felt that sexual relationships with many different people are likely to be less satisfying than making love, in the intense psychedelic sense, with a single person.

It appears then that Leary is describing L S D as an aphrodisiac only in the restricted sense of its capacity to augment sexual experiences when they occur: not as a trigger to release pent-up sexuality which would otherwise be restricted. Yet, in another passage of the same interview, he recounts that amongst the large number of priests, ministers, and monks to whom he has administered L S D, a large number were so affected that they gave up celibacy and chastity, and renounced their orders, to seek a 'mating relationship'; the reason, it is claimed, being that they had at last come face to face with their true organic selves, stripped of their more superficial beliefs and ritualized behaviour. Thus Leary appears to be postulating some modified sort of trigger effect as well as enhancement of sexual intercourse. Of course, we must take into account the possibility that those members of religious orders who took L S D did so because they were already disillusioned with their vocation and lives and were ready to try something new. Indeed, in the absence of other evidence, this seems to be the most likely explanation and it is possible that Leary himself would repudiate a trigger effect in favour of a more general one in which the individual simply came to terms with a new social and interpersonal role.

Certainly there was no evidence of libidinous impulses being let loose at the psychedelic training centre which Leary and his associates established in an hotel at Zihuatanejo in Mexico. One disinterested medical observer, Downing (1965), stated that the women there reported no change in their erotic drives, although one spoke of a lessening of inhibitory shame. But the men reported an actual lessening in their erotic drive attendant upon repeated use of L S D which amounted, in two cases, to erectile impotence. Downing, working with an admirable thoroughness, checked these statements against behaviour by making inquiries amongst the ever-observant hotel employees and confirmed that the sexual activities of the participants certainly appeared to be less than they would expect from the average party of people away on holiday.

Downing's findings are just what Louria (1970) would expect. He claims that L S D is actually an anti-aphrodisiac in that, though it may increase mental eroticism, this is not matched by an appropriate physical counterpart and that, when sex does take place, the augmentation occurs simply in terms of illusions and distortions of time, shape, and size. Thus breasts and genitals may *seem* vast and vivid and time immensely extended but, of course, this is no more than a grotesque, subjective, distortion of reality. Needless to say, one could equally argue that the sensation *is* the reality, but Louria appears to reject this line of thinking and, instead, concludes that the aphrodisiac claims made for the drug are unfounded, but that they continue to be promoted by proselytizers as a bait with which to attract others to become users. Stafford and Golightly (1967) also came to the opinion that LSD is not an aphrodisiac in the more usual sense, but that it may be helpful in removing frigidity, reticence, inhibitions and poor sexual relationships, and that it may offset boredom and produce real sensual and interpersonal improvements. Much the same conclusion was arrived at by the Canadian Commission of Inquiry (1970), though they also made the point that, even though LSD is by no means sex-specific, its behavioural consequences may be profound – some finding sex more satisfying whilst others appear to lose their interest in it.

Cannabis, too, has been described as being a useful substance to quell sexual desires. Taylor (1969) came out strongly in saying that ganja (cannabis) is a clear sexual inhibitor and cites as supporting evidence the fact that it is used for this purpose by Indian priests. However, Dwarakanath (1965) reports that paradoxically, as well as being smoked by yogis and fakirs for meditative and religious purposes, cannabis is also very widely prescribed by practitioners of traditional medicine as an aphrodisiac. Schultes (1969a) also describes its use in India – referring to its value in religion, folk-medicine, and as an aphrodisiac. But Carstairs (1954) cautions us that things are not always all that they seem for concoctions of cannabis are often made up also containing a favourite aphrodisiac and de Ropp (1958) also refers to the oriental practice of adding a pinch of nux vomica or cantharides. Indeed, Dwarakanath writes of the preparation of aphrodisiacs containing cannabis, though there seems no doubt that this material is regarded as a potent stimulant in itself. However, it does not necessarily follow that any observed aphrodisiacal properties always derive solely from the cannabis used.

Turning to another of the drugs, and on a slightly different tack, la Barre (1938), confirming the findings of other research, himself concluded that the mescaline which is taken in the form of peyote by North American Indians appears to have no specific influence on sexuality in any way. In fact, the association of this drug with religious practices resulted, according to Barron, Jarvik, and Bunnell (1964), in a common belief that the substance was an anaphrodisiac. But, they concluded, the hallucinogens are neither sexual stimulators nor inhibitors – they simply change the perception of events in a way which depends upon set, setting, dosage and the user. And this is surely the point; all the evidence we have looked at so far must be regarded as contingent upon these factors when we draw our conclusions. The results presented are full of *apparent contradictions* which might be quite simply resolved if only it was possible to control these variables, or at least to have a reasonable working knowledge of them. For example, Leary made a very telling point in the interview earlier referred to when he stated that LSD may, because of the novelty and potency of the situation, make it difficult or impossible to enter into a sexual relationship during perhaps the first ten sessions, but that this would depend upon both the setting and the partner involved. If this is so, it would follow that statements about stimulant qualities should also be accompanied by some information about the prior relationships of the people taking drugs together, as well as about their stage of usage. If the individuals are relative strangers, or at an early stage of experimentation, then sexual abandon is probably a less likely sequel than if they are already sexually familiar with one another and experienced in the use of the drug. However, no such refined analysis yet appears to exist so we must cautiously make what we can of our existing information, paying less attention to the idiosyncratic, and more to the broadly based survey.

Tart (1971) was responsible for one such study in which sex was one element in a broader evaluation of the sensory, emotional, and intellectual effects of using cannabis. Making contacts and preserving anonymity is always a problem, especially when enormous prison sentences could be involved, so Tart chose as his instrument a questionnaire. His subjects were American students and to these he distributed 750 questionnaires with stamped addressed envelopes. The students were given these and asked to pass them along until they fell into the hands of 'experienced' marijuana users: that is, people who had used it on at least a dozen occasions. This procedure resulted in the return of 153 completed documents, of which 72 per cent of the respondents had also used LSD. His results were very positively in favour of sexual enhancement. Subjects commonly held that their sexual appetite was increased in contexts where they would normally be responsive, though not in ones where they would not, and that the quality of their physical and interpersonal sensitivity was very much increased. Characteristically, too, they reported that orgasm developed new, and very pleasurable, qualities.

Goode (1969, 1970), also found this sort of result in questioning 200 marijuana users, noting that it was the women more than men who seemed to respond with an increased sexual interest. But it was the *regular* users who were the most sexually stimulated – it perhaps being the case that, as with LSD, infrequent users are more distracted by the range and variety of other sensory effects. Goode, in looking for reasons why cannabis should have such apparent aphrodisiac effects, felt that aphrodisiac myth itself played a part: thus, when a man and woman took cannabis together, there was already a covert understanding and expectation. Moreover, the general sensuality and feelings of euphoria in the context of a taboo adventure may themselves be expected to contribute towards uninhibited sexual relationships. Also women, being hedged by more restraints against displaying frank sexuality, may find it easier to shed them if they can find some 'excuse' for their behaviour, thus 'letting themselves go' in the comforting assurance that it is the drugs, and not they, who are responsible.

But, whatever the reason, the best evidence available certainly suggests that many of the psychedelics do bear an intimate relationship to the human sexual response. It is by no means clear though whether such drugs themselves produce erotic desire for, after all, they are mainly used by young people at a stage in life when their sexual drives are at the maximum anyway. But, despite some contrary evidence which may well reflect nothing more than differing types of set, setting, dosage, and personality, the bulk of evidence strongly suggests that the psychedelic drugs may, at the very least, serve to sweep aside guilt, modesty, and restraint, and to enhance the sensual element in a way that makes sex less self-conscious and more physically satisfying than is often otherwise the case. Whether these effects represent, as the conclusion might seem to suggest, an unqualified good, or whether they also contain or suggest an unacceptable threat to society by promoting promiscuity or sensuality at the cost of other values, is by no means clear. Such value judgements cannot, in any case, be derived directly from the evidence, but one could wish that more information on this topic was available. Whether or not the psychedelics are ever legalized, one needs such data for both scientific purposes and as part of a properly based empirical rationale for our decisions.

8 Crime and Aggression

Probably the most widely known 'fact' about the connection between violence and psychedelic substances is that it was hashish that induced the madness, and provoked the atrocities, of the 'Assassins'. As has already been mentioned in another context, their story was first told by Marco Polo after he had passed through that part of Persia where 'The Old Man of the Mountains' had established his fortress to counter not only the Crusaders but also a large proportion of his own secular and religious kin. The now well-known tale which was unfolded told of a Muslim religious leader who, through cunningly stage-managed tastes of 'Paradise', was able to manipulate the behaviour of his followers and introduce widespread assassination as the instrument of his influence. The main historical facts, that the sect was responsible for considerable guerrilla activity and the assassination of many prominent people, is a matter of record – as is the fact that the group flourished between the years A.D. 1090 when it was established in Alamut, a Persian mountain fortress, and 1272 when its once widely spread possessions were finally regained and its head quarters destroyed by the Mongols and local forces.

Marco Polo arrived on the scene some fifteen years after this dissolution had taken place and brought back with him the story which has become the basis for the most extensively used *evidence* that hashish, or cannabis, is the cause of ungovernable violence. The story that was retold as proof of this association was how 'The Old Man' had given hashish to his disciples and how, under the effects of suggestibility and the malevolence which was thus evoked, they were sent on their missions of murder – which they performed with unprecedented ferocity and in-humanity. Such a view was presented as fact by Kingman (1927) in the early stages of the American movement against marijuana; his emphasis being placed on the 'hypnotic-like suggestibility' which could be used to sweep away all normal mental restraints. The story was told and re-told, losing nothing, and was paralleled by many other versions which might be said to culminate in the virtually unchallenged statements of U S Narcotics Commissioner H. J. Anslinger who, in making his prominent contributions to the anti-marijuana legislation of 1937, used the tale as *proof* that cannabis led to violence and murder. The tale, being so captivating and filled with circumstantial associations, still flourishes to some degree: even the scholarly Schultes was still in 1969(a) able to write of the Assassins that 'excited to their nefarious work by ingesting hashish, a form of cannabis, they would carry out murder for pay'.

The idea that hashish was the mainspring of the Assassins' behaviour, and indeed the source of their very name (i.e. haschischin), had begun in the nineteenth century and by the twenties and thirties of this century was the spearhead of political and legislative propaganda. But this cavalier approach to history has inevitably resulted in a backlash: people are now going back over the evidence to re-establish the real facts (Grinspoon, 1971; Mandel, 1966).

The first thing that comes out of such analyses of the basic material is that Marco Polo never referred to the use of hashish by the Assassins: only two drugs appear in his tale, a narcotic used to render young men unconscious while they were transported in and out of the gardens of 'Paradise' and the conduits flowing with wine which they found in there. But the gardens contained other heady delights too, in the form of beautiful women, music, and the soothing charms of a rich garden in a region of mountainous waste. The purposes of this 'Paradise' can only be inferred from what we can suppose would be the needed 'props' for a self-styled prophet and secular leader, but the marijuana-prohibitionists have tended to think of it as a place where young men could be intoxicated with hashish and sensual stimulation and then, in a state of derangement and hyper-suggestibility, could be despatched to engage in murder and mayhem.

However, the *original* account tells us of how 'The Old Man' would have his disciples drugged and brought out from the garden and then asked, in front of other young men, where they had been. The disciples would reply that they had come from 'Paradise', a reward promised *to the other young men* regardless of whether they lived or died in following their master's orders. In other words, it appears that the gardens of 'Paradise' were the *reward* for savage behaviour – not its precurser and that it was to *enter* that blissful place which incited the Assassin, and not that he had been converted into a murderous fanatic by the drugs received there.

Actually, the only certain link which exists between the use of hashish and the Assassins lies in the presumption that their name, the 'Haschischin', derives from the name for the drug. Yet, even though hashish was a common enough commodity in those days, the original tale makes no suggestion that this drug played any part in the lives of the Assassins. It seems reasonable to discount the popular etymological speculations of the nineteenth century, and the subsequent corruptions of this tale, in favour of the more parsimonious conclusions of the distinguished Arabic translator, Edward Fitzgerald, who thought that the name of the sect most probably derived from the name of their leader, Hasan.

A traveller's tale of hundreds of years ago, about a then already defunct extremist group, may seem scarcely to merit even so limited a discussion in this necessarily brief overview of the relationship between aggression and the psychedelics. But, given the fact that this particular case has achieved so prominent a place in the literature – with hardly a relevant summary or report overlooking this 'evidence' and which therefore still continues to colour opinion – it does seem worth underlining some of the less often quoted details.

Also from historical sources comes another much quoted relationship between the psychedelics and violence, that of the Viking 'Berserkers'. Their name, deriving either from that of their mighty folk-lore hero Berserker or, as Blum *et al.* (1970a) assert, from the description 'ber sark' ('the wearers of bearskin'), either way refers to men of excessive ferocity – even by the standards of the Dark Ages. Two theories are used to explain the Berserkers and their behaviour: one holds that they were a warrior elite, violent and given to bouts of excessive drinking; the other account claims that they were simply men driven to murderous frenzy, to going 'berserk', through drinking potions made from the fly agaric mushroom – *Amanita muscaria*. The evidence on this subject is extremely sparse but, as Cohen (1965) observes, a similar psychedelic potion is known to be still in use amongst the Koryak nomads of Siberia – though they seem to derive only peaceful and visionary pleasures from it! On the whole, it looks much more likely that it was alcohol rather than a psychedelic substance which resulted in people going 'berserk' and committing all the vicious and destructive acts with which we are, alas, still all too familiar.

Like the historical evidence, that which derives from anthropological sources also has its problems, though it, too, is well represented in the scientific literature. For example, de Ropp (1958) gives us accounts of such occasions as the Yurupari whipping ceremony – in which Colombian Indian youths whip one another to a state of exhaustion after taking caapi, a psychedelic substance derived from a form of vine. There is also the 'Feast of Gifts' in the Indian village of Panuré – where the individual singled out to drink the caapi will rush around hitting at doors and walls and shouting that this is what he would do to his enemies.

In both cases the behaviours are very stereotyped and give one the impression that, far from being uncontrolled outbursts, they are very controlled and structured affairs. Moreover, they take place within most complex cultural frameworks and only the most incautious would wish to use such 'evidence' in the case against the psychedelics. Nevertheless, as we have seen, it has been quite customary to abstract these tenuous fragments from the historical and anthropological record and present them in support of a viewpoint. This would be perfectly acceptable if one could be sure that the facts and the causal links in these examples had been properly evaluated by those competent to do so but, as this seldom seems to be the case, it is better to forgo such circumstantial material and concentrate on those situations where one knows much more about the relevant facts.

One area where we *should* be able to assemble very complete data is that deriving from psychiatric sources – cases where the use of these drugs has been so profound as to precipitate the individual into insane acts of violence. One of the most celebrated of these cases is that of Knudsen (1964) in which he described how one of his women patients, after a series of five L S D therapy sessions, knifed her lover to death. The circumstances of this case were that the woman, who had been seduced and made pregnant by her lover – a man who, as well as causing her an abortion, also involved her in illicit distilling of alcohol and injected her with narcotics – had become seriously mentally disturbed and thus was in need of treatment. During the treatment she revealed aggressive and homicidal feelings towards her lover and, *three days after* the final L S D session, she murdered him.

The clinicians concluded that, though she was obviously not under the *toxic* influence of the drugs she received, they dared not rule out the possibility that the L S D had resulted in some diminution of her self-restraint. But, given the fact that the woman was already a psychiatric case, and the time factor involved in the crime, one can see that even a well-documented case like this one may still end with a question-mark. The main problem is, of course, that it really isn't possible, on the evidence, to decide whether the crime was due to the drug or the condition of the patient – or to some indefinable combination of the two. In such circumstances, it is right to issue cautions but it would be wrong to suppose that the evidence demonstrated causal connections.

On the other hand, there is ample evidence that patients who 'freak-out' on L S D or a similar substance often exhibit quite violent behaviour which, except in the case of the profoundly psychiatrically ill, usually occurs during the first few hours after ingestion. At this time, the paranoia, mania, or depression may on occasion lead to very violent behaviour: both outwardly directed and in terms of suicide and self-damage (Advisory Committee on Drug Dependence, 1970; Louria, 1968). However, as was apparent in chapter 5, many of the cases falling into this category were very disturbed and aggressive personalities prior to taking drugs and thus they present the same difficulty in interpretation as we have already encountered with Knudsen's case.

But it is cannabis much more than the major psychedelics which has been held responsible for precipitating cases of violent insanity. This again is a matter which has already been taken up in the consideration of pathogenic outcomes but some comment is obviously called for at this point. The US Federal Bureau of Narcotics has no doubts at all about the violent madness which marijuana may cause and Grinspoon (1971) presents a nice example of their 'documented cases'. This particular one refers to the murder of two women by a man who then committed suicide by slicing himself to pieces: the 'evidence' that it was a case of murder whilst under the influence of marijuana being that the examining doctor could think of no other explanation for the man's resistance to the shock of his self-mutilation!

Needless to say, these sort of inferences would be comic if the situation were not so tragic, yet this sort of nonsense continues to be retailed – mainly still by the American prevention agencies and especially by past collaborators of ex-commissioner Anslinger. For example, Williams (1967), in his text on drugs and police science, states unequivocally that marijuana causes crime and degeneracy by disrupting and destroying the brain with the result that 'no act is too fantastic or horrible for users of marijuana'. And Munch (1966) continues the theme in his presentation of potted cases taken from the files of the Federal Bureau of Narcotics for the years 1921 to 1964. These 'case histories', some three score or so of them, are tabulated under headings ranging from bigamy to rape and burglary to murder and are intended to be 'objective evidence' which *proves* the causal relationship between marijuana use and a wide range of crimes. Most of these case notes describe a violent incident, the sentence imposed, and a link with marijuana use but they are not in any way critically appraised – just catalogued in such a way as to shock and persuade the reader that marijuana has been proved to cause wholesale crime.

Unfortunately, propaganda exercises of this sort have very frequently found their way into the scientific literature, though the effect has not been reciprocal for, when Mayor La Guardia's committee of professional scientists and doctors reported back that they had found no direct evidence to link marijuana with the commission of crimes of violence, Mr Anslinger condemned the report. In a statement of totalitarian loftiness, he disposed of it by saying 'The Bureau immediately detected the superficiality and hollowness of its findings and denounced it.' Having criticized them, it is still difficult not to feel that these confident prohibitionists are acting in good faith but, when they go beyond their function as executives and claim a superior expertise in assessing social, psychological and psychiatric dynamics, one might feel that the time has come to re-assess their credentials.

Young (1971), a sociologist, expresses very well the social scientist's dismay at the facile logic which takes an association for an explanation and points out that, whether the event concerned is a Manson-type slaying or a Vietnam massacre, causality is only established by a proper regard for all the forces at work – cultural and sub-cultural values, the psychological and psychiatric status of the individuals concerned, and the circumstances which attended the violent outburst – as well as the evidence relating to the use of drugs.

How good intentions without appropriate critical expertise may mislead is evident in an example cited by Grinspoon (1969). This case, used by the Federal Bureau of Narcotics, concerned a man who had confessed to murdering a friend whilst under the influence of marijuana but when the man was medically examined it transpired that he was a psychopathic liar and that there was no evidence of his ever using *any* form of drug. The psychiatrist concerned in this case, Walter Bromberg, had himself made a careful study of the criminogenic effects of marijuana (Bromberg, 1934), including a review of material referring to thousands of cases dealt with by the courts. He found the usual association between criminals and the use of marijuana but his analysis led him to conclude that there was no evidence that marijuana *caused* criminal behaviour but that, in the psychopathic and socially inadequate individuals who frequently use it, it does seem to reduce their inhibitions and allow the expression of the aggressive and sadistic elements of their personalities. He felt that alcohol was probably more powerful in this respect but, nevertheless, did not give marijuana a completely clean bill of health.

Bromberg's conclusion that cannabis, though perhaps a 'breeder of crime' only when used by psychopathic types, turns out to be very similar to that of another experienced clinician, Andrade (1959). Professor Andrade, writing of his ten years' experience as medical superintendent of a Brazilian asylum for the criminally insane and of his contact with hundreds of cases involving marijuana, also stated that the key to such crimes was the individual not the drug. In the cases he reviewed, he traced causality back to the morbid condition of the criminal's personality – whether psychotic, neurotic, or mentally defective – and held that the use of marijuana in all these cases was either incidental, or it was the 'trigger' for aggressiveness in known dangerous characters. As an interesting extra, he recounts that, despite all efforts to prevent it, marijuana continues to be smuggled into the asylum and that, even considering the dangerous and disturbed natures of the inmates, it does not produce violence.

Doctors and scientists in other less-developed countries have also recently begun to move towards a much less condemnatory position regarding the part played by cannabis in inciting violent crime: this seems to be especially so in India where the use of this drug is particularly prevalent. In 1930, Dhunjibhoy was asserting confidently, on the basis of his own clinical experience, that excessive or prolonged use degrades the mind and predisposes the user to crime. He tells us that 'Bhang is a very useful weapon in the hands of criminals for looting ornaments from women of easy virtue, and the sweetmeat majum (also cannabis) for looting ornaments from children.' Further, he affirms that a high dose of ganja (a more potent form), *when mixed with datura seeds*, is used to fortify people for murder, rape, or violent assault, and that it will precipitate these behaviours, as well as the phenomenon of 'running amok'.

Dhunjibhoy reports how, in the company of friends, he tried a potent cannabis concoction and how, on the basis of his subsequent amnesia for the events which took place, and the account which he was given of these, he would have no hesitation in the future of accepting that people may commit acts of violence under the influence of the drug and have no memory of it later. Alas, he glosses over the incident because of 'lack of space', but it would have been fascinating to know. . . .

The Chopras, in their series of papers between 1939 and 1957, took a much more moderate view of the criminogenic dangers of cannabis and, by 1957, stated that 'The result of continued and excessive use of these drugs in our experience in India is to make the individual timid rather than lead him to commit violent crimes'. By 1969 Chatterjee was *contrasting* the state of affairs in India with that in North America and noting that, though the latter was reporting that cannabis users became violent, brutalized and criminal, this was not the experience of oriental countries. In other words, the wheel has turned full circle: the West had used evidence taken from the then scientifically un-sophisticated East to make its prohibitionist points but, as the clinical and scientific standards developed in India and elsewhere, they have become more subtle in their causal analyses and find that it is the West which now supplies the horror stories. But, of course, the West's perception of the problem has been steeped in tales of the Assassins in Persia and the Thuggees and insane of India and these, in turn, have been used as causal models to explain much of the crime and violence in our own society!

Naturally, our own degree of sophistication has also been increasing and, despite the pressures of preventative and pro-hibitionist agencies, virtually every official investigation and report – from the Indian Hemp Drug Commission of 1894, through the New York Mayor's Report in 1944, the British Advisory Committee Report of 1968, as well as the Canadian and American Government Reports of the Seventies – have all rejected a causal link between the *moderate* use of cannabis and violent crime. However, it must be noted that, though the tenor of these reports is a long way from the alarmist propaganda, they all express some reservations – either as a result of the effects of chronic or excessive dosages, or of 'significant exceptions' to the general rule – whether or not these are due to transient paranoid or panic reactions.

Schofield (1971), on the basis of his membership of the 1968 Advisory Committee on Drug Dependence (the 'Wootton Report' on cannabis) and his very extensive experience with the adjustment problems of young people, tends to ridicule the evidence which is generally used to link cannabis causally with violent crime. He discounts case-history accounts of overdose panic reactions resulting in serious crime as 'anecdotes' and disallows the claim that cannabis, because of its reputation for inducing apathy and inertia, can also lead to aggressive and violent behaviour.

One rather doubts whether Schofield would object to the proposition that the drug alcohol is equally capable of inducing torpidity, bonhomie, or great aggressiveness – depending on the person and the circumstances – yet he seems to find the same principle unacceptable in relation to cannabis. But, this rather curious quirk aside, he does argue very interestingly that cannabis is hardly the sort of drug that criminal types would choose to use and that such groups as the 'Skin Heads', 'Hell's Angels', 'Rockers', etc., tend to choose such substances as the amphetamines to provide the energy and confidence necessary for their violent way of life.

Cannabis, he argues, would not be likely to serve their ends: it might give a certain amount of 'Dutch courage' but it might also reduce their efficiency and make them lose interest in committing crimes. It might indeed, but then so might alcohol which, though undoubtedly a tremendously impairing drug, is nevertheless very widely used by street gangs and other criminals. So far as making people lose interest in committing crime, this is a very speculative notion indeed.

Barber (1970) points out there are two main viewpoints on the likely criminogenic effects of the motivational loss which often accompanies the habitual use of cannabis. One faction holds that this loss of volition results, as Schofield implies, in *less* crime as the users are 'damped-down', becoming more passive and lethargic. The other faction holds that this passivity and the 'amotivational syndrome' results in *more* crime as the users, becoming either less able or less willing to work, must subsidize themselves with criminal activities. No one doubts that some criminals do use cannabis but whether this promotes crime and violence, reduces it, or has no effect still remains an important issue for debate but the current consensus would seem to be that its criminogenic potential has certainly been over-stressed in the past.

LSD, though seen as a personally very dangerous drug and likely to precipitate psychiatric conditions which might involve short-term violent reactions, has seldom been thought of as a serious source of criminal impulses in otherwise quite healthy individuals. However, Klee (1963), working with several hundred normal volunteers, reported that the effect of LSD on many of these was to unleash marked aggressive, and even homicidal, impulses. The bulk of his subjects proved to be rather passive and withdrawn during their drug experience but, in the case of an unspecified minority, a trivial incident was enough to provoke a violent reaction. Klee concluded that, though impulse-control is not affected in most subjects, for some subjects, at least, there occurs an 'impairment of their ability to tolerate tension and delay discharge'.

Cheek and Holstein (1971), studying changes in patterns of small-group social interaction following the taking of LSD, also came up with results congruent with those of Klee. Of the four groups of four which they investigated, two of them were composed of alcoholics, one of chronic schizophrenics, and the remaining one of prisoners from a reformatory. The generalized result of the study was that LSD revealed and facilitated more loving and socially positive behaviour. But the exception was the already aggressive reformatory group who became progressively more overtly hostile with increasing doses of the drug. And, though one subject claimed that his experiences had persuaded him to give up crime as he feared he might otherwise kill some-one, one of the other subjects had to be taken back to the penitentiary as his paranoid suspicions about his wife made him threaten to escape and murder her. The remaining subjects also showed increased, though less extreme, aggressiveness and led the researchers to speculate as to the behavioural effects of this drug on the already hostile psychopathic type, people like Charles Manson.

On the other hand, Smart and Bateman's 1967 review article contained only minimal evidence to implicate LSD as a source of *consummated* crime. Of the two serious instances relevant to criminal activity, one researcher reported the case of a man who, becoming grandiose for several weeks after a 'trip', threatened his wife with a gun but, no doubt thinking better of that solution to his domestic relationships, instead took himself off to live in a desert. The other case was of a man who, after a first 'trip' of 200 to 300 mcg of LSD, attacked his two friends, one of whom escaped whilst the other was severely beaten and later fell (or was pushed) out of a fourth floor window.

Louria (1970) is able to provide us with predictably lurid examples of violence and crime. One instance concerned four students who, whilst on holiday in New York, all took some LSD. The result was that one of these students started to bite the cheek of one of the others and the victim, because of the 'anaesthetic effect' of the drug, did not stop this happening until a two-inch chunk had been bitten from his face. Commenting that there have been 'perhaps a dozen' murders attributed to LSD, he proceeds to recount the most notorious one of these – a mother who was stabbed to death, with 105 wounds, by her son who later claimed that he had taken LSD and had no memory of the crime; he was acquitted on the grounds of temporary insanity.

This last case of Louria's raises one of the most thorny issues in appraising the criminogenic effect of the psychedelics – how much credence can we put in defences based on the claim of diminished responsibility as a result of taking, or of being given, one of this class of drugs? Regardless of the status at law of drug-induced crimes, there is little doubt that such a plea tends to be treated sympathetically. Bergel and Davies (1970) described the killing of a girl in London by an American who claimed that they were both on an LSD 'trip' and that he had no knowledge of his actions. In this case, though the court convicted the man and accepted his claim of amnesia, the *charge* was nevertheless reduced from murder to that of manslaughter.

Undoubtedly a defence based on the claim that the criminal is really the *victim* has many attractions; how often it has been used is impossible to say, but it has the very great advantage that the claim can be made in the comforting knowledge that, at our present stage of chemical technology, it is virtually impossible to either prove or disprove use. However, in the most recent report on this subject – the Canadian Government's Commission of Inquiry into the non-medical use of drugs – it was concluded that, where arrests are associated with LSD, the current evidence shows them usually to be 'disturbances of the peace' types of offence, with little data to indicate that LSD plays a significant role in the commission of major crimes.

In fact, a case can be built up to argue that, not only are the psychedelics innocent of generating crime and violence, but that they have quite the opposite effect by creating calm and a sense of brotherly unity. This sort of viewpoint has been put forward by Helen Perry (1970) on the basis of her participant observation of the 1966–7 Haight-Ashbury scene. The small social revolution which took place in that area certainly did produce an ethos of love and comradeship and, she notes, the young people involved recommended at least one psychedelic 'trip' so that the 'tripper' would be able to experience this sense of oneness and thus give up the competition and materialism which carry in them the seeds of violence. Watts (1962), was equally sensitive to the peaceful possibilities of LSD and also argues, from his own experience and that of being a prominent member and intellectual of the psychedelic movement, that the prior condition of aggression – a sense of disunity – is inevitably lost in the boundary-dissolving psychedelic experience which reconciles all differences.

Perry also refers to the investigations of Slotkin (1952) who, in an investigation of Menomini peyotism came across the Indian myth that peyote was a gift of the Great Spirit, given at a time of great tribal and internecine strife, to teach the basic lesson of peace – that all men and women are brothers and sisters. From my own experience on American Indian reservations, I can only agree that this evidence is very relevant: the members of the peyote churches are indeed very law-abiding and peaceful individuals and form a sharp contrast to the large numbers with alcohol problems.

The more controlled and experimental evidence on this question of how far psychedelics make people more calm and peaceful is, as we have already seen, somewhat variable – and dependent on the nature and dosage of the particular drug concerned. Hoffer and Osmond (1967) found that, with large doses given to both normal and abnormal subjects, the reduction of tension which resulted would last anything from several days to several months and that, during this time, 'they were practically unable to become angry'. Blacker *et al.* (1968) also noted the profound non-aggressive attitudes of the chronic L S D users that they studied. These people, all volunteers and with an average score of sixty-five 'trips', were typified by a life-style which rejected many of the usual provocations to hostility – for example, they had renounced ambition, competitive games, and any sort of 'pecking order' and instead shared a set of magical-mystical beliefs which ordered their values and relationships. But the researchers' interviews with their subjects did reveal that most of these people had developed frustrated and angry relationships with their parents and that their use of L S D seemed often to be a conscious attempt to suppress or change these unpleasant emotions.

In other words, the users were basically hostile and rejecting, though apparently attempting to change this with drug use. Given their new way of life and their belief systems, one might interpret the outcome in at least two ways – either it might be assumed that the 'therapy' had obviously worked and that their aggression had been changed to gentleness, *or* it might be argued that their whole way of life was an assault on all that their parents stood for, and that their basic hostility was revealed by the way in which they humiliated and hurt their families. Short of death itself, most responsible parents could hardly conceive of anything more distressing than the prospect of their children living in poverty and promiscuity and with little apparent future, 'on drugs', and living on the wrong side of the law. If these young people had meticulously planned to hurt their parents, it is hard to imagine how they might have done so more effectively.

Which interpretation one finds most convincing is, of course, a matter of individual preference – but a study by Edwards, Bloom, and Cohen (1969) is rather suggestive on the issue of whether apparent love really masks aggression. The study, which involved a group of thirty chronic users of psychedelics and another of thirty 'normal' controls, each composed equally

of men and women, involved the subjects in undergoing standardized psychological tests (i.e. the Rosenzweig Picture-Frustration
Test and the Comrey Personality Inventory). The results showed
that the drug users were significantly more aggressive and hostile
than the control subjects – leading the experimenters to conclude
that either their sampling, or the stereotype of the gentle psychedelic user, was wrong. The investigation clearly indicated that,
just below the surface, the users were markedly aggressive and
that this may readily be demonstrated by testing.

Williams (1970) also argues that the hippie movement is really
an attempt to 'integrate their rage'; that examination reveals
them frequently to be youngsters with a high degree of pre-
existing aggression which they are attempting to handle with
repression and denial. That their 'cult of love' is basically
insincere is, he argues, apparent from the way in which they are
united by their *hostility* to the 'straight world' – at which they
direct invective and scorn, and which they work to destroy.

On the other hand, Clark (1969) is in no doubt that drugs like
LSD, mescaline and psilocybin are capable of reforming the
delinquent and making the violent gentle. In support of this view
he refers to the study in which he was involved with Dr Leary
at the Concorde Prison – where recidivists who had been exposed
to psilocybin sessions proved significantly less likely to be
re-convicted over a short-term follow-up – though whether this
improvement was due to the drug effects or the fact that the
prisoners had been singled out for special interpersonal treatment
and help is still very much a matter of contention. But he also
reports that Ken Kesey took 'Hell's Angels' into the country to
give them LSD and that, when Clark himself visited Haight-
Ashbury, a hippie told him 'we used to be afraid of them, but
now they protect us'. But though the motor cycle gangsters
have tended to exploit the hippies, they have less often been
in direct conflict with them: rather, as in Yorkville, they have
treated them as a subject race.

Whether one accepts or rejects this tale of violent motor cycle
gang members becoming gentle after a day in the country,
Louria (1970) recounts another incident in which some at least
of the participants acted more in character. The story tells of how

a girl from the 'Trans-love Commune' in Buffalo was raped by a group of motor-cyclists. The hippies, instead of approaching the police, got another motor-cycle gang 'The Road Vultures' to deal with them. An account of this incident, published by the hippies, stopped short of recounting what vengeance was wreaked – because of the danger of police action – but no doubt the episode was violent and squalid in the extreme as such affairs commonly involve maiming and murder. Louria's assessment is that this sort of happening reveals the hippie love ethic for what it is, a sham, and that the apostles of love and brotherhood are really as guilty of violence as the degenerates they incited. But then Louria is as prejudiced against psychedelics as Clark is for them and, both being very experienced in the field, they could no doubt exchange anecdotes *ad infinitum*!

Another, and perhaps even richer, area for anecdote and disturbing tales is of the criminogenic effect of marijuana on soldiers – usually those who had been caught, sentenced, and were being seen by military psychiatrists. The Americans have had this problem for some time now and as early as the Second World War (Charen and Perelman, 1946; Gaskill, 1945; Marcovitz and Myers, 1944) accounts began to be published of disciplinary problems and outbursts of violence in soldiers known to smoke marijuana.

However, the one other feature which links all of these cases is that those affected tended to be already paranoid and aggressive types or to have a previous history of criminal behaviour. For example, in Marcovitz and Myers' sample of thirty-five confirmed marijuana users, all but three of them had civilian records of prison and reformatory sentences, with attendant histories of deprivation and failure. Similarly, fifty out of the sixty studied by Charen and Perelman also had criminal records – ranging from drunkenness to murder. The background study revealed long-established psychopathic behaviour and problems at school, in the home, and at work, leading the investigators to infer that 'infractions of the law are to be expected, regardless of the use of marijuana'. Even so, it also seemed that an effect of the drug was to lessen, or even to eradicate, those anxieties which check the performance of criminal acts and, in this sense, they seemed to play a limited causal role in the lawlessness of at least some individuals.

The difficulties of the United States presence in Vietnam have resulted in an almost uncountable number of crises – political, military, economic, and so on – but involved in many of these has been the appalling escalation of drug abuse. The human problems of heroin addiction are well known, and beyond the scope of this discussion, but cannabis use has also been strongly attacked as the cause of many an American failure and débâcle.

In 1967 two American investigators (Sapol and Roffman, 1969) gave questionnaires to 584 soldiers passing through the repatriation centre at Long Binh in order to establish just how many of them had used marijuana. They found that 28·9 per cent had used it in Vietnam and 31·7 per cent had used it at least once in their lives: other studies from Chu Lai and Pleiku were cited as giving corroborative evidence – with prevalence rates of 31·3 per cent and 35 per cent respectively. In an excellent review of the statistics based on studies in US colleges, Sapol and Roffman showed that the number of young people using the drug in Vietnam was much the same as those in colleges back home and that (though one may not accept the comparability of his samples) the evidence suggested that the fact of being in Vietnam was not an adequate explanation for the high rate of use amongst military personnel.

By contrast, de Lory and Gaber (1971) do appear to feel that there were special circumstances in Vietnam which precipitated troops into heavy usage, especially the feeling that they were 'suckers not saviours' in a complicated game of politics: their apathy and cynicism, mixed with fear, boredom, and a sense of being 'out of the real world' leading them to seek some sort of emotional escape. It is claimed that, by the beginning of 1971, virtually all soldiers were smoking the drug and that the favourite brand 'Cambodian Red', at fifty cents for a packet of twenty, was both readily available and exceedingly potent.

Sapol and Roffman had found that marijuana use was positively correlated with minor disciplinary infractions and that the heavy users were more liable still. As de Lory and Gaber observed, it is perhaps only a short step from smoking marijuana in front of your sergeant to acts of insubordination and refusal to fight. There have already been innumerable reports of soldiers disobeying orders and 'fragging' (i.e. blowing up with a fragmentation bomb) officers and NCOs who insisted on taking out patrols or who made themselves unpopular in other ways. But, once again, the causal relationships are far from clear – certainly marijuana was in common use, but then so too was heroin and alcohol, and the morale problems attendant upon a political mêlée where the soldier feels that his life may be squandered in a cause which few believe in, all introduce other possible causes of unmilitary behaviour.

Thus marijuana has been held responsible for undermining soldiers' will and capacity to fight, and also of increasing their aggressiveness towards comrades who do wish to do so. By way of compounding the confusion it has also been claimed that marijuana feeds the ferocity of troops to such a degree that they will slaughter anyone they think might be an enemy, or even an enemy sympathizer. Drankenbring (1971) reports how a communications NCO of the 2nd Marine Division told editors of his journal how, during his year of duty, he had seen the corpses of several Vietnamese who had been killed by marijuana-crazed soldiers, though he had never seen any killed in an attack. Indeed, there has been a good deal of political support for the explanation that the My Lai massacre was caused by the effect of marijuana. However, though the evidence has not supported this causal link, one can see that it would be a politically adroit conclusion – strengthening the hand of drug-control agencies and putting the responsibility for such incidents back on the local inhabitants who supplied the drug!

Yet despite the fact that the US military can hardly welcome the use of any drug amongst their personnel, their position is sometimes amazingly tolerant. It seems that the effect of marijuana has not always been detrimental to their functioning and the tolerant line must have received some support in 1971 when Peter Lemon, a former infantryman in Vietnam, was decorated by President Nixon. Lemon, who was given the Medal of Honour, America's highest award for gallantry, revealed later that he had been 'stoned' on marijuana during the battle, and that it was his experience that the drug made soldiers more alert.

Anyway, and according to Destefano (1972), the general who recently came from Vietnam to take command of the US Army, Europe, has implemented a very forbearing policy towards drug-users generally, and the use of psychedelics in particular. A 'Special Action Office' has been set up to handle drug problems and a mimeograph paper is prepared under the supervision of a medical officer whose policy is to help soldiers to 'turn-on' safely, stay alive, and remain unconvicted. The intention is by no means to encourage drug-use but to put the welfare of the individual first in the face of a *fait accompli*: for example, the paper 'Cosmic Flash' contains such tips as 'mescaline is generally safer than German acid'. Cannabis use is also treated leniently – there are no courts martial for first offences, despite the fact that a similar crime in some states back in America can result in a thirty-year jail sentence!

If cannabis is coming to be *tolerated* by the US military, then the major psychedelics have sometimes received a more positive reception – though this time as potential weapons. Cookson and Nottingham (1969), in their survey of methods of chemical and biological warfare, note that as early as 1957 Assistant Army Secretary Larsen stated, in Congressional testimony, that both the USA and the USSR were currently developing psychoactive chemicals which would be capable of incapacitating entire cities, without destroying them. This information was, according to Cohen (1965), repeated by General Stubbs who told a House of Representatives Subcommittee on science and astronautics that he felt these non-lethal drugs represented a great potential in the waging of war in limited trouble areas.

No doubt such weapons have very considerable attractions: not least that one individual could carry a sufficient quantity of LSD to incapacitate an entire country. But the problems of distributing the drugs effectively to people who may be indoors at the time of an aerosol attack, or who may not have drunk the contaminated water before seeing other people affected, all make it a tricky weapon – especially as gas masks are an effective protection and antedotes are readily available. In consequence, psychedelic chemicals do not *seem* to have much of a future for use against large populations – though one never knows how these technologies are evolving.

General Creasy was particularly enthusiastic about the use of incapacitating chemicals and felt that a new age might be dawning in which war would not necessarily mean death. Cohen disagrees with this sanguine evaluation and points out that there would still remain terrible risks to infants through overdoses, to travellers through perceptual errors, and as a result of the panic which would break out. This is no doubt so, but many people might disagree with Cohen that the temporary degradation of their minds is worse than physical death and feel that, if one *is* to be involved in the lunatic business of warfare, being incapacitated for a day or so is infinitely better than radiation burns or death in a napalm blaze. But, value judgements aside, it will be effectiveness rather than humanity which is likely to determine military policy and, as one has no way of knowing how psychochemicals are evolving in relation to more conventional weapons, the question of their use in this particular form of organized violence must, for the moment, be allowed to rest whilst we ourselves now turn to more constructive applications of these drugs.

9 Creativity

The apparently simple question of whether psychedelic drugs stimulate creativity is capable of a whole host of diverse interpretations: it all depends on what you mean by 'creative'. Of course, this is a rather trite observation but perhaps excusable in view of the ways in which this rubric attempts to subsume so many very different processes. For some, 'creativity' has meant the fairly conventional notion of actually producing original things like symphonies or paintings whilst others have stretched the concept to include innovations in dress, life-styles, and ideas. However, for a very large proportion of those people interested in the problem, enhanced aesthetic *response* or experience has become a major source of evidence that psychedelics influence the creative process. And a prominent group amongst those focusing on aesthetic response are the experimenters who define the criterion, and thus the problem, as the way in which scores on their standardized tests vary during drug-induced assessment sessions. Each of these approaches may tell us *something* but it is well to remember that they are probably telling us a number of quite *different* things, and thus a generalized answer to the question of how psychedelics affect creativity is not possible unless one is prepared to accept a rather narrow definition at the outset.

It is always difficult to define a concept to everyone's satisfaction, but there are usually a number of propositions which are common to even quite divergent conceptualizations. In the case of creativity, the one criterion with which most of us would agree is that something *new* is brought into existence – whether this 'new' thing is new to the world or only new to the person who has produced it. Of course, we operate a more or less subjective hierarchy of creativity – from the person who creates what we consider to be either a particularly useful or beautiful thing and which far outstrips present practice in its innovative qualities, right down to the minor technical improvements and even the process of *making* perfectly familiar and commonplace things. Yet such a hierarchy of creativeness is difficult to apply and far from vertical, a fact which rapidly becomes apparent in cases which involve discrepancies between vision and competence, for example, – as when comparing the work of an artist who is imaginative, skilful, and productive, even though his work is done within a conventional idiom and involves little by way of innovation, with that of another artist whose output is relatively sparse, whose technique and control of the medium is poor, yet whose work represents a new and distinctive approach.

With all the wisdom of hindsight, we may say that the Gauguins of this world are more creative than their contemporary academicians but it is not so easy to recognize creative inspiration at the time when it occurs. The problem is always that of deciding what constitutes an aesthetic advance: there are always plenty of execrable artists whose work, though certainly different, is destined for a merciful oblivion because it lacks this quality. Just as all change is not necessarily progress, so all that is novel is not necessarily creative: the solution to a scientific problem that is ludicrously inept and incorrect might be *novel* but it is hardly evidence of creativity.

A piece of work is normally judged according to convention, and public and personal tastes, since it is difficult to appraise it in terms of other objective realities. The very fact that artistic criticism tends to be such a personal, variable, and indefinable matter certainly underscores the problems involved in assessing creative capacity, or changes that may take place in it – whether drugs are involved or not.

Standardized test measures are often used in the scientific study of artistic criticism, particularly by workers anxious to avoid value judgements and subjective criteria. The principle is fine, but in practice the experimental criteria are often no less subjective in the assumptions that are made about the processes involved, the measures which would adequately tap these processes, and the significance of the derived scores. Here is not the place to review the general approaches to these problems, but it is apposite, if not tremendously illuminating, to look at the work carried out in relation to the psychedelics.

One of the most celebrated, and earliest, of the attempts to study the effects of psychedelic substances on the creative process was that of Aldrich (1944). This study is of particular interest for the way it illustrates how far test measures can depart from the realities of the situation which they set out to assess and how, when the results are reported elsewhere, they continue to get even further away from the point. Aldrich's study was entitled 'The effect of a synthetic marihuana-like compound on musical talent as measured by the Seashore Test', the stated purpose of the experiment being to investigate a popular claim that the use of marijuana causes swing musicians to 'ascend to new peaks of virtuosity'.

The circumstances of the investigation were as follows: the subjects were twelve male prisoners, *two* of whom were professional musicians and all of whom were regular users of marijuana who had been imprisoned, ostensibly, for violation of the Marihuana Tax Act. There were three once-weekly sessions in which the subjects did the Seashore Tests; only on the third occasion was a drug, *pyra-hexyl*, used. The tests, presented on gramophone records, involved the subject in distinguishing between pairs of notes as to their difference in pitch, loudness, time and timbre, and in identifying similarities, differences, and changes in simple patterns of sound. Broadly speaking, the results showed that most subjects made gains, due to practice, between the first and second tests but slipped back to a lower level on the drug-involved final test – despite most of them *feeling* that they had done better on this last trial. However, the real fascination of the study lies not in the results, but in the way that they have been generalized.

Aldrich himself obviously, from what he said in his introduction, thought that he was empirically testing a popular claim that marijuana improves the ability of musicians to perform jazz or swing and this construction has been rather widely accepted in the literature. But, as Grinspoon (1971) comments, the interpretation of this work depends upon a number of assumptions. Firstly, that pyra-hexyl is the same as marijuana – a fact which is disputed – and secondly, that the tests used adequately reflect the conditions of musicians making jazz. Perhaps we could be forgiven for thinking that the situation of predominately non-musical prison inmates judging the difference between pairs of notes was rather far away from the original one of a group of musicians improvising in an atmosphere of emotional involvement and cooperative effort. The trouble is, though, that for many people a report like that of Aldrich's is taken as a direct experimental study of the creative process, with results which may be applied to creativity generally.

Pop or jazz music has undoubtedly been very closely connected with the use of cannabis for many years now, and continues to be so – as the spate of prosecutions against contemporary pop figures plainly shows. But, though Winick (1960) has convincingly traced the association of the drug with popular music, he is less persuasive in trying to show that the effects of cannabis are not closely correlated with the excellence of performance – as judged by other musicians. This would indeed be a very difficult proposition to demonstrate in any controlled sense and would require a scope of survey and degree of cooperation amongst musicians which go far beyond anything which was feasible for Winick or any other researcher.

Of greater significance, at least in a lot of people's minds, is the fact that cannabis has been closely associated with many of the best pop musicians, including the Beatles and the Rolling Stones. Of course, however many first-class performers and songwriters one mentioned in an associational sense, and the list could be very long, this would not in itself be acceptable evidence that the drugs *caused* the users to be better musicians. On the other hand, even if one only accepts that they are *associated*, it is very difficult to argue the case that cannabis tends to impair abilities. It may be so, but demonstrating the point would present some knotty problems!

Krippner (1968) reports that, in the course of one of his studies, a well-known pop recording artist disclosed that most rock groups use marijuana regularly and L S D at least once, and that much contemporary music is openly about psychedelic experiences. This point is developed by Taqi (1969) who, though careful to say that he was not necessarily making any claims about intent or conscious motivations, nevertheless pointed to a pattern of expression exceedingly congruent with covert psyche-delic communication.

He cites, for example, the songs 'Lucy in the Sky with Diamonds' which has as its initials 'LSD' – which the Beatles say is a coincidence; 'Eight Miles High' by the Byrds – which their leader, Jim McGuinn, says refers to an aeroplane flight; 'Mellow Yellow' by Donovan which is about 'electrical bananas' and might seem to refer to the then current craze for smoking banana skins; 'Acapulco Gold' by the Rainy Daze which has a title the same as a well-known high quality form of marijuana; and so on. The precedent for this sort of music came, according to Taqi, with 'Walk Right In' by the Rooftops in the winter of 1962–3 and which, for anyone knowing the lyrics, could easily be taken for an invitation to participate in the marijuana experience.

All of this is extremely unsatisfactory from a strictly scientific point of view and it might easily be argued that Taqi, Krippner, and others like them were simply projecting their own interests into quite innocent pieces of music: one can never *prove* intention in such cases. But, given that the association between the use of psychedelic drugs and the creators of some of these songs is a matter of public record, one might agree that even if the music is not likely to send hordes of teenagers straight out to buy drugs it may well help to change the climate of opinion about drug-use amongst the young and influence some of the more impression-able ones. Without wishing at this stage to get involved with the equally relevant moral, musical, and social issues which are raised, it has been argued that this usage of the mass-music media does imply another sort of 'creativity' – the creation of new standards, values and covert forms of communication within a psychedelically orientated sub-culture.

This notion of 'creativity' as applied to social matters might seem to stretch the conventional use of the concept somewhat but there is no real reason to exclude new syntheses of experience and their resultant behaviour because they are represented in daily living rather than symbolically. We have already discussed the ways in which philosophical shifts may occur in relation to psychedelic use – particularly in relation to the more extreme cases where people turn to communal living or to a 'hippie' life-style. One of the aspects of this, and one to which we have also referred, is the great concern that such people express about being creative and 'doing their own thing' – whether this is farming unpromising soil with primitive tools, building gaudy geodesic dome-houses, making ornaments and decorations, or in song and dance.

Hedgepeth and Stock (1970) have given us a good deal of the flavour of this in *The Alternative* but nowhere more amusingly than in their description of 'Heliotrope' – the hippies' own 'free university' in San Francisco which, in addition to some *almost* conventional things, also runs courses in belly dancing, Greek dance, and electronic music making. Some of the other things in their curriculum look like pure lunatic-fringe activities but one could scarcely argue that there was any shortage of the impulse to create new ways of living. Even the emphasis, so often repeated, on 'tribal living' obviously contains a strong element of wanting to achieve a much simplified way of life in which each individual can make some significant creative contribution.

What the hippies have created has turned out to be much more influential than most of them probably expected. Looking around now we see hair-styles, clothes, ornaments, posters, literature, and goodness what else besides which has its origins in the psychedelic sub-culture. And although one index of creative vigour derives simply from which innovations catch on it looks as though, even allowing that the psychedelic movement may have had more than its fair share of help from commerce and the media, it nevertheless must have contained the conditions for such growth. For, even though it may be impossible to trace with certainty the actual connection between the creative energies released by the psychedelic drugs and the sort of objects which are now so familiar to us, it would be difficult to deny that they were born and grew up together.

But *proof* of a relationship requires more than just an apparent association: it demands experimental studies. In one of these early attempts, Berlin *et al.* (1955) did set about investigating what happened to creative ability in the presence of psychedelics –

using mescaline and lysergic acid. Their concern was with painting and, in addition to the pictorial work produced, they also measured changes in muscular coordination and steadiness as indices relating to the capacity to execute the fine movements typical of graphic art: the rationale here being that impairment of basic skills would tend to indicate an overall impairment in the capacity to draw or paint.

They used four prominent graphic artists as their subjects and, as judges of the pictorial work, a panel of art critics. Scores on finger-tapping and muscular steadiness proved to be adversely effected by the drugs but the panel of judges felt that the paintings produced had greater aesthetic value than their usual work but that the bolder lines and more vivid colours used were also coupled with a generally poorer standard of technical execution. The artists themselves reported that they found the psychedelic experiences aesthetically very powerful.

A much more controlled and comprehensive study is that of McGlothlin, Cohen, and McGlothlin (1967) in which seventy-two paid, post-graduate student volunteers were assigned to one of three groups to be compared on the way in which their scores on standardized tests varied with the drug they were given. Each group was given the battery of tests – which included judging between designs which met conventional aesthetic criteria of balance and harmony and those which did not; seeing hidden figures in more complex ones; conceptual items which measured the ability to generate fluent and ingenious associations; and an assessment of imaginativeness through the capacity to invent original stories around presented pictures. Testing took place on three occasions: before the drug session, two weeks later, and again after six months. Of the three experimental groups, one received LSD at an appropriate effective dose of 200 mcg, one group received only 25 mcg of LSD – which would generally be either totally ineffective or exceedingly mild in its effects – and the third group received 20 mg of amphetamine – which should simply create an increase in psychic and physical energy.

The results of this experiment showed that there was only one significant difference – in the 200 mcg LSD group who showed an improvement in their score on spontaneous flexibility of thought, as measured by their ability to invent multiple uses for objects, and which was evident at the two-week and six-month follow-ups. However, as McGlothlin, Cohen, and McGlothlin (1964) had previously recorded negative results, they decided to change the statistical criteria in the 1967 study to more stringent ones and again declared their results negative. What is interesting is that there *were* very pronounced psychological differences in reaction to the drugs. For example, 25 per cent of the 200 mcg LSD group *felt* that they evidenced a greater degree of creativity as a result of taking the drug – as compared with 9 per cent of the amphetamine group and none in the 25 mcg group. Most interestingly of all, at the six-month follow-up nearly two-thirds of the 200 mcg LSD group asserted that they now had a greater appreciation of music, whilst nearly a half said the same in relation to visual art. These claims were supported by such behavioural indicators as the number of records which the subjects bought and the time that they spent in galleries, concerts, etc. This measure proved to be significantly greater than for either of the other two groups.

A somewhat similar study to the previous one was that of Zegans, Pollard, and Brown (1967). Paid volunteers were again used, of which nineteen were randomly assigned to receive LSD whilst eleven control subjects received a placebo. Standardized tests were once more the criteria – ones claimed by the researchers to tap 'ego resources important in their creative processes' – and which included making patterns with coloured mosaic tiles, seeing embedded figures in more complex ones, word-association tests, and the capacity of subjects to identify words and objects flashed extremely briefly on the screen of a tachistoscope.

The results showed that the LSD group did significantly better on only one test – the modified word-association test, in which the subject was scored on his ability to produce original and non-stereotyped responses to stimulus words. It transpired that the LSD group were best on expansive remote associations and worst on such restricting perceptual tasks as the tachistoscope and making mosaic patterns, thus suggesting that the effect may be to liberate creative thought whilst impeding artistic skill and focused attention. In fact, the drug-using group did perform better than the controls on *most* comparisons – but the differences did not reach a statistical level of significance. The researchers concluded, therefore, that, with relatively unselected people, the use of LSD to enhance their creative ability is not likely to be successful.

However, taking *selected* individuals is, as the study by Harman *et al.* (1966) shows, quite a different matter. This investigation involved twenty-seven male subjects, all of whom were in creative occupations – including professional engineers, physicists and architects. None of them had previously taken psychedelic drugs; all of them were judged to be psychologically 'normal', and each of them had a conceptual problem which he was currently trying to solve. The situation was quite simple: the subjects were drawn together in groups of three or four, given 200 mg of mescaline and then guided to relax, to 'turn off' their analytic faculties and to listen to music. After this came snacks and an hour of psychological testing, then three to four hours of thinking about their problems alone, followed by group interaction when experiences could be shared. One of the methodological weaknesses of this study was that, at the end of the session, there was sometimes group-working on one of the problems. The experimental report is not helpful in evaluating this possibly confounding circumstance and it might be argued that it was cooperation rather than drug effects which contributed most. A subjective report was required from the subjects some days later, plus questionnaire and interview data after three to six weeks – including information on how post-experimental creative processes had been affected, plus information on the acceptability of the solution which had been arrived at during the psychedelic session.

Comparisons were also made between each subject's score on a battery of psychological tests which he took some days before the drug session and then again during it. The tests, which included such problems as finding as many uses as possible for pictured objects, visualizing two-dimensional figures folded into solids, and distinguishing 'embedded figures', were in two equivalent, highly correlated versions. Average scores on each of the tests showed significant improvements under mescaline but, much more to the point, the objective outcomes – solutions to the real-life problems which were brought to the sessions by the subjects themselves – proved to be extremely satisfactory. The criterion of satisfactory problem solution was not just how people *felt* they had done but whether the solutions were workable and *adopted*. One subject's solution was for a private house, another's for a commercial building; there were designs for furniture and electronics, as well as a satisfactory design for a 'linear electron accelerator beam-steering device' (whatever that is!).

The subjective aspects of this study are no less fascinating. One of the features which appeared to be significant in the way people dealt with their problems was that they developed a much heightened sense of indentification with their material. As one subject expressed it, it was 'almost like *becoming* the problem' and another, working on an optical problem, recounted how he had 'spent a productive period climbing down my retina, walking round and thinking about certain problems relating to the mechanisms of vision'. At the follow-up stage, which took place weeks after the psychedelic session, it transpired that most subjects reported that they still retained the capacities developed in the experimental session. These were said to include increased concentration on the task, ability to visualize problems in their widest context, reduced inhibitions (i.e. a holding-back on nega-tive-censoring of unusual ideas), and an increased energy and decisiveness.

Stafford and Golightly (1967) also cite evidence of the useful-ness of psychedelic agents in relation to technical problems. They describe the case of a man who had spent five years on a problem connected with the design of an anti-submarine detection device and who, in one LSD session, broke through his 'block' and perfected a device which was then taken up by the US Navy. As a result of this success, it is said that further personnel were trained in the use of psychedelics as an aid in creative problem solving.

Harman *et al.* felt that their results demonstrated the value of psychedelics in facilitating problem solving by affecting the 'illumination phase' which is held, in many theories of the creative process, to be a short distinctive stage in a relatively extended operation. Pet and Ball (1968) summarized one such view of creativity which could be conceptualized into the four stages of preparation, frustration, insight and verification. In this formulation, which is representative enough, 'preparation' covers the time whilst the problem is being delineated and during which the individual works to develop the skills and knowledge necessary to solve it: this stage may be very short but it may equally take many years. 'Frustration' may develop along with the preparation though it tends to be most acute when all that can be done has been done but still the solution is elusive: this stage is characterized by emotionality, restlessness, and sometimes even by abandoning the problem. 'Insight' is the *critical* phase when solutions occur often 'in a flash', as with Newton and his apple, and may be accompanied by great exhilaration – as with Archimedes and his bath! Finally comes the sober stage of 'verification' when 'brilliant insight' must be checked against dowdy reality!

Pet and Ball believe that marijuana, at least, mimics a part only of this creative process – the insight phase – in which the subject experiences the *feeling* of understanding things and the exhilaration of discovery but, because the groundwork has not been prepared, the whole thing is delusory: the drug-user cannot express his new 'understanding' and there is nothing to verify against reality. But, in those cases where genuine creativity is associated with the use of marijuana, Pet and Ball point out that it is usually also the case that the people involved had studiously prepared themselves for their task and had been creative *before* using the drugs. This conclusion is, of course, quite congruent with the findings of the previous studies: where the drugs were given to unprepared and non-creative people the results were fairly negative – even though subjects may *feel* much more creative. But, where the studies concern people who were both creative and prepared, the results show positive enhancement of creativity.

Certainly the psychedelics have received a good deal of praise by such established artists as Baudelaire, Gautier, and Huxley, but these were people who had proved their creative powers long before they had ever used these substances. The same is true of William Burroughs but he adds something more to the argument, going beyond the use of psychedelic experience as a *subject* for literary description, when he says that his book, *The Naked Lunch*, was written at a consciousness-level opened up by the cannabis that he was smoking at the time of writing and that many of the scenes in his book derived directly from the use of this drug (Burroughs, 1961). He also found that mescaline was a positive aid to artistic sensibility, though this time mainly through heightening the aesthetic experience of music and visual art forms. Moreover, Burroughs found that the changes brought about by psychedelics were not just transient phenomena; they had tapped a level of reality in him which remained accessible thereafter. Years later, when he had long discontinued the use of cannabis itself, he found it still possible, and desirable, to evoke these same reactions and stimulating effects through the technique of 'sensory overload' with a curious word game, flickering lights and intense music.

The poet, Allen Ginsberg (1969), though far from showing any inclination to renounce cannabis himself, also makes a very strong case for its value in art. He describes how his own perceptions were enormously enhanced by smoking marijuana: how, for the first time, he truly understood and responded to the paintings of such different artists as Klee, Cézanne, and Rembrandt and how these perceptions of meaning, once achieved, remain in normal consciousness – though a 'normal consciousness' which is now much expanded. His claim is that these changes are not at all unnatural – the perceptual processes are heightened in ways that can, and do, occur quite naturally in the course of life. Love and the death of people near us are, for example, events which shake up and engage all the senses in a way which, though they may be painful, change and enrich our consciousness and stimulate the creative impulse.

It is Ginsberg's claim that these psychedelic augmentations are of profound value to creative people and that their measure lies in the 'fact' that most major contemporary artists, British and American, have been smoking marijuana for years. He specifies virtually the whole range of art forms and, in his own field, asserts 'I have gotten high with the majority of the dozens of contributors to the Don Allen *Anthology of New American Poetry 1945–1960*', and that drug-use amongst artists is the rule not the exception. Of course, Ginsberg is not demonstrating that cannabis generates creativity but, if we accept his testimony and assertions, he is certainly showing that they are not incompatible.

Yet it has been argued that the use of psychedelics *is* inimical to the creative act. Freedman (1968) argues that the very nature of the experience is such as to impair any goal-directed activity by reducing the efficiency of the integrative and synthetic functions. The merging of sensory inputs, the attention to tiny and usually disregarded detail, perceptual distortions and intensifications, though arresting, are not art. Abnormal brilliance is not the same as beauty and, indeed, the primitivization of perception which is seen in animals and men, is more suggestive of vividness than it is of subtlety and discrimination of the complex. But, most importantly, he holds that creativity demands not only perceptions but also the capacity for translating these into art forms, a capacity which is only adversely affected by the psychedelic state.

Freedman's point of view has been widely expressed in many different ways but, at its most simplified, it has been argued on the analogy with alcohol – which is suppsed to increase the desire for sex, but to reduce the ability. A good deal has been made of this aspect of psychedelic effects: for example, Barron (1963) records how four artists, who had worked throughout a drug 'trip', were extremely let down and disappointed with their productions when they looked at them again afterwards. Further, experimental studies of the cognitive and psychomotor effects of the psychedelics have frequently suggested that the impairments observed *must* result in reduced efficiency and ability in the performance of any task, whether creative or not.

But implicit in such a conclusion is the belief that effects on creativity are best measured when the subject is involved with the drug session: an inference which is vigorously rejected by many artists and psychologists alike. They argue, and I should have thought with complete justice, that such assessments are nonsense, and most certainly so if they involve inexperienced users with little control over their reactions or the situation: it takes a peculiar sort of perversity to imagine that anyone, faced with what may be the most powerful experience of his lifetime, would not be affected in his ability to perform *any* task – whether an IQ test, a test of creativity, or any other complex performance such as driving or painting. With experienced users this may be a different matter but, in any case, most artists do not work under the influence of a drug but translate their psychedelic perceptions into art forms some time later. As Masters and Houston (1968) point out, though the mind is alert during the session, coordination and motivation to work are impaired; the value of the session lies in what may be expressed about it later.

By performing experiments on changes in creative abilities as reflected in the work obtained from people struggling with shattering drug-induced states of consciousness, the researchers have, at least in the view of many artistically creative people, often come very close to making themselves appear ridiculous. Masters and Houston (1968), in what is the key text on psychedelic art, emphatically deny the basic proposition that such alterations of consciousness bestow the ability to create works of art and it looks as though the researchers are testing a hypothesis which no one seriously holds anyway. Thoughtful advocates generally seem to be saying no more than that the drugs create *experiences* which the artist may sometimes be able to transform into works of art because of his pre-existing special skills and qualities of mind. But, strange though it may seem, researchers have often been guilty of assuming that the uncreative and talentless should be miraculously transformed if there is any truth in the claim that psychedelics aid creativity – and, even in relation to artists themselves, that they should perform much better under the direct influence of drug stimulation.

Presumably, few researchers would expect a poet or writer to pen their best lines whilst a loved one was dying in their presence – though we know that such emotional maelstroms may be powerful sources of inspiration at a later time. Yet it is often blandly assumed that the appropriate measure of the creative effects of psychedelic experiences is to be obtained by trying to get the artist to work in the middle of the emotional and cognitive tempest that may be let loose in a psychedelic session. Instead, Masters and Houston compare the value of such happenings with distant travels and powerful visual experiences; just as blast-furnaces or South-Sea Islands stimulate the imagination and creative impulse for some artists, so the exotic landscape within the mind may equally serve as a rich source of inspiration for others.

In other contexts we have already said a good deal about the nature of the psychedelically evoked mental landscape, of the dissolution of those psychic boundaries, categorizing functions, and ideational barriers which normally determine our perceptions of time, space, and our relationship to the physical world, but nowhere has the importance of *eidetic imagery* been more relevantly expressed than in a paper by Masters and Houston (1971) dealing with the therapeutic situation. Eidetic imagery is a way of mentally representing events which has all the character-istics of actually *seeing* them happen: this capacity is often quite well developed in small children but, as one grows older, it gradually fades in most people. However, in psychedelic 'trips' this faculty is often regained with startling clarity.

Masters and Houston describe how the 'psychenaut' may be able to project himself imaginatively not only backwards into his own past, but right back into history: to be *present* at famous battles or events; perhaps to be at the building of the pyramids, or in the presence of great figures of the past. He may go beyond even this, *seeing* and *feeling* the very processes of evolution take place; re-living the evolutionary sequence from the primeval swamp to the creation of man.

All of these images may be of a convincing reality, vivid impact, and an intricate detail which goes far beyond anything that the subject allows as existing in his conscious knowledge. The levels of experience may also penetrate the symbolic world of myth and legend, of archetypes, gods, and fairy-tales. And, though each individual's range may be more or less limited, given these new psychological vistas, it would indeed be sur-prising if the coming together of such rich materials with inventive and original minds did not open up enormous possi-bilities for creative re-combination and description in art forms.

The images produced in psychedelic art have often resulted in its being compared with surrealism which, as Schwartz (1968) observes, is a reasonable comparison so far as it goes. Both movements are concerned with penetrating the deepest layers of the human mind and with going beyond rationality to show that apparent irrationality and paradox may hold the germs of other, no less profound, types of meaning which can reconcile such apparent opposites as life and death, real and imaginary, past and future. But, though both movements are psychologically based forms and share the same artistic goals, their main *difference* lies in the level of consciousness achieved by the artist.

The surrealists pushed back their own levels of awareness as far as they were able, leaving behind them a trail of casualties, but they were still unable to get far beyond the world of dreams and the repressed unconscious. Their frontiers lay on the borders of madness, nightmare and magic but, nevertheless, they were able to create a striking new art form of considerable aesthetic merit and psychological interest.

Eidetic imagery also played a considerable part in the work of many surrealists and is evidenced in the sparkling clarity of many a dreamlike terrain or strange classical temple. Yet, despite the impact of such paintings, they do tend to be much more static than their psychedelic counterparts which are more kinetic, vibrant, optimistic, and more concerned with creation and cosmic forces than with the despair and ghosts of a personal landscape. Indeed, Schwartz avers that the central theme of psychedelic art is *creation*, just as *salvation* is at the core of Christian art, and that its preoccupations are very much with the external realities of life, growth and evolution.

The ways in which these preoccupations are expressed are, nevertheless, not only often markedly similar to some surrealist work but also have much in common with the work of Klee, Blake, Breughel, and Heironymus Bosch: painters who displayed a 'psychedelic sensibility', though obviously not members of the movement whose defining characteristic lies in consciousnesses specifically stimulated by psychedelic drugs.

As we have already observed, a typical effect of these drugs is the fusing together of sensory experiences: with stimulation of one modality evoking responses from others. This fact has led to a characteristic form of art, one in which many types of stimulation are joined together to simulate, re-evoke, or enhance the psychedelic experience proper: a typical scenario perhaps involving poetry reading, set against a brilliantly painted background, and also involving music and stroboscopic light effects. Like the drug effect itself, the effect of this type of presentation is meant to be overwhelming and, like the drugs, meant to result in a 'sensory overload' in which normal critical thought patterns will disintegrate and be replaced by more primitive, and more spontaneous, reactions.

Not all psychedelic art is of this order; paintings like those of Ernst Fuchs, Arlene Sklar-Weinstein, and Isaac Abrams, though very distinctive, tend to be set in the conventional idioms of graphic design, whereas 'environmental paintings' like Alan Atwells' 'The Total Temple' – consisting of a room in which all the walls are painted in brilliant abstract forms and where the viewer is literally *inside* the painting – are much closer to the sensory-overload aim which is characteristic of so much psychedelic art.

However, the mixed-media creations are almost certainly its most distinctive aspect: particularly the work of such people as Jackie Cassen, Rudi Stern and Don Snyder, with their combinations of light effects, living sculpture and music. And it is here, perhaps more than anywhere else, that it becomes so extraordinarily difficult to apply the usual standards of art criticism to psychedelic creations – after all, where the art-object is a transient phenomenon, where technical standards of art are subordinate to the technological and conceptual ones, and where appreciation may imply a sharing of previous psychedelic experiences, it is hard to know what standards may be appropriately applied.

In such circumstances, we might be inclined to follow the advice of Timothy Leary (1965) and forget the trivial standards accepted in the 'scientific' studies of psychedelics and creativity, as well as the opinions of such relatively unqualified and uncreative people as psychologists and psychiatrists, in favour of the experience of artists themselves. This is exactly what was done by

Krippner (1968) in the course of a series of interviews and questionnaires with ninety-one artists, all of whom had had more than one psychedelic 'trip' – most of them having used LSD, though many other psychedelic substances had also been used. His sample included only serious artists of some status: people working in the range of media which, though painting and drawing predominated, also included poetry, lumia, music, and photography. 'Sunday painters' and the like were rigidly excluded.

Krippner's fundamental question was how the artist felt his work had been affected by his psychedelic experiences. Three felt that they had made no difference one way or the other but none thought that their work had suffered as a result – though some commented that their friends might not agree with this! The effects which the artists reported were classifiable as changes which had taken place in their content, technique, or approach to their medium.

As might have been anticipated from what was said earlier, it was found that the *content* of many artists' work (sixty-four of them) had been affected by their much enhanced eidetic imagery – sometimes involving personal material from their early memories. Religious topics, too, were an outcome of the experiences and one woman painter commented that LSD and cannabis had helped her to 'transcend the ordinary and enter into the limitless intuitions which are now the basis of everything I do in my work'. Artistic *technique* was also held to be improved by forty-nine of the artists – particularly in relation to the use of colour, where inhibitions had been overcome. Forty-seven claimed that they had changed their *approach* to their work as a result of psychedelic experiences: reporting increased subjective satisfaction and the belief that their viewpoint was not less trite and that they were currently making more profound artistic statements.

And so we come back to findings that also derive from the slightest of the empirical studies that we mentioned earlier – that people who use psychedelics develop the *feeling* that they are more creative. Alas though, this is not necessarily the same as *being* more creative and, despite the relevance of Dr Leary's advice, we are still sailing in treacherous waters as the only way of judging the evidence is by assessing the creative work produced – and this, too, is a matter of great subjectivity and taste. Almost every new school of art has been rejected and ridiculed in the beginning – some, like cubism and surrealism, violently so. The psychedelic movement is no exception to this general rule and though, as we have seen, the psychedelics seem to have provided the *impetus* for new forms of creative expression, only time will tell whether these are genuine artistic innovations or merely eccentric experiments.

10 Religion

In selecting the topics which will give an overview of psychedelic drug usage many, like the pharmacological, pathological, or social outcomes, seem to have a ready justification for inclusion but, when one gets to religion and mysticism, there may be a feeling that the issues involved are somehow less real. Yet, despite the current unpopularity of religious ideas, and the prevalent squeamishness most of us seem to share when it comes to discussing things mystical, the religious and mystical aspects of the psychedelic movement are central to our full understanding. The sub-culture is not principally concerned with social issues or good works anymore than was the primitive church: at the centre of both Christian religion and serious psychedelic drug use lies the search for spiritual growth.

The principal luminaries of the movement, men like Aldous Huxley, Timothy Leary, and Alan Watts, were all individuals consciously concerned with promoting mystical states of mind and exploring the nature of God. Leary is perhaps more a man of his times in that he has also been vigorous in promoting social and mental health ends but the social, political, and philosophical directions, though important, are not regarded as the epicentre of the movement: rather they are valued spin-offs.

Within the movement, as within the church, there are many opinions about what are the most important and fundamental qualities, beliefs or practices. Some stress practice, the good life, good works, and ritual observances; others place the greater emphasis on their beliefs – as derived either directly from personal revelation and insight or indirectly from accounts of the experiences of others. Christianity is largely in this latter category – drawing its fundamental beliefs from the testimony of others: only rarely is personal and direct revelation a regular part of the Christian experience. Indeed, this missing core has even become a virtue such that one's beliefs and commitment are held to be the more creditable just because they *are* acts of faith. By contrast, the psychedelic way has little faith in scripture, the revelations of others, or canon law.

The institutional churches have many centuries of domestication behind them now: plenty of time for skilful propagandists. theologians and church logicians to give some semblance of reconciliation between the logic of the mechanical world and the alogic, revelation, and miracles that are at the real centre of faiths like Christianity. But the attempt to reconcile the irreconcilable, though perhaps motivated by the generous wish to bring feelings and experiences within the ken of those who have not known them, has now resulted in a quasi-logical system of such an unconvincing sort as to undermine the credibility of what it purports to promote – spiritual or divine revelation. The claims of the psychedelic movement are no less incredible to most people – though for opposite reasons: instead of relying on dubious argument it simply denies the relevance of logic and reasoning in this entire sphere.

Now to propose that there may be an association between religion and the use of *any* drug – even alcoholic communion wine – is very near to blasphemy for many people. That cherished and sustaining beliefs should be equated with 'mind bending' drugs – ones which have been widely publicized as being related to hallucinations, delusions, and insanity itself – may seem to the average person to be an absurdity, and an offensive one at that. Most of us would find it difficult to accept that psychedelic experiences can lead to genuine religious inspiration, because such a hedonistic and short-cut approach is so divorced from customary religious practice. Yet this is what many intelligent and experienced people are claiming and we must therefore examine their evidence.

Alas though, the rules of evidence are less stringent in all cases touching religious matters than they are in science or even jurisprudence and it should be remembered that the shortcomings of the evidence relating to drug-induced experiences are not too dissimilar from those where no drugs are involved. In the end, the 'data' usually turns out to be a matter of faith, or belief in the experience of others, or else a personal experience which we accept ourselves without the need for justification. However, there is also a growing area of empirical study of religious phenomena: interviews, questionnaires with large groups, and controlled studies with religious and chemical variables being manipulated. These approaches are of particular interest in assessing both psychological meaning and behavioural change in relation to pharmacologically induced experiences. But if we are to consider the psychedelics in relation to religion we should perhaps define our terms, as we have already done with the drugs, and devote a moment or two to considering what should be included under the religious/mystical rubric.

Most usually it is held that a central defining characteristic of religion is the belief in a superhuman controlling power. Typically this belief centres on a personal god, a quasi-person, who demands both worship and a code of behaviour. Certainly such an axiom is a reasonable starting point for the description of, say, Christianity or Islam but it is inadequate or misleading in many other cases. For example, many experiences are, and have been throughout recorded history, regarded as being of a religious sort but without necessarily seeming to imply either a personal god or a primitive pantheism. These experiences or revelations are instead mystical – they relate to ecstatic states of awareness and knowledge. In fact, though, they usually *do* occur within the context of either a religious conviction or, in the case of conversions, within the context of a pre-existing religious imagery and framework. Indeed, mystical experience is the very core of religion itself: without the visions of John the Baptist, Jesus, and Paul there would have been no Christianity. And, without the visions of Moses, Elijah, Isaiah, and others, what conceivable religious relevance would the Old Testament have beyond its mythical and historic value to a Middle Eastern people? Change the names and places and the same holds true of all religions.

Despite the crucial value of the mystical experience to the established religions, it is they who are most condemnatory and harsh about new mystical movements: inquisitors in all ages find their life's work in discrediting and punishing the very processes on which their own lives and beliefs depend. And one is not just thinking of the Spanish Inquisition type of situation, but all 'defenders of the faith' – including the gentle parish priest or minister who is totally distrustful of, and even repelled by, any contemporary examples of mystical experience. This is not to argue that all experiences which are claimed as mystical and divinely inspired are worthy, but simply to point out the paradoxical relationship which exists between religion and mysticism – being at the same time both its most cherished asset and its greatest perceived source of threat. Being aware of this paradox, Christian churches have been at pains to specify what is, and what is not, true revelation, psychedelic drugs apparently constituting one of the more recent, and pressing, reasons for trying to define the ways in which accepted revelations differ from those now being reported.

However, the simplest pragmatic solution to a difficult situation is simply to deny the validity of any drug-induced state of mind as being, by definition, a psychological aberration and therefore not of religious significance. Another solution is to back those people who would totally ban the substances and thus remove the source of the problem. Both solutions have been well favoured by most churches. But banning has proved to be ineffective and the existing documentary evidence is such as cannot be ignored – especially as scholars have shown that the qualities which typify 'religiously induced' mysticism, i.e. prayer, fasting, mortification, etc., are so very similar to those reported in drug-induced states. The only honest thing for any churchman to do is to dispassionately consider whether psychedelic experiences are, as they are often claimed to be, of a similar type of those accepted as valid within his own church. Happily, there are a number of such people at work and their comparisons and conclusions make fascinating reading.

Probably one of the most arresting of the empirical studies of the relationship between 'religious mysticism' and psychedelic experience was the one conducted by Walter Pahnke in 1966. Pahnke himself is something of an unusual phenomenon, having a wide range of qualifications, including medicine and theology, and is thus uniquely equipped to understand and integrate the mental, physical, and spiritual aspects inherent in such an investigation. His first task, before starting his empirical experiment, was to define the characteristics of accepted mystical states of consciousness by reference to available accounts. The writings of the mystics themselves and other analysts of these states, for example William James (1902) and W. T. Stace (1960), yielded a comprehensive phenomenological typology of nine categories which included the feeling of unity or 'oneness' with all creation, the dissolution of the time–space context of awareness, feelings of joy, love, sacredness, deeper reality, alleged ineffability, and persisting positive changes in attitudes and behaviour. Having specified the qualities which typify 'true' mystical consciousness, he then turned to examining the nature of the psychedelic experience.

The subjects for the experiment were twenty Christian theological students who were first examined physically, psychologically, and in terms of their previous religious experience. None had previously taken any form of psychedelic drug and they were carefully prepared for this session in order to give them confidence and reduce anxieties. The experimenters who undertook this preparation were not, themselves, familiar with the mystical typology which had been derived for comparative purposes and they were thus not able to influence unconsciously the subject's experiences and reports. The setting for the study was a private chapel screened off from the main part of a church in which a two and a half hour Good Friday service was taking place. The subjects were able to hear the service; a situation which was thought to be optimal for conducting an experiment with the subjects emotionally and intellectually orientated towards religious matters.

The crucial part of the study was that it was a 'double-blind' situation in which subjects were matched in pairs with only one of each pair receiving psilocybin, the other receiving a psychologically inactive substance which produced some minor transient bodily effects which might suggest that it was psychoactive. But neither Pahnke nor the subjects knew which individuals had received what until after the study.

Content analysis of tape recordings of experiences, written accounts, interviews, group discussions, questionnaires and a follow-up after six months all yielded the evidence to evaluate whether the 'mystical' effects were simply due to suggestibility (i.e. did these effects also occur in the individuals not receiving psychedelic material?), and whether the experiences could be seen as being mystical in the same way as those of the 'true mystics'.

The result showed that both groups got a great deal spiritually from the experience but that those who had received the psilocybin were the ones who had profound and 'typical' mystical experiences. The effect was therefore not due to pure suggestibility within an emotionally powerful context. Of those who received the drug, eight out of ten still felt that their lives had been profoundly enriched after a six-month interval. The powerful psychological states reported by these subjects, when compared with those of the mystics, strongly suggested that they were of the same genre. Pahnke concluded that the psychedelic drugs represent a potentially powerful research tool for studying mystical states of consciousness – without prejudice to their 'reality' – and that they are perhaps a valuable new adjunct to carefully supervised spiritual retreats.

Other studies, like that of Downing and Wygant (see Blum, 1965), have been less concerned with the nature of the mystical phenomena and relatively more concerned with the ways in which religious belief is modified by having taken psychedelics. In this case forty-two subjects, including psychiatric patients and normals, were given LSD and their responses monitored by questionnaire. The results showed that there was a greatly felt improvement in positive feelings towards God, their Church, and its teaching as well as personal improvements such as feeling more secure, trusting, and tolerant. The investigators noted that there occurred no polar changes in people's basic beliefs: no one gained or lost their religious faith – but existing ones became more positively humane or religious. They concluded that nothing was added which had not previously been there, and that nothing which had been present was subtracted. Studies like these are only examples drawn from a wide literature. The findings vary with the nature of the group observed and with their set and setting, the most striking effects occurring when the subjects are consciously religiously focused and in a religious context. Yet even in quite unpropitious circumstances the number of positive mystico-religious experiences reported is still surprisingly high.

But if the Christian community is unhappy about the claimed relationship between the experiences of the saints and those of the contemporary psychenaut, they are a great deal *more* unhappy about the relationship which one biblical scholar claims to be the case. John Allegro, in his book *The Sacred Mushroom and the Cross* (1970), argues that the entire Christian religion is actually based upon a misunderstanding of the recorded myths of an ancient psychedelic mystery cult. Had the claim been made by an insubstantial mystifier then it might be dismissed out of hand as yet another crank theory, but Allegro is a distinguished academic philologist who worked in a department of theology. He was the first British representative on the international editorial team responsible for preparation for publication of the Dead Sea Scrolls. His contentions therefore deserve to be considered.

It is Allegro's thesis that many of the religions of the Near East derive from a common source – a primitive fertility cult which arose in ancient Sumer. The cult was concerned with the worship of a divine penis, the organ which was supposed to fertilize mother earth and thus produce the necessary substances of life. And, because mushrooms resemble the penis, they were magically identified with the penis-god and were therefore treated as sacred objects which were only to be used sacramentally. They were commonly referred to as 'The Son of God'. One of these available fungi, the fly agaric (*Amanita muscaria*), having powerful psychedelic properties, created visions which were thought to be of a divine origin and, in consequence, a powerful cult developed around the use of this mushroom – a cult which diffused throughout that part of the world and to which was ascribed a range of different local myths and stories. Many *apparently* different religious groups were formed throughout the Near East but, it is argued, behind the clamorous differences is very often the original Sumerian fertility cult and the sacred mushroom.

Allegro goes on to argue that, by studying the language and accounts of the early mystery cults, one can trace a direct link from the very ancient past, through the Old Testament, to Christianity – although he argues that the content, if not the form, of Christianity actually ante-dated Christ by many centuries. The breath-taking conclusion at which he finally arrives is that Jesus and the apostles never existed at all: they are merely parts of a cultic fable about the properties of the sacred herbs and that Christ, the 'Son of God', was the cryptogram for fly agaric. The teachings and convictions arising from mystical psychedelic experiences were, it is supposed, given the narrative form familiar to us only in order to disguise their real meaning from enemies.

It is further argued that one effect of the mushroom's use was to provoke the Jews to rebellion against the Roman occupational forces and thus to precipitate the national dissolution which followed in A.D. 66. In order to preserve the traditions of the cult, a seemingly innocuous vehicle, the story of Jesus, was constructed by the sect and their mysteries encoded in a form acceptable to their enemies, i.e. a spiritual saviour who accepted the temporal authority of the Romans. But the scheme failed disastrously: the 'Christians' were destroyed in vast numbers and only the form, not the content, of the mysteries survived. Therefore, Allegro concludes, the entire Christian story is revealed as nothing more than the external form of an ancient deception.

Assessing this case is enormously difficult for anyone other than another philologist or etymologist and those who do specialize in this same area tend to be religiously committed. Allegro charges them with suppression and bias and they, in turn, charge him with poor scholarship and a worse capacity for inferential reasoning. Certainly though, the case makes intriguing reading and the linguistic coincidences (or usages) do seem to yield a consistent logic compatible with the case for amanita. One of his most convincing pieces of evidence is a photograph of an early Christian fresco of Adam and Eve in the Garden of Eden in which the sacred mushroom appears as the 'Tree of Good and Evil'. But one's capacity for seeing relationships is sometimes very taxed indeed and one is inclined to feel that the case has been pushed far too far.

However, even Allegro's critics tend to agree that the fly agaric was the basis of many Middle Eastern mystery cults of the sort described, though they deny that these bear any relationship to Christianity. And so the matter rests for the time being. Whether

Allegro's thesis is finally rejected or accepted in whole or in part, it has caused a great deal of light to be thrown on the place of one psychedelic substance in the evolution of religious practices.

Allegro is not, though, the only investigator postulating sacred mushrooms as the prime source of ancient religions. Since 1957, the Wassons have been developing their own case for amanita as the centre of many religious cults – some still extant ones having the oldest continuous history of any religious practice in the world whilst others, like the Eleusinian Mystery, have not so successfully withstood the test of time (Wasson, 1961). As with Allegro's argument about the Judeo-Christian faith, the Wassons' arguments are mainly philological and tangential but they, too, make arresting reading.

The Christian church has other sources of embarrassment deriving from the use of psychedelics. One such is the use of peyote by ostensibly Christian groups amongst the American Indians. Deriving from aboriginal Mexican sources, the use of peyote spread very rapidly throughout the American tribes from about 1870 onwards. La Barre (1938), in his book *The Peyote Cult*, presents a most detailed treatment of this phenomenon which, according to Farb (1969), derived much of its virulence from the religious and social hiatus created by the failure of the Ghost Dance. The beliefs surrounding the cult of the Ghost Dance contained the final hopes for establishing Indian supremecy. Wodziwob's vision of the return of the Great Spirit and the dead ancestors in a train, of the great explosion, the destruction of the whites, and the inheritance of their material culture, had received bitter blows in the failure of the prophesy and the suppression of their rebellion. Peyotism represented a potent way of symbolically re-establishing a cultural freedom and reviving bruised beliefs and myths.

Early peyotism, as with the Mescalero Apache, the Kiowa, and the Comanche, was purely aboriginal in its values and beliefs, being without Christian content. But as the cult diffused throughout the tribes, it came to include more and more of the Judeo-Christian tradition until just before the First World War when the original Indian rites were attracting what La Barre refers to as 'government trouble', it became propitious to modify them or at least to interpret them in a way more acceptable to the ruling Christians.

Most prominent amongst the trimmers was Jonathan Koshiway, an ex-evangelist of the Church of Latter Day Saints, whose efforts had, by 1914, resulted in an Indian Peyote Church being registered in Oklahoma as the 'First-Born Church of Christ' and subsequently in the emergence of the 'Native American Church' which came to encompass more than fifty different Indian groups. This new church organization was registered under the great seal of the U S Secretary of State in 1918 and its present strength is variously estimated at anywhere between 50,000 (Pahnke, 1966) and 225,000 (Barron, Jarvik, and Bunnell, 1964).

Farb (1969) states that 'the road to peyote' is nowadays of a Christian orientation though rejecting official Christian sects. The imagery of the ceremonies contains many allusions to Christ's life, his divine nature, and to the miracles. The bible and the crucifix are also often very much in evidence. Also, like the Christian churches, the Native American Church has social organizations like men's and women's fellowships. Yet la Barre, writing in 1938, felt that this all added up to no more than a very superficial cosmetic change from the original peyote cult. However, the resemblance continues to grow and many of the basic peyote tenets of brotherly love, gentleness, and temperance are quite compatible with idealized Christianity. But perhaps the closest ceremonial convergence, and the greatest source of Christian unease, is the use of peyote as the Eucharistic Sacrament. Instead of the symbolic meal of bread and wine, peyotists take their cactus dried or in the form of tea as the body and blood of Christ. Whatever the pros and cons, the experiences which follow must surely seem more congruent with the great religious event being celebrated.

Not only the Christian church but also the United States, the world's most technically advanced country and greatest supporter of religious missionaries, appears somewhat embarrassed by the existence of the peyote cult. Yet the peyote cult, precariously protected from extinction by the terms of the American Constitution, continues to grow – and to irritate anti-psychedelic drug propagandists by revealing no evidence whatsoever of any mental, moral, or physical deterioration due to the long-term use of mescaline in the form of peyote. Moreover, the ceremonies are not wild, nor sexual, nor even spectacular: they are rather typified by personal revelation taking place within a quiet, sober, and subdued atmosphere of contemplation (Osmond, 1971).

Many attempts have been made to deny members of peyote churches their constitutional right to practice religion as they choose. So far, the attacks have not been successful, though nearly so. Williams (1967) recounts a case of the arrest and conviction of three Navajo for possessing peyote for religious purposes: their conviction was only finally quashed by the California Supreme Courts in a split decision (1964). It was held that the application of the narcotics laws in the case of religious use contravened the First Amendment of the US Constitution.

Not all religious use of peyote is as peaceful as the Native American Church though. In his remarkable book *The Teachings of Don Juan: A Yaqui Way of Knowledge*, Carlos Castaneda (1970), a post-graduate student of anthropology, describes how he met, and ultimately became apprenticed to, a Mexican 'brujo' or sorcerer. In the course of his long apprenticeship he was taught the power of many psychedelic substances and, over a number of years, there was opened up for him a world which contained not only wonderful perceptions but also terrifying visions. On three occasions he came into the presence of 'Mescalito', the god of the peyote, and on many other occasions was convinced that his life was in very great danger.

Not surprisingly he broke off his apprenticeship but, some time after writing his book and completing his research thesis, he returned to spend a further period of time with Don Juan (Castaneda, 1971). Again miraculous happenings were also accompanied by terrifying events and Castaneda once more felt his life to be in great danger from powerful dark forces. His accounts, written as anthropological records, are a unique description of the sort of unrecorded mysteries which must lie at the centre of very many of the ancient religious cults. The disturbing thing is that, in the end, Castaneda feels unable to set aside his experiences as being simply subjective. No doubt one should expect this though of substances demonstrably capable of inspiring religions.

The history of the psychedelics abounds with examples of religious cults derived from the use of one drug or another. Even cannabis has a long and distinguished history in that respect and has been used by ruling factions as a tool of manipulation – even to the extent of becoming the centre of an established religion! The explorer von Wissman described how in 1888 he visited the Belgian Congo and found that Kalamba-Moukenge, the Chief of the Balouba, in order to consolidate his kingdom, caused to be destroyed the cultic forms and practices of the subject tribes and replaced them by a universal practice based on the use of hashish (Andrews and Vinkenoog, 1967; Blum, 1969). In fact, such became their fondness for smoking the drug, that the Kalamba came to refer to themselves as the 'bena-Riamba' or 'sons of the hemp plant'.

On the subject of local tribal usage one could go on for a very long time indeed. Cohen (1965) lists some of the substances in common use in the Amazon basin where they are used as snuffs, drinks, and smokes to create ecstatic and other non-normal states of consciousness – though their religious, as opposed to temporal, significance is more difficult to detect in societies where no such distinctions are conceived. De Ropp (1958) probes deeply into drug use in more advanced societies in Mexico and South America. His book can be recommended as an excellent source of information on primitive and ancient practices, including the use of drugs in divination and European witchraft. However, for the best coverage and for the wider historical perspectives, the reader is recommended to look at Blum's *Society and Drugs* (1969).

But, of the great world religions, it is Hinduism which is probably the most overtly associated with psychedelics. What is less clear, though, is just which drugs were involved. For example R. Gordon Wasson in his book *Soma: Divine Mushroom of Immortality* (1969) showed that a tenth of the *Rig-Veda* concerns a psychedelic referred to as 'Soma'. Wasson identifies this as *Amanita muscaria* but Basham (1961) thinks it was probably cannabis. However, the most important point is not so much *which* psychedelic it was but that a psychedelic substance should evidently play, or have played, so prominent a part in one of the great religions. Of course, though amanita has currently little or no place in Indian religious affairs, cannabis is much enjoyed by the Hindu religious caste, the Brahmins (Carstairs, 1954). And Chatterjee, writing in 1969, refers to the especially prevalent usage of this drug by mendicants and sadhus – who hold that it is an aid to concentration and meditation and that it frees the mind from wordly bonds. No doubt the tradition of psychedelic drugs in Indian religion, as well as their current availability in that country, helps to make India a place of pilgrimage for young psychedelic users and also helps commend the prevailing religious beliefs and forms to them.

However, the religious use of psychedelics in our own society requires more complex explanation, examples from other cultures serving only to show that the association is not excepttional and that there is a venerable universal tradition. It may even be the case that our own secular success, based firmly on empirical and pragmatic modes of thought, has been at the expense of other psychologically important processes. The rationalization of work, education, and even traditional religion has, it might be argued, resulted for many of us in an unfulfilled psychological hunger: the need for a personal, ecstatic faith in something. What this 'something' is we can perhaps explore in a moment, but this sort of thing appears to have been part of man's psyche from time immemorial.

That the use of psychedelic materials is quite commonly for religious purposes is surely beyond doubt: the historical world picture attests to this usage, as does the contemporary one. The interim report of the Canadian Government Commission of Inquiry into the non-medical use of drugs (1970) has also observed that a 'considerable degree of religiosity has pervaded the pychedelic drug movement of the 1960s, playing a major role in the function of such drugs in other cultures'. This being the case, who are the principle religious guides of these young people and where are they leading them? The answer to this would seem to be that generally acceptable guides seem to be particularly scarce. For those people who accept the framework of an existing system there is no real need for other religious leadership. In fact, though, probably only a tiny minority of the regular psychedelic users maintain an overt link with a religious body and participate in regular worship: a very much larger number use these systems purely as a *context* for their explorations.

Indeed, the users of psychedelics often draw on the tangible or conceptual trappings of existing systems. Items such as crucifixes or the Tantric hymns are often used though this seldom implies any real belief in the Christian creed or in the reality of Shiva. But certain of the underlying principles, teachings, philosophies and examples may be accepted and used by the individual as a best approximation to his own beliefs and experiences at any moment in time. The external forms are often felt to be particularly useful as an imaginative and meditational starting point, though no undertaking of arriving at the same finishing point is given.

Christianity, perhaps because its image is now so tarnished by its deplorable and much more widely known history, is generally not a preferred context. Also the association with Victorian dirges, platitudinous sermons, and stereotyped and archaic litanies has created difficulties in containing the volcanic religious experiences which psychenauts report. What is missing is the great sense of awe and mystery and the possibility of expressing and discussing these events in a constructive rather than a pious or censorius manner. Eastern religions, being more orientated towards personal mystical experiences, have attracted many converts. Even so, the greater number of users are almost certainly not converts or adherents to any formal system, but supplement their religious education by reading the works of contemporary writers on religion who also use psychedelics.

In this respect, Aldous Huxley probably deserves a much greater influence than he has actually achieved but, as it is, his main impact upon the psychedelic scene is due to his essays *The Doors of Perception* and *Heaven and Hell*. To a lesser extent is his last novel, *Island*, an influential work, and his prophetic early work, *Brave New World*, is generally only of antiquarian interest to a minority of the psychedelic drug-users. But in another of his early works, *The Perennial Philosophy*, Huxley has summarized the bulk of his mystical searchings in an intellectual form. He did this by starting from a belief that mystical experience is the same in all times, amongst all men, and in all religions: only the circumstances and the metaphor are different. His readings, particularly of Christian, Hindu, Sufi, and Buddhist mystics, had suggested this basic similarity and his book represents a comparative study which attempts to show the reconciliation of what had been thought dissimilar.

Years later, after he had himself experienced psychedelically induced states of consciousness, he concluded that these were quite congruent with the wide ranging mystical forms that he had distilled into his book. Moreover, it was only at this stage in his life that he felt himself truly able to comprehend what he had intellectually grasped and recorded earlier. In other words, he was identifying psychedelically induced states with those of the accepted religious mystics. Alas, it seems that relatively few of the religiously inclined users of psychedelics actually refer back to Huxley's exposition of the *philosophia perennis*, preferring to concern themselves only with the writings which followed his revelation and which, in my own view, are not completely comprehensible unless one also looks at his intellectual and religious development through his earlier writings. Indeed, it is only by reference to these works that Huxley could be really significant as a religious teacher.

Paradoxically, one of the writers who has been most influential in pointing back to these earlier works is also one of Huxley's most vehement critics. R. C. Zaehner, a Professor of Eastern Religions and Ethics at Oxford, actually entered the (to him) unfamiliar field of mysticism just to refute and discredit Huxley's claims. In his view, Huxley is simply an example of an intellectual with religious needs whose experiments with pathological and non-normal states of consciousness were the vehicle of self-deception. But worse, Zaehner sees Huxley's claims as striking at the very roots of all religion unless refuted. And, as Huxley commanded so much respect as a writer and thinker, it was the more important that his claims be dealt with by a religious apologist.

Zaehner's (1957) refutation of Huxley (1954), judging by his use of language, appears to have its own intemperate qualities when he criticizes Huxley for absurd arrogance, manic-type misjudgement, and outrageous claims. He presumes that Huxley's experiences and conclusions were very largely an artifact of his preoccupation with Hindu and Buddhist works – though how Zaehner, or indeed any of the 'accredited mystics' themselves, could be free of such sensitization is not clear. However, Zaehner did have the courage to take the drug himself, though his own experiences were not of a mystical nature but rather amusing and manic – but then he is a specialist in that non-mystical system Zoroastrianism! Even so, the nature of his critique leaves a great deal to be desired: it proceeds using equivocation, nonsequiturs, and a personal attack upon Huxley, inferring that he was a rather unstable and shallow intellectual who could not, or would not, distinguish between madness and mystical experience. Yet, despite these regrettable features, Zaehner's book contains much else that is of interest and relevance to this discussion.

Amongst the other important thought leaders must be counted Walter Pahnke, already referred to, and Walter Clark, author of *Chemical Ecstasy: Psychedelic Drugs and Religion* (1969) and a one-time collaborator with Timothy Leary. Pahnke, though having produced some of the most interesting empirical and conceptual work on the religious implications of psychedelic drug usage, has not yet presented a readily available corpus of his work and is therefore probably not very influential in a direct sense – though his work has been very important in the thinking and writings of many who are communicating more directly with users and others in the intellectual scene. Amongst these, Walter Clark is a very good example.

Clark, a Professor Emeritus of the Psychology of Religion, is perhaps ideally qualified to assess the psychological status of these non-normal states and to appraise their relationship to religious experience. Like William James (1902), he accepts that there exists a whole multitude of levels, or 'special types', of consciousness and that 'normal consciousness' and the consciousness of dreams are simply some of these types. The mystics have reported other forms of consciousness, as have many people who are neither mystics nor drug-users but who have, perhaps, glimpsed them as a result of great emotional, physical, or intellectual stress.

The question which Clark approaches in psychological and behavioural terms is whether such experiences share the same profound qualities as the accepted religious ones. He, too, measures them against Stace's (1960) seven criteria of 'true mysticism' and then sifts the empirical evidence relating to psychedelically stimulated states. In so doing, he comes to accept the equivalence of the experiences of 'true' mystics and some of the states induced by psychedelics. He also finds himself very much in sympathy with the conclusion of Huxley, Pahnke, and others and also with the much more general conclusions about the nature of mystical levels of reality as described by Carl Jung. There is no doubt of Clark's own acceptance of these drugs, which he regards as 'triggers' to release what is already within the individual. For him they are midwives of spiritual understanding; they facilitate but do not create anything: only what pre-existed can find expression.

In evaluating the religious effect of the psychedelic experience, Clark places a good deal of importance on the question of whether people's lives are actually changed in a direction which is congruent with established religious teachings. Broadly, he concludes that this does seem to be the case: people's personal and social lives do seem to become more compassionate and reverent – especially where drug-usage takes place in the context of religious seeking. Using the drugs for 'kicks' does not necessarily preclude the triggering of such latent responses, nor does being an intellectual atheist necessarily preclude revelation, but it is less common.

One of the major *problems* with psychedelic drug-use which Clark foresees is that its effects may result in a religious quietism – as opposed to the activism, the philosophy of participation and good works, which is recommended by the Christian church. 'Dropping-out' *may* mean the abandoning of sterile forms as part of spiritual renewal but, in many cases, it really means a form of negativism and preoccupation with self. This quietism and a rather fatalistic outlook is typical of oriental religions but, as Clark points out, even Buddha deferred entering Nirvana until his service to others through teaching had been completed. However, the typical religious seeker using psychedelic means has embraced a rather selective and eclectic picture of eastern religions, generally preferring to overlook the less palatable requirements and observances. This, Clark sees as a source of great religious error: churches and theologies may often be irksome and even misguided but, without some such responsible framework and source of discipline, grasping for mystical ecstasy may become a degenerate form of self-indulgence.

As a Christian, he rather naturally feels that recourse to other, culturally alien, religions would be a mistake and feels that a greater psychological support is available in the familiar symbolism and forms of Christianity. But easier said than done: the Christian community is naturally suspicious of drug-users. Indeed, as Clark observes, the only circumstance in which most Christians are prepared to discuss drugs is to condemn them. If Clark is right about this, the possibility of Christians achieving a spiritual leadership and supplying religious guidance is sadly being missed.

Who, then, will accept the roles of leadership and spiritual guidance? The answer is probably nobody – though tips may be given by some of the more articulate of the psychedelic movement's leadership. Timothy Leary (1965) seems to come out fairly clearly in favour of people rejecting the existing forms of religion and of setting up their own alternative: to this end he offers a number of tactics, as he has also done in the social or community setting. For example, at Zihuatanejo, a training centre established in Mexico by Leary and his associates (Blum, 1965), spiritual guidance of others was absolutely central to the purpose of the group calling itself IFIF – International Federation for Internal Freedom. And, though religious guidance, in the sense of conventional religious instruction, played very little part in this organization, it was only because a religious significance was assumed to attach to everything. In fact, many of the participants held theological degrees and thus might be expected to have readily available frameworks in which to fit their own experiences.

But Leary and his colleagues also recognized that a very specific guidance was required to help the individual cope with what might otherwise be an overwhelming and disorientating experience. As they pointed out in their summarized rationale of the training centre (Leary, Alpert and Metzner, 1965), consciousness may only ever be understood by reference to metaphor – whether scientific, literary, or theological – and it is the case that the most appropriate ones for psychedelic states of consciousness are drawn from religious sources. The purpose of a metaphorical account is to provide a map and orientation for mind-travellers who have been projected into the unfamiliar. The metaphor most favoured was drawn from Mahayana Buddhism in the form of *The Bardo Thödol – The Tibetan Book of the Dead*. Leary, Metzner, and Alpert (1964), using the Evans–Wentz translation of the original, themselves re-wrote the text in more modern English, relating the content to the psychedelic experience.

The original text was ostensibly related to what one is to expect at the moment of death, during the intermediate period, and then during rebirth. However, Leary and his associates point out that the book had an esoteric meaning as well as the exoteric one of being a manual for the dying. Further, not only is the text actually about ego-death and rebirth to a cosmic consciousness, but this is exactly what the psychedelic experience is all about. Accordingly, they present, and reinterpret, the bardos as stages in a psychedelic session – giving practical advice on how to deal with all that happens. Naturally this text is extremely highly valued amongst the religiously inclined users of the major psychedelics. But, though the tactical steps are well guided, the work does not necessarily imply any specific religious allegiances, and spiritual guidance at the strategic or belief-system level is not provided.

Indeed, such a structuring is probably completely antithetical to Leary's own value-system. His philosophy is much more accessible than his religious ideas but, no doubt, he would say that it is a useless and utterly misleading linguistic game trying to make such a distinction anyway. Perhaps his position on religion is best summarized in his advice to devote one's entire life to the religious search: to 'turn-on' with whatever 'sacrament' succeeds in directing attention away from the staged games of life. The ultimate purpose is ecstatic visionary contact with the divine: a state achievable only within the 'temple of god' which resides in the individual's own body.

Undoubtedly one of the most erudite and influential religious thinkers of the psychedelic movement is Alan Watts. His life is devoted to religious matters, and, when he criticizes religious forms, it is not out of indifference or dislike but seemingly because of his caring. For example, in his book, *The Joyous Cosmology* (1962), he highlights one of the sources of the Christian church's failure when he says that 'it is *crowd*, not group orientated'. The individual's focus is concretely upon the backs of necks and upon the face of a leader who struggles to explain the abstract and ideational.

By contrast, Watts himself is enormously enthusiastic about the feelings of 'oneness' and the experiences deriving from psychedelics: indeed *The Joyous Cosmology* is based on a composite of many of his own psychedelic experiences. Central amongst his conclusions is the belief that there is no difference between this type of induced state and the accepted experiences of the mystics and also the idea, often thought to be so clear a sign of madness amongst Westerners, that both the self and others are divine.

He refers to people seen in a psychedelic encounter as being really avatars of Brahma, Vishnu and Shiva simply pretending to be ordinary mortals: a not unusual psychedelic conclusion though rather uncommonly symbolized. However, Van Dusen's (1961) summary comes much closer to the conventional when he describes his own experiences of 'satori' or enlightenment which resulted from the use of LSD. The value of *The Tibetan Book of the Dead* is again stressed in the transition from ego-death to that state of revelation in which one apprehends the godhead of the self and of others and that heaven is with us all the time in what is usually perceived as the mundane present.

One of Watts' own more conventional metaphors is the equating of psychedelic drugs with the microscope – both of which are held to reveal a pre-existing reality. This scientific metaphor is particularly congruent with Watts' optimism that, one day, scientifically derived psychedelics will become the 'sacrament' of a new religion which will unite science with non-science to create a vastly richer world, and cosmological view, than anything which is now possible.

But, whatever lies in the future, there is a current lack of constructive ideas to guide the present. Watts, and many like him, appear to hold that the sense of oneness inherent in the religious ecstacy of the psychedelic experience will prove to be a quite effective basis for creating enduring social organizations – and a good deal more reliable than the games of competitive social egos. Perhaps Watts is right but many people would also feel with Clark (1969) that simply dwelling on personal experiences, unless geared to a framework of purpose and agreed meaning, may easily deteriorate into futility through excessive talk about the ineffable. This is not to downgrade the significance of the experiences: indeed, Professor Clark freely admits that a large, perhaps the greater, portion of his own understanding of religion has come directly from his use of psychedelics. But guidance is also necessary if the user is to achieve spiritual growth rather than a deepening superstitiousness.

Alas, the users of psychedelics are not all like Clark, Huxley, or Watts and though these may be influential thinkers, they are not typical members of the psychedelic scene. What is typical would be difficult to say but, though the range is wide and the scene changes rapidly with time, there are also some generic similarities which seem to persist.

The work of Gopala Alampur, though carried out during 1967–8 in the very small bohemian suburb of Yorkville in Toronto, nevertheless still contains something of the distinctive flavour of 'hippiedom'. Alampur, an anthropologist, took on the role of participant observer – dressing like, and living with, the 'villagers' who occupied the few streets which comprised their community. His notes, chronicling the emotional and physical attempts at survival of a mixed group of hippies, motor-cycle gangsters, drug pushers, week-enders, and the like, also contain a good deal about the religious aspirations of the hippie psyche-delic users. He stresses their search for a spiritual identity and their disillusionment with, and rejection of, the religion and ethics of their culture and parental generation. Instead, they look to the mysterious East and to mysticism generally. Alampur himself, just because he was an Indian, was asked by many to become their 'guru' or spiritual teacher! Almost anything unfamiliar seems to enjoy a special status in the psychedelic movement and 'religion' and 'mysticism' would have to be very

widely defined in order to compass some of the occult preoccupations such as astrology, numerology, and magical lore
which abound.

Alampur concludes that, despite the conversational forms of
the hippie community, which very often contain apparently
sophisticated and complex notions from Buddhism and Hinduism,
this generally signifies no more than an acquaintance with the
jargon. There is little real underlying knowledge, only the words,
trappings, and forms being assimilated. Recondite books on the
subject are frequently carried but seldom read; little effort goes
into learning and the attempt to understand – much more into
trying to make an impression and creating an 'image'.

Now, whilst Alampur's account may be fairly representative of
the bulk of youthful psychedelic users, there is also a much more
serious minority – as evidenced by some of the writings to which
we have referred. However, though such writers have created an
exciting and appealing vision of the human and divine spirit, this
may or may not be substance of a real religious revival: the results
and not just the pious words will show whether it is.

Spinks (1963) develops this point in his book *Psychology and
Religion*, and goes on to trace a basic similarity between the
practices of the ascetic mystics in both tribal cultures and the
Christian church and the users of the psychedelic drugs. For,
though the former employ most disagreeable forms of self-torture,
fasting, and deprivation whilst the latter use rather agreeable
chemical means, both are attempting to achieve the same desirable states of consciousness by means of changed body chemistry.
He concludes that, just because unusual states of awareness are
derived through abnormal bodily states, this does not necessarily
invalidate the quality of the result: it is the end-product which
must be judged, not the means.

If, he continues, the result of whatever means creates spiritual
buoyancy in the individual and leads him to help others to shed
egocentricity, then the events must be judged to signal a genuine
spiritual experience. But the crunch comes in judging the effects,
in establishing criteria to judge by, in specifying who we should
choose as exemplars, and in deciding what to make of the many

fakes, failures, and mentally sick who adhere to any religious movement.

This sort of difficulty makes the assessment of psychedelics extremely difficult but Zaehner, in developing his arguments against their use, makes two points which are apposite in judging the likely effect of widespread usage. In the first place, he draws attention to the practical problems of organizing a society comprised of ecstatics who have lost the more usual material and interpersonal motivations. There is no doubt much in what he says, yet, on the other hand, these are perhaps just the sort of problems which Christianity itself would raise if it was implemented to any degree.

Zaehner's second objection is that the psychedelics often appear to lead people to believe that they have transcended good and evil and so, instead of guiding their lives by ethical practices in order to achieve spiritual reward, they may give up ethical commitment and become amoral. One could certainly point to many amoral and immoral concomitants of psychedelic drug use, or the practice of any religion for that matter, but then one could equally point to the opposite in either case. This argument is, however, another facet of the vexing discussion of whether morality can exist without religion, but it does serve to bring us back to traditional theological concerns and opinions. And so, having presented something of the history, evidence, and arguments, it must finally be left to the individual to draw his own conclusions as to whether psychedelic drugs lead or mislead us in religious matters.

In a most delightful reinterpretation of the Adam and Eve story, an American physician, Ivan Bennett (1971), identifies the fruit of the 'Tree of Knowledge of Good and Evil' as a psychedelic drug – a notion which would surely delight John Allegro and explain his early Christian picture of Adam and Eve standing beside a giant fly agaric mushroom in the Garden of Eden! However, Bennett is not concerned with the idea of Christianity as an esoteric code but with how well the 'evidence' in Genesis is congruent with the 'Forbidden Fruit' being some sort of psychedelic. Being satisfied that the evidence is good, he goes on to call

Adam and Eve 'the first hippies' – whose forbidden food made them fully aware of the world for the first time.

Reading the biblical story for oneself will yield the 'clues' and one can see that the allegory, and mankind's social and religious strivings ever since, fit the picture of our sense of paradise lost and our attempts to regain it. One way in which people have sought to return is, paradoxically, by using these same mind-altering drugs which were supposed to have led to the 'fall'. Bennett concludes that all such attempts are doomed to failure, that it is man's lot to live with the 'divine discontent' which keeps him struggling with his environment and any temporary relief, even achieved through these same drugs, is both deceiving and dangerous. Others hold that the key which opened the 'exit' door also fits the one marked 'entrance'. They, too, will have to judge for themselves.

11 Retrospect

We began by posing the question of what place, if any, psychedelic drugs are likely to have in our present and future society and now, having spent ten chapters in considering the ways in which people are affected by these substances, we should be in a better position to come to some conclusions.

Perhaps, though, the first point about which we should remind ourselves is that the psychedelics are already a part of our society and that they exert a not inconsiderable influence, directly or indirectly, on a great many lives. What the prevalence of use is, judged on national or international standards, would be a matter of pure speculation but there is little doubt that, in most Western societies, we are talking about a quite significant minority of young people. Precise estimates based on a representative sampling of entire populations are very difficult to make because of the enormous cost of this type of epidemiological research; most studies extend only to a sample drawn from, say, a given city, university, or military unit. Yet, even allowing that such studies are very imperfect, patchy in distribution, and biased towards concentrated urban areas, the number and proportion of users identified is usually surprisingly high.

For example, our own investigation in Glasgow of the prevalence of drug abuse amongst the sixteen- to twenty-four-year-old group, though based on 'target' groups like students, delinquents, casualty cases, pupils in school, etc., showed a remarkably high usage in a centre which we had initially supposed to have very little such activity. Unfortunately, completely random sampling from an entire population is a practical impossibility with research which requires substantial face-to-face contact time and which, moreover, involves the subject in revealing information about drug-use for which he *could*, in theory, be sent to prison. In these circumstances a street-corner survey of the BBC audience research type is obviously not a possibility, any more than is a door-to-door study of the census type. In consequence of sampling only within defined groups, our results cannot be generalized to all people of that age group in Glasgow but, as the research report will indicate in due course, the degree of usage is substantially greater for a whole range of categories of young people than most of us might have supposed. Furthermore, it transpired that it was the psychedelics which took pride of place – with cannabis at the head of the list and LSD seemingly gaining ground amongst those still at school.

That psychedelics play some part in the present social scene is obvious, but to understand their popularity will involve some feeling for the supposed value of these substances in the lives of users. Obviously though, it would be naïve to expect that the part played would be the same in all cases. For example, we might 'explain' the prevalent use of cannabis by saying that people use it because they see it as a safe and inexpensive source of pleasure, merriment and relaxation. And this may well completely account for why many people believe that they use cannabis; but in circumstances where the drug is used in moderation and when the user finds cost unimportant, there may be other reasons why the user chooses cannabis, which may cost him his freedom, instead of alcohol.

Our own research findings indicated clearly that distinctive personality patterns are involved and, though our results are still awaiting their turn to appear in the technical literature, they have have shown quite consistently that those who used drugs were significantly different from those who did not in that they scored much more highly on test measures of neuroticism, psychoticism, and anxiety. In other words, the users of drugs appeared to be compensating for their relatively greater subjective distress and feelings of inadequacy by using these substances to offset psychological tension and interpersonal problems. From what we know of cannabis, this drug might serve very well in this role whereas the major psychedelics presumably have some other qualities to offer – quite possibly connected with the urge for adventure and experiment, but perhaps also to achieve that *sense* of profound understanding and wisdom which must be a great source of comfort for people who are otherwise plagued by feelings of inadequacy, ambivalence, and self-distrust.

Of course it would be over-optimistic of us to expect all-embracing explanations of the use and usage of the 'psychedelics' as such – even if we were dealing with only one drug rather than so many. But, of the innumerable attempts which have been made to understand these problems, many of them do share a common belief that the age of the user is of some significance.

If we look at the scene as a whole, and despite an older *intellectual* leadership, the illegal use of psychedelics is mainly the prerogative of the teens and early twenties, with the greater emphasis on the just post-adolescent stage. These young people, caught between the biological pressures of adolescence and the social pressures of transition from a world of dependency to that of adult autonomy, are frequently subject to a state of turmoil typified by a lack of self-definition and resulting in a great fluidity and ambivalence of attitudes, moods, and beliefs. This ambivalence itself relates also to the *self-concept* and there is a tendency for the young person to swing from extremes of nihilism and self-abasement to those of omnipotence and grandeur. Thus the pseudo-identities of this stage of development not untypically relate to both the social outcast or minority-group member, and the saviour of society – perhaps symbolically as the omniscient mystic, philosopher, and persecuted or misunderstood poet, or more directly, as the all-wise and omnipotent revolutionary. Variations on the theme will depend upon circumstances and may be more gang- than society-orientated but, eitherway, they tend to connote a degree of rebellion, aggressiveness, and sexuality which society demands to see controlled.

Naturally enough, this developmental pattern is neither universal nor is it completely confined to people of a given age-group. But it does seem to afflict the young particularly hard and one reasonable explanation of the attraction of psychedelic drugs is that, in addition to providing euphoric experiences and release from psychological tensions, they differ from alcohol in that they are positively useful in modifying the effects of the sexual and aggressive impulses by both reducing sexual conflicts, inhibitions, and guilt, as well as damping down the destructive and aggressive tendencies of this stage of development.

The very fact of using illegal drugs is also, in itself, the source of a valued common bond between individuals who are otherwise wrestling with feelings of alienation. Some writers have noted that there seems to exist a vast, though undefined, 'youth club' based upon psychedelic drug-use, the members of this club being united by a common *argot*, or in-group vocabulary, and by their own 'prophets' and 'saints', clothes and ornaments, books and posters, poetry and music. And, of course, in addition to the idealistic and humanitarian elements expressed, there is also the powerful effect of being bound together through sharing the same common enemy – the 'square world' with its authority structures and materialism.

The issue of anti-materialism has been given a good airing elsewhere but, for whatever age-group, it is one which recurs regularly as being a fundamental part of the psychedelic scene. A number of strands seem to be related here: in the first place, there is the discovery that ecstatic pleasure is a most satisfying and necessary psychological requirement, and one which is not usually adequately met by the processes of conventional living and material achievement. This belief is also widely coupled with a feeling that the measures of success in a materialistic society are judged on fraudulent scales, where status role-playing and possessions weigh more heavily than philosophical, ethical, and religious qualities.

No doubt this is so, but the assertion has created much hostility from society at large because of its concern that the sense of meaning and fulfilment which the psychedelics often evoke may undermine *any* sort of cultivated or advanced society by amputating the will to achieve. This view sees people as being diminished by never getting down to the qualities and demands of the 'real' world and, moreover, preventing others from doing so because of the economic dependency of large numbers of 'lotus eaters'.

And probably one of the most disturbing facts about psychedelics is that their use *has* so often been associated with a loss of the motivation to participate usefully in the mundane work of the world, the satisfactions of the drug-induced experiences sometimes becoming vocations in themselves rather than new perspectives for living a good and socially acceptable life. But even allowing that this is so, it is probably equally true that most of the young people who at some time use one or another of these drugs are *not* profoundly affected by the experiences – at least not in any obvious behavioural sense. Undoubtedly there are some users who do turn their avocation into a vocation, just as there are in many fields, but society usually contrives to absorb such people unless their numbers become excessive.

Complacency in dealing with any sort of drug abuse would be obvious folly but one should perhaps not be *too* alarmed at the number of young people who are *at some time* experimenting with psychedelics. Fortunately, these substances are not capable of inducing any physical dependence and it looks very much as though most of those who dabble with them do so for only a very short while and then carry on as before. Indeed, even many of the regular users seem quite quickly to reach a stage where they are ready to move on to 'transcendental meditation', or mortgage repayments, and leave drug use behind. For most young users, the psychedelics probably represent no more than an occasional outing to a super-psychological fairground of colourful and unusual sensations and though, for some, the commitment plainly becomes much greater and long-term, I suspect that it would be wrong for the rest of us to get the situation out of perspective. In most cases we are very likely only observing a contemporary *rite de passage* and should be very careful not to fixate it by our clumsy handling of the situation.

What, though, of the other reasons for which psychedelics are used? The euphoria and perceptual enrichment need no explanations as motives and we have also seen how many unbalanced individuals experiment with their consciousness as a mode of intuitive therapy or escape. But we are still left with the question of whether the 'consciousness expansion' of the psychedelics is of any *positive* value or whether it is completely bogus and simply an episode of subjectively satisfying 'unsanity' and intriguing illusion.

Regrettably, it would be virtually impossible to answer this question in terms of rules of evidence and theories of meaning which were acceptable to both sides. Take, for example, creativity as one of the only two areas which stands a reasonable chance of producing objective evidence of the positive qualities of psychedelic 'trips'. In this case, it was all too obvious that the question of value to graphic artists was bedevilled by the fact that the supporters of this view and the critics differ in their aesthetic viewpoints. And coming to any conclusions on the subject is made worse by a dearth of research in the entire area, not least in the case of problem solving where solutions could be objectively and independently assessed.

On the other hand, the positive value of psychedelic states of consciousness is much more readily apparent in relation to psychotherapy. In this case, though there is still a good deal of disagreement between supporters and critics as to whether these drugs represent any new and remarkable effective therapeutic breakthrough, the evidence does seem to be more unequivocal in suggesting that psychedelic states are extremely valuable in certain cases. And if these states *are* capable of relieving great mental anguish and instability, even if not uniquely so, this might justify the conclusion that they have some positive psychological aspects – at least within carefully controlled circumstances.

As we have seen, the evidence supporting the notion that the psychedelics are highly pathogenic substances proves, except possibly in the case of cannabis, to be very mush overstated. But, given that certain risks do attend the *unsupervised* use of all of these drugs, we may still ask whether it is right to throw away the baby with the bath water.

After all, such tremendously useful medicines as morphine, aspirin, and penicillin all carry a certain risk in use – indeed most people would probably be quite horrified to learn of the serious, or even lethal, reactions which may follow from the use of such warmly regarded and trusted drugs as aspirin and penicillin. And, without a doubt, if a small number of untoward reactions was made the criterion for rejecting *any* drug, whether or not it had been properly used, then our available medicines would be drastically reduced as there is probably hardly a single powerful medicament which does not carry some degree of risk under certain circumstances.

In fact, from a scientific and medical point of view, it is a source of considerable exasperation to many investigators and practitioners when such important new chemicals are fairly arbitrarily condemned despite the fact that the record indicates that they may be the first generation of a range of profoundly useful tools for both therapy and the investigation of the mind. This sort of control is particularly annoying when one thinks of the innumerable experimental surgical and medical procedures which carry degrees of risk which are of many magnitudes greater than those involved with the psychedelics.

However, though the clinical application of such drugs as L S D may not involve unusual or unacceptable risks, the evidence relating to unsupervised use indicates that the risk to the individual becomes greater, and the social acceptability of the risk presumably diminishes, as the purpose of use moves away from treatment. Yet by no means everyone would accept this point of view, and it is sometimes argued that people have a perfect right to pursue their own ends so long as they are not harming others in doing so. Moreover, runs the user's argument, because something has been dubbed a 'drug' it doesn't necessarily follow that it is only to be valued as a medicine, or that it may be annexed as the sole prerogative of the medical profession. The psychedelics are, it is argued, a significant part of their social, philosophical, and religious way of life and, whether other people think them misguided or not, free, adult citizens should have the right to please themselves within the sort of limits of age and health set for, and by, other potentially hazardous activities such as driving a car or flying an aeroplane.

Pursuing the analogy with other activities like sailing, climbing, sky-diving, exploring, etc., in which the individual accepts that he may be killed or injured, it is pointed out that the very elements of danger and discovery involved are ones which society applauds in people like Livingstone, Mallory or Scott – even when these adventurous souls perish in the pursuit of their rather unusual aims. Psychedelic explorers argue, with disarming logic, that if society feels it to be its duty to ban psychedelics in order to protect those people who would use them, they must also rationally ban, say, small boat sailing as this indisputably causes hundreds of deaths every year.

The young, inexperienced, or otherwise vulnerable are perhaps easily answered, but there remain circumstances which do justify a careful examination of the claims put forward in support of the more general, if controlled, usage of psychedelics. For example, in the United States there are still thousands of people belonging to the Native American Church who are tenuously managing to hold onto their Constitutional right to use mescaline as a sacrament, and there are many more who demand the same freedom of action on the basis of this precedent. In the same vein, many mature private citizens who wish to explore the roots and recesses of their minds for philosophical or creative purposes also resent this curtailment of their liberty. Finally, there are the clinicians and professional research workers who wish to investigate thoroughly the possibilities opened up by these materials for studying the workings of the human mind.

Speaking as a scientist myself, I should naturally like to see the excessive restrictions which govern research into psychedelic effects relaxed to a great extent. And, as such research requires the help of subjects, there would be the opportunity for many would-be explorers, providing that they were mature and in good mental and physical health, to undertake their explorations within supportive and safe conditions. Naturally, this sort of arrangement would not meet the requirements of those people whose demand is for virtually unrestricted freedom, but then those who ask for the moon seldom expect to be given it.

Some of the major psychedelics are so potentially dangerous that no sane society would ever contemplate their use outside of a laboratory. Minor ones, like cannabis, may well achieve the same sort of currency as alcohol – providing no serious side-effects are established – and others, like LSD, mescaline and psilocybin, whilst most unlikely ever to be other than closely restricted, *could* become much more widely used again. After all, the massive sanctions and controls which now surround the use of these latter drugs were largely precipitated by such dramatic, but unsubstantiated, claims that LSD produces genetic or congenital disasters of the 'thalidomide' type. Society must, quite naturally, act with all appropriate caution when it foresees danger to its members but, judging from the more sober reflections of recent official reports, it seems possible that the psychedelics might soon achieve at least some degree of rehabilitation.

It may be that, at some time in the future, we shall see psychedelic centres for experimental mysticism, creative thinking, philosophical speculation, and so on. I rather doubt it, though the rate and way in which society is now changing clearly makes any sort of prediction a chancy affair. However, I should be surprised, and disappointed, if our present policy in respect of controlled psychological exploration was to be permanently maintained. Controversial or not, the inner space of the human mind will continue to be probed and mapped, just as we are doing with the outer space which surrounds us all. And, if it should seem that psychedelics have unique qualities in this respect, then there will be continuing pressures to use them.

As citizens, we are all concerned in the making of laws, even though we are never directly consulted. But for all that, it is still our opinion on the subjects of legislation which finally decides whether, and how, such enactments are applied, and how well they succeed. The psychedelics, being a realm in which there is a hotly debated and shifting social and legal perspective, represent one of those areas where, because of the way in which the present laws are being attacked and disregarded, particular attention must be paid. All of these drugs raise different questions but cannabis stands out most obviously from the rest because of the strong arguments which are now being made to have it legalized. The other psychedelics involve less dramatic manoeuvres but they, too, are potent parts of our present social scene and their future is no less in need of re-definition.

It has not been the purpose of this book to mould people's opinions on these issues but rather to present some of the information on which we may each shape our own. Certainly there are many important scientific and medical considerations which must be weighed but, as so many of the other issues raised have such large ethical and moral components, their solution must finally rest upon subjective truths no less than facts.

Of course, as with censorship or the introduction of any sort of social control, acting on other people's behalf for what we believe to be their own good may be judged as tyranny. But, on the other hand, there comes a point at which failing to apply one's know-ledge in the service of others is simply a mark of indifference, despair, or irresponsibility. The balance is a delicate one but, whatever we do or do not do, we are involved and accountable.

References

Aaronson, B., and Osmond, H. (eds.) (1971), *Psychedelics: The Uses and Implications of Hallucinogenic Drugs*, Hogarth Press.

Aberle, D. F. (1966), *The Peyote Religion Among the Navaho*, Aldine.

Advisory Committee on Drug Dependence (1968), *Cannabis*, HMSO.

Advisory Committee on Drug Dependence (1970), *The Amphetamines and Lysergic Acid Diethylamide (LSD)*, HMSO.

Alampur, G. (1969), 'The Yorkville Subculture: a study of the life styles and interactions of hippies and non-hippies', field notes subsequently prepared by R. G. Smart and D. Jackson for Addiction Research Foundation, Toronto, 1969.

Aldrich, C. K. (1944), 'The effect of a synthetic marihuana-like compound on musical talent as measured by the Seashore Test', in S. E. Grupp (ed.), *Marihuana*, Merrill, 1971.

Alexander, G. J., Miles, B. E., Gold, G. M., and Alexander, R. B. (1967), 'LSD: injection early in pregnancy produces abnormalities in off-spring of rats', *Science*, vol. 157, p. 459.

Allegro, J. M. (1970), *The Sacred Mushroom and the Cross*, Hodder & Stoughton.

Allen, J. R., and West, L. J. (1968), 'Flight from violence; hippies and the green rebellion', *Amer. J. Psychiat.*, vol. 125, pp. 354–70.

Alnaes, R. (1964), 'Therapeutic application of the change in consciousness produced by psycholytica (LSD, psilocybin, etc.)', *Acta Psychiat. Scand.*, suppl. 180, vol. 40, pp. 397–407.

Ames, F. A. (1958), 'A clinical and metabolic study of acute intoxication with cannabis sativa and its role in the model psychoses', *J. ment. Sci.*, vol. 104, pp. 972–99.

Ananga Ranga of Kalyana Malla, trans. Sir Richard Burton and F. F. Arbuthnot, Kimber, 1963.

Andrade, O. M. (1959), 'The criminogenic action of cannabis (marihuana) and narcotics', *Bull. Narcot.*, vol. 16, pp. 23–8.

224 References

Andrews, G., and Vinkenoog, S. (eds.) (1967), *The Book of Grass: An Anthology on Indian Hemp*, Peter Owen.

Anslinger, H. J. (1943), 'The psychiatric aspects of marihuana intoxication', *J. Amer. Med. Assn*, vol. 121, pp. 212–13.

Anslinger, H. J., and Tompkins, W. F. (1953), *The Traffic in Narcotics*, Funk & Wagnalls.

Barber, T. X. (1970), *LSD, Marihuana, Yoga, and Hypnosis*, Aldine.

la Barre, W. (1938), 'The peyote cult', *Yale University Publications in Anthropology*, no. 19, Yale University Press.

Barron, F. (1963), *Creativity and Psychological Health*, Van Nostrand.

Barron, F., Jarvik, M. E., and Bunnell, S. (1964), 'The hallucinogenic drugs', *Sci. Amer.*, vol. 210, pp. 29–37.

Basham, A. L. (1961), 'Soma', in G. Andrews and S. Vinkenoog (eds.), *The Book of Grass: An Anthology on Indian Hemp*, Peter Owen, 1967.

Baudelaire, C. (1858), 'An excerpt from the Seraphic Theatre', trans. N. Cannon, in D. Solomon (ed.), *The Marijuana Papers*, Panther, 1969.

Beattie, R. T. (1968), 'Nutmeg as a psychoactive agent', *Brit. J. Addict.*, vol. 63, pp. 105–9.

Bender, L. (1970), 'Children's reactions to psychotomimetic drugs', in D. D. Efron (ed.), *Psychotomimetic Drugs*, Raven Press.

Bender, L., and Siva-Sankar, D. V. (1968), 'Chromosome damage not found in leukocytes of children treated with L S D-25', *Science*, vol. 159, p. 749.

Bennett, I. F. (1971), 'Drug abuse: who and why?', *J. Indiana State Med. Assn*, vol. 64, pp. 407–9.

Berg, R. H. (1969), 'Warning: steer clear of T H C', *Look Magazine*, 15 April.

Bergel, F., and Davies, D. R. A. (1970), *All about Drugs*, Nelson.

Berlin, L., Guthrie, T., Weider, A., Goodell, H., and Wolff, H. (1955), 'Studies in human cerebral function: the effects of mescaline and lysergic acid on cerebral process pertinent to creative activity', *J. nerv. ment. Dis.*, vol. 122, pp. 487–91.

Bialos, D. S. (1970), 'Adverse marijuana reactions: a critical examination of the literature with selected case material', *Amer. J. Psychiat.*, vol. 127, pp. 819–23.

Blacker, K. H., Jones, R. T., Stone, G. C., and Pfefferbaum, D. (1968), 'Chronic users of LSD: the "acidheads"', *Amer. J. Psychiat.*, vol. 125, pp. 341–51.

Blewett, D. (1971), 'The psychedelics and group therapy', in B. Aaronson and H. Osmond (eds.), *Psychedelics*, Hogarth Press.

Bloomberg, C. (1971), 'The far-out city', *Observer Colour Supplement*, 25 April, pp. 15–18.

Blum, R. (1965), *Utopiates: The Use and Users of LSD-25*, Tavistock.

Blum, R. (1969), 'A history of cannabis', in R. H. Blum (ed.), *Society and Drugs*, vol. 1, Jossey-Bass.

Blum, R., *et al.* (1970a), *Society and Drugs*, Jossey-Bass.

Blum, R., *et al.* (1970b), *Students and Drugs*, Jossey-Bass.

Blumenfield, M., and Glickman, L. (1967), 'Ten months' experience with LSD users admitted to the county psychiatric receiving hospital', *New York State J. Med.*, vol. 67, pp. 1849–53.

Bozzetti, L., Goldsmith, S., and Ungerleider, J. T. (1967), 'The great banana hoax', *Amer. J. Psychiat.*, vol. 124, pp. 678–9.

Brill, N. Q. (1969), 'Marijuana problem', *Psychiat. Dig.*, July, pp. 9–19.

Bromberg, W. (1934), 'Marihuana intoxication', *Amer. J. Psychiat.*, vol. 9, pp. 303–30.

Browning, L. S. (1968), 'Lysergic acid diethylamide: mutagenic effects in drosophila', *Science*, vol. 161, pp. 1022–3.

Bruyn, H. B. (1970), 'Drugs on the college campus', *J. School Health*, February, pp. 91–7.

Burroughs, W. S. (1961), 'Points of distinction between sedative and consciousness-expanding drugs. Address presented to the American Psychological Society, 6th September', in D. Solomon (ed.), *The Marijuana Papers*, Panther, 1969.

Busch, H. A., and Johnson, W. C. (1950), 'LSD-25 as an aid in psychotherapy', *Dis. Nerv. Syst.*, vol. 11, pp. 241–3.

Campbell, A. M. G., Evans, M., Thomson, J. L. G., and Williams, M. J. (1971), 'Cerebral atrophy in young cannabis smokers', *Lancet*, vol. 7736, pp. 1219–24.

Campbell, D. R. (1971), 'The electroencephalogram in cannabis associated psychosis', *Canad. Psychiat. Assn. J.*, vol. 16, pp. 161–5.

Canadian Government Commission of Inquiry (1970), *The Non-Medical Use of Drugs: Interim Report*, Penguin, 1971.

Carstairs, G. M. (1954), 'Bhang and alcohol: cultural factors in the choice of intoxicants', *Q. J. Stud. Alcohol*, vol. 15, pp. 220–37.

Castaneda, C. (1970), *The Teachings of Don Juan: A Yaqui Way of Knowledge*, Penguin.

Castaneda, C. (1971), 'Further conversations with Don Juan', *Esquire*, vol. 75, pp. 3, 89, 164–8.

Chapple, P. A. L. (1966), 'Cannabis – a toxic and dangerous substance– a study of eighty takers', *Brit. J. Addict.*, vol. 61, pp. 269–82.

Charen, S., and Perelman, L. (1946), 'Personality studies of marihuana addicts', *Amer. J. Psychiat.*, vol. 102, pp. 674–82.

Chatterjee, M. L. (1969), 'Mind expanders', *J. Indian Med. Assn*, vol. 53, pp. 201–4.

Cheek, F. E., and Holstein, C. M. (1971), 'Lysergic acid diethylamide tartrate (LSD-25) dosage levels, group differences, and social interaction', *J. nerv. ment. Dis.*, vol. 153, pp. 133–47.

Cheek, F. E., Newell, S., and Joffe, M. (1970), 'Deceptions in the illicit drug market', *Science*, vol. 167, p. 1276.

Cheek, F. E., Newell, S., and Sarett, M. (1969), 'The down-head behind an up-head – the heroin addict takes LSD', *Int. J. Addict.*, vol. 4, pp. 101–19.

Cheek, F. E., Sarett, M., and Newell, S. (1969), 'The illicit LSD group and life change', *Int. J. Addict.*, vol. 4, pp. 407–26.

Chopra, I. C., and Chopra, R. N. (1957), 'The use of cannabis drugs in India', *Bull. Narcot.*, vol. 9, pp. 4–29.

Chopra, R. N., and Chopra, G. S. (1939), 'The present position of hemp-drug addiction in India', *Indian med. res. Memoirs*, vol. 31, pp. 1–119.

Chopra, R. N., Chopra, G. S., and Chopra, I. E. (1942), 'Cannabis sativa in relation to mental diseases and crime in India', *Indian J. med. Res.*, vol. 30, pp. 155–171.

Claridge, G. (1970), *Drugs and Human Behaviour*, Allen Lane The Penguin Press.

Clark, D., and Nakashima, N. (1968), 'Experimental Studies of marihuana', *Amer. J. Psychiat.*, vol. 125, pp. 379–84.

Clark, J. (1971), 'The use of psilocybin in a prison setting', in B. Aaronson and H. Osmond (eds.), *Psychedelics*, Hogarth Press.

Clark, W. H. (1969), *Chemical Ecstasy: Psychedelic Drugs and Religion*, Sheed & Ward.

Clark, W. H., and Funkhouser, G. R. (1970), 'Physicians and researchers disagree on psychedelic drugs', *Psychology Today*, vol. 3, pp. 48–50, 70–73.

Cohen, M. M., Marinello, M. J., and Back, N. (1967), 'Chromosomal damage in human leukocytes induced by lysergic acid diethylamide', *Science*, vol. 155, p. 1417.

Cohen, S. (1960), 'Lysergic acid diethylamide: side effects and complications', *J. nerv. ment. Dis.*, vol. 130, pp. 30–40.

Cohen, S. (1965), *Drugs of Hallucination*, Secker & Warburg. Also published as *The Beyond Within: The LSD Story*, Atheneum, 1966.

Cohen, S. (1966), 'A classification of LSD complications', *Psychosomatics*, vol. 7, pp. 182–6.

Cole, J. O., and Katz, M. M. (1964), 'The psychotomimetic drugs: an overview', in D. Solomon (ed.), *LSD: The Consciousness-Expanding Drug*, Putnam.

Cookson, J., and Nottingham, J. (1969), *A Survey of Chemical and Biological Warfare*, Sheed & Ward.

Crow, W. B. (1969), *The Occult Properties of Herbs*, Aquarian Press.

Curtis, C. (1971), 'What went wrong with the hippie dream', *Observer Colour Supplement*, 21 February, pp. 6–13.

Dally, P. (1967), *Chemotherapy of Psychiatric Disorders*, Logos Press.

Denson, R. (1969), 'Complications of therapy with lysergide', *Canad. Med. Assn J.*, vol. 101, pp. 659–63.

Destefano, T. (1972), 'Drugs and GIs in Europe', *Drugs and Society*, vol. 1, pp. 21–3.

Dhunjibhoy, J. E. (1930), 'A brief resumé of the types of insanity commonly met with in India, with a full description of "Indian hemp insanity" peculiar to the country', *J. ment. Sci.*, vol. 76, pp. 254–64.

Downing, J. J. (1965), 'Zihuatanejo: an experiment in transpersonative living', in R. Blum (ed.), *Utopiates: The Use and Users of LSD-25*, Tavistock.

228 References

Downing, J. (1969), 'Attitude and behavior change through psychedelic drug use', in C. T. Tart (ed.), *Altered States of Consciousness*, Wiley.

Downing, J. J., and Wygant, W. (1965), 'Psychedelic experience and religious belief', in R. Blum (ed.), *Utopiates: The Use and Users of LSD-25*, Tavistock.

Drankenbring, W. F. (1971), 'Marijuana on trial – new evidence', *The Plain Truth*, vol. 36, pp. 22–3.

Dwarakanath, S. C. (1965), 'Use of opium and cannabis in the traditional systems of medicine in India', *Bull. Narcot.*, vol. 17, pp. 15–19.

Eddy, N. B., Halbach, H., Isbell, H., and Seevers, M. H. (1965), *Drug Dependence: Its Significance and Characteristics*, World Health Organisation.

Edwards, A. E., Bloom, M. H., and Cohen, S. (1969), 'The psychedelics: love or hostility potion?', *Psychol. Rep.*, vol. 24, pp. 844–6.

Egozcue, J., Irwin, S., and Maruffo, C. A. (1968), 'Chromosomal damage in LSD users', *J. Amer. Med. Assn.* vol. 204, pp. 214–18.

Ellis, H. (1898), 'Mescal: a new artificial paradise', *Contemp. Rev.*, vol. 73, pp. 130–41.

Faillace, L. A., Snyder, S. H., and Weingartner, H. (1970), '2, 5-dimethoxy-4-methylamphetamine: clinical evaluation of a new hallucinogenic drug', *J. nerv. ment. Dis.*, vol. 150, pp. 119–26.

Faillace, L. A., Vourlekis, A., and Szara, S. (1970), 'Hallucinogenic drugs in the treatment of alcoholism: a two-year follow-up', *Comp. Psychiat.*, vol. 2, pp. 51–6.

Farb, P. (1969), *Man's Rise to Civilization: As Shown by the Indians of North America, from Primeval Times to the Coming of the Industrial State*, Secker & Warburg.

Favazza, A. R., and Domino, E. F. (1969), 'Recurrent LSD experience (flashbacks) triggered by marihuana', *Univ. Mich. Med. Cent. J.*, vol. 35, pp. 214–16.

Fraser, J. D. (1949), 'Withdrawal symptoms in Cannabis indica addicts,' *Lancet*, vol. 2, p. 747.

Freedman, D. X. (1968), 'On the use and abuse of LSD', *Arch. gen. Psychiat.*, vol. 18, pp. 330–47.

Frosch, W. A., Robbins, E. S., and Stern, M. (1965), 'Untoward reactions to lysergic acid diethylamide (LSD) resulting in hospitalization', *New Eng. J. Med.*, vol. 273, pp. 1235–9.

Frosch, W. A., Robbins, E., Robbins, L., and Stern, M. (1967), 'Motivation for self-administration of LSD', *Psychiat. Q.*, vol. 41, pp. 56–61.

Gaskill, H. S. (1945), 'Marihuana, an intoxicant,' *Amer. J. Psychiat.*, vol. 102, pp. 202–4.

Gautier, T. (1846), 'The Hashish Club', trans. R. J. Gladstone, in D. Solomon (ed.), *The Marijuana Papers*, Panther, 1969.

Geber, W. F., and Schramm, L. C. (1969), 'Effect of marihuana extract on fetal hamsters and rabbits', *Toxic appl. Pharmacol.*, vol. 14, pp. 276–82.

Geert-Jörgensen, E., Hertz, M. Knudsen, K., and Kristensen, K. (1964), 'LSD treatment', *Acta Psychiat. Scand.*, Suppl. 180, pp. 373–82.

Geert-Jörgensen, E. (1968), 'Further observations regarding hallucinogenic treatment', *Acta Psychiat. Scand.*, Suppl. 203, pp. 195–200.

Ginsberg, A. (1969), 'First manifesto to end the bringdown', in D. Solomon (ed.), *The Marijuana Papers*, Panther.

Glickman, L., and Blumenfield, M. (1967), 'Psychological determinants of "LSD reactions"', *J. nerv. ment. Dis.*, vol. 145, pp. 79–83.

Goode, E. (1969), 'Marijuana and sex', *Evergreen*, vol. 66, pp. 19–20.

Goode, E. (1970), *The Marijuana Smokers*, Basic Books.

Grinspoon, L. (1969), 'Marihuana', *Sci. Amer.*, vol. 221, pp. 17–25.

Grinspoon, L. (1971), *Marihuana Reconsidered*, Harvard University Press.

Halloran, J. (ed.) (1970), *The Effects of Television*, Panther.

Harman, W. W., and Fadiman, J. (1971), 'Selective enhancement of specific capacities through psychedelic training', in B. Aaronson and H. Osmond (eds.), *Psychedelics*, Hogarth Press.

Harman, W. W., McKim, R. H., Mogar, R. E., Fadiman, J., and Stolaroff, M. J. (1966), 'Psychedelic agents in creative problem solving: a pilot study', *Psychol. Rep.*, vol. 19, pp. 211–27.

Havens, J. (1964), 'Memo on the religious implications of the consciousness-changing drugs', *J. Sci. Study Relig.*, vol. 3, pp. 216–26.

Hedgepeth, W., and Stock, D. (1970), *The Alternative: Communal Life in New America*, Collier-Macmillan.

Hekimian, L. J., and Gershon, S. (1968), 'Characteristics of drug abusers admitted to a psychiatric hospital', *J. Amer. Med. Assn*, vol. 205, pp. 125–30.

Hensala, J. D., Epstein, L. J., and Blacker, K. H. (1967), 'LSD and psychiatric inpatients', *Arch. gen. Psychiat.*, vol. 16, pp. 554–9.

Hirschhorn, K., and Cohen, M. M. (1967), 'Nonpsychic effects of lysergic acid diethylamide', *Ann. intern. Med.*, vol. 67, pp. 1109–11.

Hockman, C. H., Perrin, R. G., and Kalant, H. (1971), 'Electroencephalographic and behavioural alterations produced by △¹-tetrahydrocannabinol', *Science*, vol. 172, pp. 968–70.

Hoffer, A. (1971), 'Treatment of alcoholism with psychedelic therapy', in B. Aaronson and H. Osmond (eds.), *Psychedelics*, Hogarth Press.

Hoffer, A., and Osmond, H. (1967), *The Hallucinogens*, Academic Press.

Hollister, L., and Hartman, A. (1962), 'Mescaline, lysergic acid diethylamide and psilocybin: comparison of clinical syndromes, effect on colour perception and biochemical measures', *Comp. Psychiat.*, vol. 3, pp. 235–41.

Hungerford, D. A., Taylor, K. M., Shagass, C., LaBadie, G. U., Balaban, G. B., and Paton, G. R. (1968), 'Cytogenetic effects of LSD-25 therapy in man', *J. Amer. Med. Assn*, vol. 206, pp. 2287–91.

Huxley, A. (1932), *Brave New World*, Chatto & Windus.

Huxley, A. (1950), *The Perennial Philosophy*, Chatto & Windus.

Huxley, A. (1954), *The Doors of Perception*, Penguin, 1971.

Huxley, A. (1956), *Heaven and Hell*, Penguin, 1971.

Huxley, A. (1962), *Island*, Chatto & Windus.

Huxley, L. A. (1968), *This Timeless Moment*, Farrar, Strauss & Giroux.

Indian Hemp Drugs Commission Report (1894), Simla and Calcutta, Government Central Printing Office.

Irwin, S., and Egozcue, J. (1967), 'Chromosome abnormalities in leukocytes from LSD-25 users,' *Science*, vol. 157, p. 313.

Isbell, H. (1959), 'Comparison of the reactions induced by psilocybin and LSD-25 in man', *Psychopharmacologia*, vol. 1, pp. 29–38.

Izumi, K. (1971), 'LSD and architectural design', in B. Aaronson and H. Osmond (eds.), *Psychedelics*, Hogarth Press.

Jacobsen, E. (1968), 'The hallucinogens', in C. R. B. Joyce (ed.), *Psychopharmacology: Dimensions and Perspectives*, Tavistock, 1971.

Jacobson, C. B., and Magyar, V. L. (1968), 'Genetic evaluation of LSD', *Clin. Proc. child. Hosp.*, *Distr. Columbia*, vol. 24, pp. 153–61.

James, W. (1902), *The Varieties of Religious Experience*, Longman.

Johnsen, G. (1964), 'Three years experience with the use of LSD as an aid in psychotherapy', *Acta Psychiat. Scand.*, Suppl. 180, pp. 383–8.

Jørgensen, F. (1968), 'Abuse of psychomimetics', *Acta Psychiat. Scand.*, Suppl. 203, pp. 205–16.

Kama Sutra of Vatsyayana, trans. Sir Richard Burton and F. F. Arbuthnot, Kimber, 1963.

Kaplan, H. S. (1971), 'Psychosis associated with marijuana', *New York State J. Med.*, vol. 71, pp. 433–5.

Kast, E. C. (1964), 'Pain and LSD-25: a theory of attenuation and anticipation', in D. Solomon (ed.), *LSD: The Consciousness-Expanding Drug*, Putnam.

Kast, E. C., and Collins, V. J. (1964), 'Lysergic acid diethylamide as an analgesic agent', *Anaesthesia and Analgesia*, vol. 43, pp. 285–91.

Kast, E. C. (1971), 'A concept of death', in B. Aaronson and H. Osmond (eds.), *Psychedelics*, Hogarth Press.

Keeler, M. H. (1967), 'Adverse reaction to marihuana', *Amer. J. Psychiat.*, vol. 124, pp. 7–13.

Keeler, M. H. (1968), 'Motivation for marihuana use: a correlate of adverse reactions', *Amer. J. Psychiat.*, vol. 125, pp. 386–90.

Keeler, M. H., and Reifler, C. B. (1967), 'Grand mal convulsions subsequent to marihuana use', *Dis. nerv. Syst.*, vol. 28, pp. 474–5.

Keeler, H., Reifler, C. B., and Liptzin, M. B. (1968), 'Spontaneous recurrence of marihuana effect', *Amer. J. Psychiat.*, vol. 125, pp. 384–6.

Kingman, R. (1927), 'The green goddess: a study in dreams, drugs, and dementia', *Med. J. Rec.*, vol. 126, pp. 470–75.

Klee, G. D. (1963), 'Lysergic acid diethylamide (LSD) and ego functions', *Arch. gen. Psychiat.*, vol. 8, pp. 461–75.

Klein, J., and Phillips, D. L. (1968), 'From hard to soft drugs: temporal and substantive changes in drug usage among gangs in a working-class community', *J. Health soc. Behav.*, vol. 9, pp. 139–45.

Klüver, H. (1926), 'Mescal visions and eidetic vision', *Amer. J. Psychol.*, vol. 37, pp. 502–15.

Knudsen, K. (1964), 'Homicide after treatment with lysergic acid diethylamide', *Acta Psychiat. Scand.*, Suppl. 180, vol. 40, pp. 389–95.

Kramer, R. A., and Pierpaoli, P. (1971), 'Hallucinogenic effect of propellant components of deodorant sprays', *Pediatrics*, vol. 48, pp. 322–3.

Krippner, S. (1968), 'The psychedelic artist', in R. E. L. Masters and J. Houston, *Psychedelic Art*, Weidenfeld & Nicolson.

Krippner, S. (1969), 'The psychedelic state, the hypnotic trance, and the creative act', in C. T. Tart (ed.), *Altered States of Consciousness*, Wiley.

Kruskal, W. H., and Haberman, S. (1968), 'Chromosomal effect and L S D: samples of four', *Science*, vol. 162, pp. 1508–9.

Laurie, P. (1967), *Drugs: Medical, Psychological, and Social Facts*, Penguin.

Leary, T. (1965), *The Politics of Ecstacy*, Paladin, 1970.

Leary, T. (1966), *Psychedelic Prayers*, Poet's Press.

Leary, T. (1968), *High Priest*, World, New York.

Leary, T., Alpert, R., and Metzner, R. (1965), 'Rationale of the Mexican psychedelic training center', in R. Blum (ed.), *Utopiates: The Use and Users of LSD-25*, Tavistock.

Leary, T., Litwin, G. H., and Metzner, R. (1963), 'Reactions to psilocybin administered in a supportive environment', *J. nerv. ment. Dis.*, vol. 137, pp. 561–73.

Leary, T., Metzner, R., and Alpert, R. (1964), *The Psychedelic Experience: A Manual Based on the Tibetan Book of the Dead*, University Books, New York.

Leff, R., and Bernstein, S. (1968), 'Proprietary hallucinogens', *Dis. nerv. Syst.*, vol. 29, pp. 621–6.

Levine, J. (1969), 'L S D – a clinical overview', in P. Black (ed.), *Drugs and the Brain*, Johns Hopkins Press.

Levine, J., and Ludwig, A. M. (1967), 'The hypnodelic treatment technique', in H. A. Abramson (ed.), *The Use of LSD in Psychotherapy and Alcoholism*, Bobbs-Merrill.

Levine, J., Ludwig, A. M., and Lyle, W. (1963), 'The controlled psychedelic state', *Amer. J. clin. Hypnosis*, vol. 6, pp. 163–4.

Levy, N. J. (1968), 'The use of drugs by teenagers for sanctuary and illusion', *Amer. J. Psychoanal.*, vol. 28, pp. 48–58.

Lienert, J. (1966), 'Mental age regression induced by lysergic acid diethylamide', *J. Psychol.*, vol. 63, pp. 3–11.

Lindesmith, A. R. (1969), 'The marijuana problem: myth or reality?', in D. Solomon (ed.), *The Marijuana Papers*, Panther.

Lingeman, R. R. (1970), *Drugs from A to Z: A Dictionary*, Allen Lane The Penguin Press.

de Lory, A. and Gaber, I. (1971), 'Drugs in Vietnam', *Drugs in Society*, vol. 3, pp. 9–12.

Loughman, W. D., Sargent, T. W., and Israelstam, D. M. (1967), 'Leukocytes of humans exposed to lysergic acid diethylamide: lack of chromosomal damage', *Science*, vol. 158, pp. 508–10.

Louria, D. B. (1968), 'Abuse of lysergic acid diethylamide – an increasing problem', in C. W. M. Wilson (ed.), *Adolescent Drug Dependence*, Pergamon.

Louria, D. B. (1970), *The Drug Scene*, Corgi Books.

McGlothlin, W. H. (1969), 'Cannabis: a reference', in D. Solomon (ed.), *The Marijuana Papers*, Panther.

McGlothlin, W. H., and West, L. J. (1968), 'The marihuana problem: an overview', *Amer. J. Psychiat.*, vol. 125, pp. 370–78.

McGlothlin, W. H., Cohen, S., and McGlothlin, M. S. (1964), 'Short-term effects of LSD on anxiety, attitudes, and performance', *J. nerv. ment. Dis.*, vol. 139, pp. 266–73.

McGlothlin, W. H., Cohen, S., and McGlothlin, M. S. (1966), 'Personality and attitude changes in volunteer subjects following repeated administration of LSD', *Excerpta Medica Int. Cong. Rep.*, vol. 129, pp. 425–34.

McGlothlin, W. H., Cohen, S., and McGlothlin, M. S. (1967), 'Long-lasting effects of LSD on normals', *Arch. gen. Psychiat.*, vol. 17, pp. 521–32.

Mandel, J. (1966), 'Hashish, Assassins, and the Love of God', *Issues in Criminol.*, vol. 2, pp. 149–56.

Maple, E. (1965), *The Dark World of Witches*, Pan.

Marcovitz, E., and Myers, H. J. (1944), 'Marihuana addiction in the army', *War Medicine* (Chicago), vol. 6, pp. 382–91.

Marshman, J. A., and Gibbins, R. J. (1970), 'A note on the composition of illicit drugs', *Ontario Med. Rev.*, September, pp. 1–3.

Masters, R. E. L. and Houston, J. (1966), *The Varieties of Psychedelic Experience*, Holt, Rinehart & Winston.

Masters, R. E. L., and Houston, J. (1968), *Psychedelic Art*, Weidenfeld & Nicolson.

Masters, R. E. L., and Houston, J. (1971), 'Toward an individual psychedelic psychotherapy', in B. Aaronson and H. Osmond (eds.), *Psychedelics*, Hogarth Press.

Mayor's Committee on Marihuana (1944), *The Marihuana Problem in the City of New York: Sociological, Medical, Psychological, and Pharmacological Studies*, Cattell Press.

Metzner, R. (ed.) (1968), *The Ecstatic Adventure*, Macmillan Co.

Metzner, R. (1971), *Mushrooms and the Mind*, in B. Aaronson and H. Osmond (eds.), *Psychedelics*, Hogarth Press.

Miras, C. (1965), 'Some aspects of cannabis action in hashish: its chemistry and pharmacology', *C I B A Foundation Study Group*, no. 21, Churchill.

Mogar, R. E. (1969), 'Current status and future trends in psychedelic (L S D) research', in C. T. Tart (ed.), *Altered States of Consciousness*, Wiley.

Munch, J. C. (1966), 'Marihuana and crime', *Bull. Narcot.*, vol. 18, pp. 15–22.

Netz, B., Jonsson, C. O., and Bergqvist, S. (1963), 'Effects of lysergic acid diethylamide (L S D-25) on normal subjects in a schizophrenia discriminating test battery', *Scand. J. Psychol.*, vol. 4, pp. 143–8.

O'Shaughnessy, W. B., (1842), 'On the preparation of the Indian hemp, or gunjah', *Trans. Med. Psychic. Soc. Cal.*, vol. 8, pp. 421–61.

Osmond, H. (1957), 'A review of the clinical effects of psychotomimetic agents', *Ann. N. Y. Acad. Sci.*, vol. 66, pp. 418–34.

Osmond, H. (1971), 'Peyote night', in B. Aaronson and H. Osmond (eds.), *Psychedelics*, Hogarth Press.

Osmond, H., and Hoffer, A. (1967), 'A programme for the treatment of alcoholism: L S D, malvaria and nicotinic acid', in H. A. Abramson (ed.), *The Use of L S D in Psychotherapy and Alcoholism*, Bobbs-Merrill.

Pahnke, W. N. (1966), 'Drugs and mysticism', *Int. J. Parapsychol.*, vol. 8, pp. 295–320.

Pahnke, W. N. (1969), 'The psychedelic mystical experience in the human encounter with death (The Ingersoll Lecture)', *Harv. Theol. Rev.*, vol. 62, pp. 1–21.

Perry, H. (1970), *The Human Be-In*, Allen Lane.

Pet, D. B., and Ball, J. C. (1968), ' Marihuana smoking in the United States', in S. E. Grupp (ed.), *Marihuana*, Merrill, 1971.

Puharich, A. (1959), *The Sacred Mushroom*, Doubleday.

Reich, C. (1970), *The Greening of America*, Allen Lane The Penguin Press, 1971.

Reininger, W. (1946), 'Historical notes', in D. Solomon (ed.), *The Marijuana Papers*, Panther, 1969.

Report on Public Health and Medical Subjects, No. 124 (1970), *Amphetamines, Barbiturates, L S D and Cannabis: Their Use and Misuse*, H M S O.

de Ropp, R. S. (1958), *Drugs and the Mind*, Gollancz.

Rosenthal, S. H. (1964), ' Persistent hallucinosis following repeated administration of hallucinogenic drugs', *Amer . J. Psychiat.*, vol. 121, pp. 238–44.

Rothlin, E. (ed.) (1961), *Proceedings of the Second Meeting of the Collegium Internationale Neuro-Psychopharmacologicum, Basle, July 1960*, Elsevier.

Sandford, J. (1972), *In Search of the Magic Mushroom*, Peter Owen.

Sapol, E. and Roffman, R. A. (1969), ' Marijuana in Vietnam', *J. Amer. Pharm. Assn*, new series vol. 9, pp. 615–18, 630.

Savage, C. (1964), 'L S D, alcoholism and transcendence', in D. Solomon (ed.), *L S D: The Consciousness-Expanding Drug*, Putnam.

Savage, C., Fadiman, J. Mogar, R., and Allen, M. H. (1966), 'The effects of psychedelic (L S D) therapy on values, personality, and behaviour', *Int. J. Neuropsychiat.*, vol. 2, pp. 241–54.

Savage, C., Kurland, A. A., Unger, S., and Shaffer, J. W. (1969), 'Therapeutic applications of L S D', in P. Black (ed.), *Drugs and the Brain*, Johns Hopkins Press.

Schneider, W. L. (1967), 'Some consequences of the L S D revolution', *Psychedel. Rev.*, vol. 9, pp. 51–7.

Schofield, M. (1971), *The Strange Case of Pot*, Penguin.

Schultes, R. E. (1940), 'The aboriginal therapeutic uses of *Lophophora williamsii*', *Cactus and Succulent J.*, vol. 12, pp. 177–81.

Schultes, R. E. (1963), 'Botanical sources of the new world narcotics', *Psychedel. Rev.*, vol. 1, pp. 145–66.

Schultes, R. E. (1969a), 'Hallucinogens of plant origin', *Science*, vol. 163, pp. 245–54.

Schultes, R. E. (1969b), 'The plant kingdom and hallucinogens (part 1)', *Bull. Narcot.*, vol. 21, pp. 3–16.

Schultes, R. E. (1969c), 'The plant kingdom and hallucinogens (part 2)', *Bull. Narcot.*, vol. 21, pp. 15–27.

Schultes, R. E. (1970), 'The plant kingdom and hallucinogens (part 3)', *Bull. Narcot.*, vol. 22, pp. 25–53.

Schwartz, B. N. (1968), 'Context, value and direction', in R. E. L. Masters and J. Houston, *Psychedelic Art*, Weidenfeld & Nicolson.

Scott, M. E. (1971), 'The flashback phenomenon', *Virginia Med. Month.*, vol. 98, pp. 317–20.

Settlage, C. F. (1970), 'An editorial postcript: on papers dealing with "Anomie, alienation, and adolescence"', *J. Amer. Acad. Child Psychiat.*, vol. 9, pp. 278–81.

Sherwood, J. N., Stolaroff, M. J., and Harman, W. W. (1962), 'The psychedelic experience – a new concept in psychotherapy', *J. Neuropsychiat.*, vol. 4, pp. 69–80.

Skakkebaek, N. E., Philip, J., and Rafaelsen, O. J. (1968), 'LSD in mice: abnormalities in meiotic chromosomes', *Science*, vol. 160, pp. 1246–8.

Slotkin, J. S. (1952), 'Menomini peyotism: a study of individual variations in a primary group with a homogeneous culture', *Trans. Amer. Phil. Soc.*, vol. 42, pp. 572–3.

Slotkin, J. S. (1956), *The Peyote Religion: A Study in Indian–White Relations*, Free Press.

Smart, R. G., and Bateman, K. (1967), 'Unfavourable reactions to LSD: a review and analysis of the available case reports', *Canad. Med. Assn J.*, vol. 97, pp. 1214–21.

Smart, R. G., and Bateman K, (1968), 'The chromosomal and teratogenic effects of lysergic acid diethylamide: a review of the current literature', *Canad. Med. Assn J.*, vol. 99, pp. 805–10.

Smart, R. G., and Jackson, D. (1969), *The Yorkville Subculture: A Study of the Life Styles and Interactions of Hippies and Non-Hippies*, Addiction Research Foundation, Toronto (mimeographed volume prepared from the field notes of Gopala Alampur).

Smart, R. G., and Jones, D. (1970), 'Illicit LSD users: their personality characteristics and psychopathology', *J. abnorm. Psychol.*, vol. 75, pp. 286–92.

Smart, R. G., Storm, T., Baker, E. F. W., and Solursh, L. (1966), 'A controlled study of lysergide in the treatment of alcoholism', *Q. J. Stud. Alcohol*, vol. 27, pp. 469–82.

Smith, D. E. (1968), 'Acute and chronic toxicity of marijuana', *J. Psychedel. Drugs*, vol. 2, pp. 37–47.

Smith, D. E., Luce, J., and Dernburg, E. A. (1970), 'Love needs care: Haight-Ashbury dies', *New Society*, vol. 16, pp. 98–101.

Snyder, S. H. (1971), 'Work with marijuana: 1. Effects', *Psychol. Today*, vol. 4, pp. 37–40, 64–5.

Solomon, D. (ed.) (1964), *LSD: The Consciousness-Expanding Drug*, Putnam.

Solomon, D. (ed.) (1969), *The Marijuana Papers*, Panther.

Sparkes, R. S., Melnyk, J., and Bozzetti, L. (1968), 'Chromosomal effect *in vivo* of exposure to lysergic acid diethylamide', *Science*, vol. 160, pp. 1343–4.

Spinks, G. S. (1963), *Psychology and Religion*, Methuen.

Stace, W. T. (1960), *Mysticism and Philosophy*, Lippincott.

Stafford, P. G., and Golightly, B. H. (1967), *LSD: The Problem-Solving Psychedelic*, Award Books.

Taqi, S. (1969), 'Approbation of drug usage in rock and roll music', *Bull. Narcot.*, vol. 21, pp. 29–35.

Tart, C. T. (ed.), (1969), *Altered States of Consciousness*, Wiley.

Tart, C. T. (1971), 'Work with marijuana: 2. Sensations', *Psychol. Today*, vol. 4, pp. 41–4, 66–8.

Taylor, J. (1970), *Satan's Slaves*, New English Library.

Taylor, N. (1969), 'The pleasant Assassin: the story of marijuana', in D. Solomon (ed.), *The Marijuana Papers*, Panther.

UCLA Interdepartmental Conference (1970), 'The marijuana problem', *Ann. int. Med.*, vol. 73, pp. 449–65.

Unger, S. (1963), ' Mescaline, LSD, psilocybin, and personality change,' *Psychiatry*, vol. 26, pp. 111–25.

Unger, S. (1964), ' LSD and psychotherapy: a bibliography of the English-language literature', in D. Solomon (ed.), *LSD: The Consciousness-Expanding Drug*, Putnam.

Ungerleider, J. T., Fisher, D. D., Goldsmith, S. R., Fuller, M., and Forgy, E. (1968), 'A statistical survey of adverse reactions to L S D in Los Angeles County', *Amer. J. Psychiat.*, vol. 125, pp. 352–7.

Unwin, J. R. (1968), 'Illicit drug use among Canadian youth: Part 1', *Canad. Med. Assn J.*, vol. 98, pp. 402–7.

Unwin, J. R. (1969), 'Non-medical use of drugs with particular reference to youth', *Canad. Med. Assn J.*, vol. 101, pp. 72–88.

Van Dusen, W. (1961), 'L S D and the enlightenment of Zen', *Psychologia*, vol. 4, pp. 11–16.

Wakefield, E. M. (1958), *The Observer's Book of Common Fungi*, Warne.

Warnock, J. (1903), 'Insanity from hasheesh', *J. ment. Sci.*, vol. 49, pp. 96–110.

Wasson, R. G. (1958), 'Hallucinogenic mushrooms of Mexico', *Trans. N. Y. Acad. Sci.*, vol. 21, pp. 325–39.

Wasson, R. G. (1961), 'The hallucinogenic fungi of Mexico: an inquiry into the origins of the religious idea among primitive peoples', *Harv. Univ. Bot. Mus. Leaflet*, vol. 19, pp. 137–62.

Wasson, R. G. (1969), *Soma: Divine Mushroom of Immortality*, Harcourt, Brace & World.

Wasson, R. G., and Wasson, V. P. (1957), *Mushrooms. Russia and History*, Pantheon.

Watt, J. M., and Breyer-Brandwijk, M. G. (1936), 'The forensic and sociological aspects of the dagga problem in South Africa', *S. Afr. med. J.*, vol. 10, pp. 573–9.

Watts, A. W. (1947), *Zen Buddhism*, Buddhist Society.

Watts, A. W. (1962), *The Joyous Cosmology: Adventures in the Chemistry of Consciousness*, Pantheon.

Watts, A. W. (1964), 'A psychedelic experience: fact or fantasy ?', in D. Solomon (ed.), *L S D: The Consciousness- Expanding Drug*, Putnam.

Watts, A. W. (1967), *This is it: And Other Essays*, Collier.

Watts, W. D. (1971), *The Psychedelic Experience: A Sociological Study*, Sage Publications.

Weil, A. T., Zinberg, N. E., and Nelsen, J. M. (1968), 'Clinical and psychological effects of marijuana in man', *Science*, vol. 162, pp. 1234–42.

Welpton, D. F. (1968), 'Psychodynamics of chronic lysergic acid diethylamide use', *J. nerv. ment. Dis.*, vol. 147, pp. 377–85.

West, L. J. (1970), 'Contribution to UCLA Interdepartmental Conference: The Marijuana Problem', *Ann. int. Med.*, vol. 73, pp. 449–65.

Williams, J. B. (ed.) (1967), *Narcotics and Hallucinogens*, Glencoe Press.

Williams, F. S. (1970), 'Alienation of youth as reflected in the hippie movement', *J. Amer. Acad. Child Psychiat.*, vol. 9, pp. 251–63.

Wilson, C. W. M., and Linken, A. (1968), 'The use of cannabis in relation to the adolescent', in C. W. M. Wilson (ed.), *The Pharmacological and Epidemiological Aspects of Adolescent Drug Dependence*, Pergamon.

Winick, C. (1960), 'The use of drugs by jazz musicians', *Social Problems*, vol. 7, pp. 240–53.

Yielding, K. L., and Sterglanz, H. (1968), 'Lysergic acid diethylamide (LSD) binding to deoxyribonucleic acid (DNA)', *Proc. Soc. Exper. Biol. Med.*, vol. 128, pp. 1096–8.

Young, J. (1971), *The Drugtakers: The Social Meaning of Drug Use*, MacGibbon & Kee.

Zaehner, R. C. (1957), *Mysticism Sacred and Profane*, Oxford University Press.

Zegans, L. S., Pollard, J. C., and Brown, D. (1967), 'The effects of LSD-25 on creativity and tolerance to regression', *Arch. gen. Psychiat.*, vol. 16, pp. 740–49.

Zellweger, H., McDonald, J. S., and Abbo, G. (1967), 'Is lysergic acid diethylamide a teratogen?', *Lancet*, vol. 2, pp. 1066–8.

Index

Drugs
Medical, Psychological, and Social Facts

Peter Laurie

What are the known facts about the 'dangerous' drugs?
What actual harm, mental or physical, do they cause?
Which of them are addictive, and how many addicts are there?

Peter Laurie has talked with doctors, policemen, addicts, and others
intimately involved with this problem. He has tried some of the drugs
for himself and closely studied the medical literature (including
little-known reports of American research). The result of his inquiries
into the pharmacological uses and social effects of drugs today
appears in this book. Now re-issued in Pelicans, it has already been
through five printings as a Penguin Special.

Originally published before the Wootton Report, *Drugs* was the first
objective study to offer all the major medical, psychological and social
facts about the subject to a public which is too often fed with alarmist
and sensational reports. For this second edition in Pelicans
Peter Laurie has added fresh information and statistics concerning
English users of drugs and noted changes in the law.

Drugs and Human Behaviour

Gordon Claridge

It is certain that someone under the influence of a drug will pick up this book. The drug may be a tranquillizer, supposed to relieve anxiety, or a sedative, intended to bring on sleep; or it may be self-prescribed, such as alcohol or caffeine. Whatever the drug, its psychological and physiological effects are likely to be far-reaching.

Recent advances in the understanding of drug action are the subject of Gordon Claridge's lucid study, about which the *British Hospital Journal* wrote: 'With a poverty of adequate literature on the subject, Dr Claridge's book may be viewed as a pioneer work on the effects of drugs on human behaviour.'

'The author looks at sleep and wakefulness, memory and learning, psychological effects, hallucinogens, variation of response, drugs and mental illness, the social use of drugs and alcoholism and drug addiction. Importantly the book is a study of drug effects through observation of human, rather than animal, reaction.'